Media Influence on Opinion Change and Democracy

Manuel Goyanes • Azahara Cañedo
Editors

Media Influence on Opinion Change and Democracy

How Private, Public and Social Media Organizations Shape Public Opinion

Editors
Manuel Goyanes
Universidad Carlos III de Madrid
Getafe, Madrid, Spain

Azahara Cañedo
Universidad de Castilla-La Mancha
Cuenca, Spain

ISBN 978-3-031-70230-3   ISBN 978-3-031-70231-0   (eBook)
https://doi.org/10.1007/978-3-031-70231-0

© Springer Nature Switzerland AG 2024

This work is subject to copyright. All rights are solely and exclusively licensed by the Publisher, whether the whole or part of the material is concerned, specifically the rights of translation, reprinting, reuse of illustrations, recitation, broadcasting, reproduction on microfilms or in any other physical way, and transmission or information storage and retrieval, electronic adaptation, computer software, or by similar or dissimilar methodology now known or hereafter developed.
The use of general descriptive names, registered names, trademarks, service marks, etc. in this publication does not imply, even in the absence of a specific statement, that such names are exempt from the relevant protective laws and regulations and therefore free for general use.
The publisher, the authors and the editors are safe to assume that the advice and information in this book are believed to be true and accurate at the date of publication. Neither the publisher nor the authors or the editors give a warranty, expressed or implied, with respect to the material contained herein or for any errors or omissions that may have been made. The publisher remains neutral with regard to jurisdictional claims in published maps and institutional affiliations.

This Palgrave Macmillan imprint is published by the registered company Springer Nature Switzerland AG.
The registered company address is: Gewerbestrasse 11, 6330 Cham, Switzerland

If disposing of this product, please recycle the paper.

Dedicated to the Spanish public university system, where we have been educated and which funds us.

Contents

1 Opinion Change and Democracy in Private Media, Public Service Media, and Social Media Platforms: An Introduction 1
Manuel Goyanes and Azahara Cañedo

Part I Opinion Change and Democracy in Private Media 9

2 The Shift in Media Power: How Media Capture Is Changing the Game 11
Marius Dragomir

3 Misinformation Campaigns, Populism, and the Role of Journalism 27
Michael Hameleers

4 Journalistic Role Performance and Its Effects 45
María Luisa Humanes

5 Big Data, Artificial Intelligence and Their Effects: The Birth of an Alert Society 65
João Canavilhas

Part II Opinion Change and Democracy in Public Service Media   81

6   Public Value and Liberal Democracies: The Potential of Public Service Media as Islands of Trust in the Digital Public Sphere   83
    Marta Rodríguez-Castro

7   Public Service Media and National Resilience in the Age of Information Disorders: A Two-Dimensional Conceptualization for Policy-Making   99
    Auksė Balčytienė and Minna Aslama Horowitz

8   The Role of Public Service Media in Democratic Engagement: An Audience Perspective   117
    Marcela Campos Rueda

9   Citizenship on the Public Service Internet: Citizens' Media Contribution to Reimagining Digital Democratic Communication   131
    Luciana Musello

Part III Opinion Change and Democracy in Social Media Platforms   149

10   Origin and Evolution of the News Finds Me Perception: Review of Theory and Effects   151
    Homero Gil de Zúñiga and Zicheng Cheng

11   From Mass Media to Social Media: Political Persuasion in the Field of Communication   181
    Beatriz Jordá and R. Lance Holbert

12 Fake News Exposure and Political Persuasion   197
    Samuel Toledano, Sheila Guerrero Rojas, and Alberto
    Ardèvol-Abreu

13 Content Sharing Dynamics and Political Polarization
    in Social Media   215
    Natalia Aruguete

Notes on Contributors

Alberto Ardèvol-Abreu is Associate Professor in the Department of Communication Sciences and Social Work at the University of La Laguna. His research focuses on the implications of new media-related phenomena for democracy and political participation. His studies cover various aspects, including conspiracy beliefs, disinformation, citizen journalism, political polarization, and political discussion. He has received important recognition for his work, including the best article award on politics and information technologies from the American Political Science Association, the Robert M. Worcester Award from the World Association for Public Opinion Research, and the Drago Latina 2013–2017 Award for the most cited article in five years.

Natalia Aruguete holds a PhD from La Universidad Nacional de Quilmes (UNQ) She is a professor at the Universidad Nacional de Quilmes and the Universidad Austral, and a member of CONICET (Argentina's Federal Agency for the development of Science and Technology). She has published four books and fifty articles studying the relationship between traditional media and social media, with particular attention to the effect of political agendas, media agendas, and the public. Her last book is *Nosotros contra ellos. ¿Cómo trabajan las redes para confirmar nuestras creencias y rechazar las de los otros?* (Siglo XXI Editores).

Auksė Balčytienė is Professor of Journalism and Communication at the Department of Public Communications and senior researcher at the Vytautas Kavolis Transdiciplinary Research Institute of Vytautas Magnus

University, Lithuania. She is also Co-Chair of the UNESCO Chair on MIL for Inclusive Knowledge Societies and a Leader of the Baltic Research Foundation for Digital Resilience (DIGIRES, http://digires.lt). Her research and practical interests lie in uncovering of disinformation, raising media awareness, and developing governance policies for engaged and dialogic communication and resilient citizenship.

Marcela Campos Rueda is a media researcher and practitioner with a successful career as an international media executive. She holds a PhD in Media Research from Universidad Carlos III of Madrid. Her research focuses on public service media (PSM) from an audience perspective, citizenship building, and gender parity in media. Campos Rueda's work has been published in renowned journals such as *Journalism*, *Journalism Studies*, and the *International Journal of Communication*.

João Canavilhas holds a PhD from the Universidad de Salamanca. He is an associate professor at the Universidade da Beira Interior (Covilhã, Portugal) and a researcher at Labcom—Communication & Arts. His research focuses on the intersection of communication and new technologies, particularly in the impact of portable devices, artificial intelligence, and disinformation processes in journalism. Between September 2013 and June 2021, he was Vice-Rector for Teaching and Internationalization (UBI).

Azahara Cañedo is Associate Professor at the Faculty of Communication, University of Castilla-La Mancha, Spain. From the critical research perspective of the Political Economy of Communication, she has developed a specialized profile in the study of the value of public service media. She is also interested in the working conditions in Communication and the influence of power structures on the functioning of the media industry. Her work has been awarded both the 2022 Article of the Year Award by the *European Journal of Communication* and the 2020 Prize for the Best Dissertation in Communication by the Spanish Association of Universities with Degrees in Information and Communication, ATIC.

Zicheng Cheng holds an MA from Boston University and is a PhD candidate at Donald P. Bellisario College of Communications at Pennsylvania State University, where she is an active member of the Democracy Research Unit (DRU). Her research interests include digital journalism and political communication on digital media.

Homero Gil de Zuñiga holds a PhD in Politics from Universidad Europea de Madrid and a PhD in Mass Communication from University of Wisconsin—Madison, serves as Distinguished Research Professor at University of Salamanca where he directs the Democracy Research Unit (DRU), as Distinguished Professor of Media Effects & AI at Penn State University, and as Senior Research Fellow at Universidad Diego Portales, Chile. His work deals with the development of theoretically driven research, aiming to shed empirical social scientific light on how social media, algorithms, AI, and other technologies affect society and democracy.

Marius Dragomir is Director of the Media and Journalism Research Center. He is a professor at Central European University (Austria) and is also a researcher at the University of Santiago de Compostela (Spain). He was the director of the Center for Media, Data, and Society in Budapest and managed the global research and policy portfolio of the Program on Independent Journalism in London. Throughout his career, he has specialized in the study of media and communication regulation, digital media, public service media governance, broadcasting, journalism business models, and ownership regulation. He is currently leading a dozen research projects, among them Media Influence Matrix, Media and Journalism Funding Project, and State Media Monitor.

Manuel Goyanes is Associate Professor of Research Methods at Universidad Carlos III de Madrid. His interdisciplinary work revolves around theoretically designing, and empirically testing, cutting-edge quantitative and qualitative methodological procedures to scientifically address challenging aspects of social science inquiry.

Sheila Guerrero Rojas is a PhD candidate in the Department of Cognitive, Social, and Organizational Psychology at the University of La Laguna. She holds a BA in Advertising and Public Relations from the University of Nebrija, Spain and an MA in Audiovisual Communication and Advertising from the Autonomous University of Barcelona, Spain. Presently, she is engaged in research on Persuasive Communication at the University of La Laguna, Spain. Her research interests revolve around the psychological impacts of uncivil discussions and political communication on social media.

Michael Hameleers is Associate Professor in Political Communication at the University of Amsterdam, in the department Amsterdam School of

Communication Research (ASCoR). His research interests include (right-wing) populism, mis- and disinformation, and polarization. In his ongoing work, he aims to unravel how disinformation as both a genre and label fuels polarization along epistemic lines. He has published extensively on the effects of populist communication and disinformation, as well as the discursive construction of both phenomena.

R. Lance Holbert is Director of the Leonore Annenberg Institute for Civics and Research Professor within the University of Pennsylvania's Annenberg Public Policy Center. His political communication research focuses on democratic outcomes of media use. He is former Editor-in-Chief of the *Journal of Communication* and an International Communication Association Fellow. His recent field-general work focusing of theory development has appeared in such outlets as *Communication Theory*, *Human Communication Research*, and *ANNALS of the International Communication Association*.

Minna Aslama Horowitz is a docent at the University of Helsinki, a researcher at the Nordic Observatory for Digital Media and Information Disorder (NORDIS, https://nordishub.eu/), and a fellow at St. John's University, New York. She researches information harms and epistemic rights from the perspective European media policy, in particular those related to public service and media and information literacy.

María Luisa Humanes is Professor of Journalism at Rey Juan Carlos University. She holds a PhD in Communication from the Complutense University of Madrid and a Postgraduate Specialization in social research and data analysis techniques. She has previously taught at the Complutense University (1996–1997) and the University of Salamanca. Her research interests include communication theories and methods, the professionalization of journalism, and the analysis of journalistic discourse. Presently, she leads the Spanish team in the Journalistic Role Performance project.

Beatriz Jordá is a PhD candidate in the Department of Communication at Carlos III University of Madrid and an adjunct professor in the English department of Saint Louis University, Madrid Campus. She is also a former visiting scholar in the University of Gothenburg. Following both qualitative and quantitative methodologies, her research focuses on the study of persuasion in social media around political and social issues. Her recent work has appeared in journals such as *Journalism, the International Journal of Communication* or *PloS one*.

Luciana Musello is Lecturer in Media and Communication at Universidad San Francisco de Quito (USFQ) in Ecuador. Her research addresses the relationship between digital technologies, communication and society. Her interests include digital labor, the platformization of cultural production, and emerging business models for news media. She is also interested in the influence of power structures on internet infrastructure, democracy, and public service media. As a practitioner, she has managed the social media communication strategy of both academic and cultural initiatives in Ecuador.

Marta Rodríguez-Castro is Assistant Professor at the School of Communication Sciences of the Universidade de Santiago de Compostela (Spain), where she is part of the research group Novos Medios. Her main research lines involve public service media, which she studies from the perspective of public value creation and media policy. Her work has been published in journals such as *Journalism Studies, European Journal of Communication, Comunicar*, and *Journal of Information Policy*. She was visiting fellow at the Center for Media Data and Society at the Central European University (then in Budapest) and at the Hans-Bredow-Institut (Hamburg). She is part of the leadership team of the International Association of Public Media Researchers (IAPMR), and a member of the expert community at the Media and Journalism Research Center.

Samuel Toledano is Associate Professor in Journalism at the University of La Laguna. His academic career has focused on the right of free speech as a core value for democracies and the responsibility of the news media, public authorities, and political parties in protecting their citizens' right to be informed. He worked several years as a journalist for news agencies and newspapers in Spain and New York and as a political communication adviser and election observer in Latin America and Central Asia.

List of Figures

Fig. 7.1	Two dimensions of national resilience. Note: processed by the author	101
Fig. 13.1	COVID-19 and risk perception in Argentina. (Note: Least squares model describing differences)	219
Fig. 13.2	Original Tweet (*left*) and Correction as "True" or "False" (*right*). (Note: The figure shows the treatment when the authority issuing the original tweet is Infobae. Other rotations used the same tweet but alternated (rotated) the authorities of that post among Página|12, La Nación, and Clarín)	222
Fig. 13.3	Original post by @INFOen140, verification by Chequeado, and responses to the fact-check. (Note: The figure shows the treatment when the original tweet is issued by Infobae. Other rotations used the same tweet but alternated (rotated) the sources of the post among Página|12, La Nación, and Clarín)	225

LIST OF TABLES

Table 6.1   Theoretical approach to PSM's contribution to
            strengthening the digital public sphere   89
Table 8.1   Expectations-evaluations discrepancies   121
Table 10.1 Question wording for NFM and its subdimensions in the
            USA, Italy, and Portugal   158
Table 10.2 NFM confirmatory factor analysis comparison of a single
            factor vs. three-factor models   159

CHAPTER 1

Opinion Change and Democracy in Private Media, Public Service Media, and Social Media Platforms: An Introduction

Manuel Goyanes and *Azahara Cañedo*

As with any scholarly endeavor, the ultimate aim of this book is to understand, describe, reason, theorize, and—although often not explicitly stated or directly achieved—intellectually influence. Our focus is on the nature and effects of political persuasion, as it affects opinion change processes in democratic societies, within three of today's most pertinent media ecologies: public service media, private mass media, and social media platforms. The distinctions among these domains demand a nuanced understanding of the media's nature that enables the persuasive process, as well as the characteristics of those who persuade and are persuaded. The theoretical and empirical exploration of the dynamics of persuasion in mass media, along with its effects on public opinion, represents a major undertaking

M. Goyanes (✉)
Universidad Carlos III de Madrid, Getafe, Madrid, Spain
e-mail: mgoyanes@hum.uc3m.es

A. Cañedo
Universidad de Castilla-La Mancha, Cuenca, Spain
e-mail: azahara.canedo@uclm.es

© The Author(s), under exclusive license to Springer Nature Switzerland AG 2024
M. Goyanes, A. Cañedo (eds.), *Media Influence on Opinion Change and Democracy*, https://doi.org/10.1007/978-3-031-70231-0_1

1

traditionally associated with the social sciences in general and communication studies in particular. This book is grounded in, and aspires to modestly contribute to, this specific theoretical tradition.

The study of political persuasion has its roots in ancient Greece, notably in the seminal works of Aristotle and his "Rhetoric." In more recent times (1940–1950), Carl Hovland's studies furthered the understanding of the factors influencing the persuasive process. Additionally, during the 1940s, scholars such as Lazarsfeld and Berelson, in their seminal work *The People's Choice* (1948), provided new conceptual frameworks to examine the processes and mechanisms of political persuasion through their two-step flow of communication. In more contemporary scholarship, the Agenda-Setting hypothesis by Maxwell McCombs and Donald Shaw (1972) stands as perhaps the most influential contribution to the study of political persuasion, demonstrating how mass media shape public perceptions of issue salience, thereby establishing the public agenda.

Beyond these contributions, which can be considered the most influential in the field of communication so far, political persuasion has been the subject of study across a myriad of disciplines interested in opinion change, from psychology to political science. However, the recent surge in interest in political persuasion is fundamentally driven by the emergence—primarily on social media platforms but also within traditional media—of actors, channels, alternative discussion forums, and conspiracy theories aimed at influencing public opinion for political and chrematistic reasons, or merely social impact. These actors often trigger changes in opinions based on false or misleading arguments. This new informational paradigm is shaped, among many other factors, by the dissolution of traditional media gatekeepers on social media platforms and the proliferation of fake news and disinformation campaigns as tools for manipulation or political persuasion to achieve desired outcomes. In this context, falsehood and deception have increasingly become instruments of political communication.

However, the significant potential of social media as ecosystems for the dissemination of disinformation campaigns should not obscure the responsibility of both traditional media and new digital-native media in the current, unchecked media environment. In recent years, we have witnessed how major media outlets, both private and public, have progressively polarized their perspectives under the influence of emergent populist politics, defending political positions that are often difficult to reconcile with their purported editorial standards. This trend suggests that traditional media have increasingly transformed into instruments of the political communication system, serving propagandistic rather than informational purposes. Furthermore, the dynamics of the post-truth era, coupled with escalating political interference in the media—exacerbated by the precarious financial conditions of many traditional media organizations—have resulted in many such entities prioritizing the interests of the political class over their fundamental role as the fourth estate.

This book aims to explore the processes of political persuasion within three distinct media environments: public media, private media, and social media platforms. The differentiation among these environments is both relevant and necessary, as the dynamics of persuasion are significantly shaped by the affordances and modes of interaction inherent to each setting. For instance, on social media, shifts in political opinion through persuasive arguments (whether true or false) typically occur through political discussions, information dissemination, or expressions of political viewpoints. Conversely, in traditional media, such shifts are often precipitated unidirectionally. Additionally, the interaction dynamics on social networks enable direct connections—often public, though sometimes private, as exemplified by platforms like WhatsApp—between persuaders and the persuaded, resulting in complex relationships that obscure the understanding of the reach and efficacy of persuasion. Thus, this volume endeavors to enhance the comprehension of the persuasive process by constructing a theoretical and empirical framework that integrates the diverse dimensions of the media landscape and persuasive efforts.

As a result of this division into distinct media ecologies, the book adopts a structure that reflects this theoretical approach. Consequently, the volume features contributions from some of the foremost experts on persuasion in public media, private media, and social media. The selection of authors to explore and explain the dynamics of persuasion has been a complex process, given that most of them have long-term commitments and stable schedules. Furthermore, within the current academic framework, the format of publishing book chapters is not the most conducive to measuring scientific performance. Therefore, we would like to express our sincere gratitude to all the authors for their contributions to this volume, recognizing the significant effort they have made to provide their insights and adhere to the publisher's deadlines.

The book embarks on its journey by examining the first media scenario: private media. In this initial section, the book features four compelling chapters that provide theoretical insights into the state and processes of political persuasion. Chapter 2, "The Shift in Media Power: How Media

Capture Is Changing the Game" by Marius Dragomir, explores the significant transformation of the media landscape driven by technological advancements. This shift has disrupted traditional media revenue models, forcing print media to close and broadcasters to adapt. The chapter delves into the concept of media power, highlighting its historical roots and current complexities, emphasizing the undue influence wielded by large media corporations. Media capture, a phenomenon where political and economic interests control media content, is scrutinized for its detrimental impact on journalism, market competition, and democracy, posing severe threats to media diversity and pluralism.

Chapter 3, "Misinformation Campaigns, Populism, and the Role of Journalism" by Michael Hameleers, addresses the pervasive challenges of misinformation. Highlighting its impact on democracy, Hameleers defines misinformation as comprising intentional falsehoods (disinformation) and unintentional inaccuracies (misinformation). The chapter explores how misinformation manifests through perceptions of information accuracy, populist attacks on mainstream media, and the dissemination of inaccurate information. It underscores the erosion of trust and polarization in society. Through theoretical analysis, the chapter offers insights into combating misinformation's detrimental effects.

Chapter 4, "Journalistic Role Performance and Its Effects" by María Luisa Humanes, delves into the evolving relationship between journalism and its audience. While traditional journalism studies often overlook audience dynamics, Humanes emphasizes their pivotal role in shaping journalistic practices. Drawing from Shoemaker and Reese's hierarchy of influences analysis, the chapter highlights how audience interests influence journalistic routines. As media landscapes evolve, audiences become more active participants in content creation and consumption. Humanes explores how these changes impact audience perceptions and expectations of journalism. Unlike previous literature focusing on biases and misinformation, this chapter explores how the fulfillment of media functions affects audience trust and credibility perceptions. By prioritizing audience perspectives, Humanes seeks to advance audience studies beyond industry concerns.

In Chap. 5, "Big Data, Artificial Intelligence and Their Effects: The Birth of an Alert Society" by João Canavilhas, the evolving landscape of public opinion in the digital age is explored. The chapter discusses how traditional media's role in shaping public discourse has shifted with the rise of new media platforms, big data, and artificial intelligence. Canavilhas analyzes how these technologies influence the dissemination of information and the personalization of content, leading to the creation of an "alert society." This society is characterized by personalized messages delivered through smartphones, shaping individual actions and perceptions.

The second media scenario (persuasion and public service media) starts with Chap. 6, "Public Value and Liberal Democracies: The Potential of Public Service Media as Islands of Trust in the Digital Public Sphere" by Marta Rodríguez-Castro, which delves into the challenges faced by liberal democracies in the digital age, particularly concerning disinformation and the erosion of trust in the public sphere. Using Spain's prime minister Pedro Sánchez's unprecedented decision to reflect on his position amid allegations against his wife as a backdrop, the chapter explores the role of public service media (PSM) as "islands of trust" in navigating the digital public sphere. It argues that PSM, operating under a public value strategy, can counteract the threats to democracy by reinforcing excellence, universality, diversity, independence, citizen participation, and social justice. Through this lens, the chapter offers insights into revitalizing the public sphere and strengthening democracy.

Chapter 7, "Public Service Media and National Resilience in the Age of Information Disorders: A two-dimensional Conceptualization for Policy-Making," by Auksė Balčytienė and Minna Aslama Horowitz, delves into the critical role of PSM in fostering national resilience against information disorders in the digital age. The chapter proposes a two-dimensional conceptualization of resilience, encompassing structural considerations ("Information resilience") and individual epistemic capacities ("Epistemic resilience"). It emphasizes the pivotal role of PSM in providing reliable, diverse, and fact-based information to combat disinformation, enhance media literacy, and foster informed citizenship. Highlighting the challenges posed by the evolving media landscape, the chapter calls for a discursive policy shift to position PSM at the forefront of ensuring democratic resilience and public opinion formation.

Chapter 8, "The Role of Public Service Media in Democratic Engagement: An Audience Perspective," discusses Marcela Campos Rueda's work. The chapter explores PSM's pivotal role in democratic engagement, focusing on audience perspectives. It traces PSM's evolution from public service broadcasting (PSB) to public service media, highlighting challenges posed by technological advancements and societal shifts. Emphasizing citizen centrality, it advocates for adaptive practices in policymaking and content creation. The chapter delves into Spanish citizens' expectations of PSM, noting discrepancies between expectations and performance evaluations. Addressing concerns of independence amid political interventions, it proposes strategies to enhance credibility. Furthermore, it examines the impact of populist discourse on citizen attitudes and emphasizes fact-based discourse to counter misinformation. Finally, it advocates for a sustainable approach integrating audience insights to ensure PSM's continued democratic efficacy.

In Chap. 9, "Citizenship on the Public Service Internet: Citizen's Media Contribution to Reimagining Digital Democratic Communication," Luciana Musello delves into the dynamics of digital democratic communication. She highlights the shift of political discourse to corporate social media, prompting PSM to vie for citizens' communicative space. Amid this, the emergence of the public service Internet (PSI) offers a noncommercial digital infrastructure aimed at revitalizing democratic engagement. Musello advocates for aligning PSM with a "citizens' media" agenda, drawing from Latin American perspectives on citizenship and communication. By empowering users and emphasizing grassroots participation, the chapter seeks to challenge the dominance of corporate platforms and foster active citizenship in the digital realm.

The last block of contributions (persuasion and social media) starts with Chap. 10, "Origin and Evolution of the News Finds Me Perception: Review of Theory and Effects," by Homero Gil de Zúñiga and Zicheng Cheng, exploring the "News Finds Me" (NFM) perception, and examining how social media's rise has shifted news consumption from active seeking to passive receiving. The chapter reviews the origins, theories, and effects of NFM, highlighting how reliance on peers and algorithms influences perceived political awareness, often without intentional effort.

Chapter 11, "From Mass Media to Social Media: Political Persuasion in the Field of Communication" by Beatriz Jordá and R. Lance Holbert, explores the evolution of political persuasion research. The chapter examines the shift from traditional mass media to the current focus on social media's effects. It highlights how social media both reinforces preexisting beliefs and fosters political attitude change. The authors argue for a holistic approach to persuasion, considering its complexity and the interplay between attitude formation, reinforcement, and change. They also recommend future research directions, including narrative persuasion, entertainment content, and a broader view of persuasion.

Authored by Samuel Toledano, Sheila Guerrero Rojas, and Alberto Ardèvol-Abreu, Chap. 12 delves into the pervasive influence of fake news on political persuasion. Drawing on historical contexts and modern examples and entitled "Fake News Exposure and Political Persuasion," it explores how disinformation distorts truth, erodes trust in media, and fuels political polarization. Highlighting cognitive biases like motivated reasoning, the chapter underscores the dangers of misinformation in shaping public opinion and political behavior. It also examines potential solutions, from media literacy to fact-checking, in safeguarding democratic discourse against the onslaught of falsehoods.

Finally, in Chap. 13, "Content Sharing Dynamics and Political Polarization in Social Media," Natalia Aruguete analyzes the role of political and affective polarization in people's interactions on social media platforms. From a Latin American perspective, focusing on the Argentinean case, a democracy currently experiencing turbulent times, the author examines how moods and preconceived ideas influence the interpretation of news and messages on social media. In addition, she analyzes the relationship between the way the message is presented and the affective reactions it provokes in the users.

All in all, this book confirms that the media are and always should be a pillar of democratic societies. In this sense, we recognize that understanding their key role in shaping public opinion is crucial to upholding democratic values and promoting an informed citizenry. We therefore encourage our readers to remain vigilant in a changing media environment.

PART I

Opinion Change and Democracy in Private Media

CHAPTER 2

The Shift in Media Power: How Media Capture Is Changing the Game

Marius Dragomir ⓘ

THE MANY SHADES OF MEDIA POWER

The media landscape has undergone a profound transformation over the past couple of decades, largely driven by technological advancements. Media enterprises now rely heavily on the burgeoning tech industry to disseminate their content, as a growing segment of the population have turned to social media for information and entertainment. This shift has had a substantial impact on the advertising revenue that traditionally sustained privately owned media outlets, forcing them to confront a challenging business environment. Many print media organizations have shuttered or downsized significantly, while prominent broadcasters have had to restructure their strategies in order to stay competitive amid the influx of new content creators in the market.

M. Dragomir (✉)
Media and Journalism Research Center, Tallinn, Estonia

Central European University, Vienna, Austria

University of Santiago de Compostela, Santiago de Compostela, Spain
e-mail: mdragomir@journalismresearch.org

© The Author(s), under exclusive license to Springer Nature Switzerland AG 2024
M. Goyanes, A. Cañedo (eds.), *Media Influence on Opinion Change and Democracy*, https://doi.org/10.1007/978-3-031-70231-0_2

The myriad of these transformations has precipitated a restructuring of the news supply chains, fundamentally altering the power dynamic within global media markets.

The concept of media power has been thoroughly examined in scholarly works. It was initially associated with the advent of innovative technologies, which shaped historical events and sparked various trends, ranging from the influence of books on the Reformation to the role of the press in American democracy (de Tocqueville, 1838/2003) and the impact of media on the evolution of modernity in Europe (Tarde, 2010). By the 1920s, media technologies had emerged as a significant force, forming a "new constellation of power" (Starr, 2004: 385).

Over the course of the last eight decades, a solid body of literature of media power has been written, its focus shifting away from technologies toward a "new collective media logic that expresses the salience of information, symbols, and knowledge in the contemporary world" (Freedman, 2014: 5). The influence wielded by the media holds considerable sway across various sectors, encompassing politics, economics, and culture.

The inherent power of the media can prove advantageous in certain circumstances. Journalists employed by influential media organizations, for instance, benefit from enhanced safeguards against external assaults, whether emanating from governmental entities or private enterprises. These protections enable journalists to fulfill their professional obligations with autonomy, shielding them from undue influences or intimidations.

Conversely, media moguls consolidating considerable power through the expansion of their media empires exert significant influence in politics, business, and society at large (Street, 2001). Their capacity to influence elections by either championing or denigrating particular political factions and figures is undeniable. Furthermore, they have the ability to manipulate market dynamics by selectively criticizing certain enterprises over others (Noam, 2018). Ultimately, they have a profound capacity to mold public opinion and preferences by endorsing or disparaging ideas and values (Knee et al., 2009).

The significant influence exerted by large media companies is a natural progression as these privately held entities seek to leverage their competitive edge and financial prowess to outmaneuver rivals and enhance their bottom line. The issue arises when this influence becomes consolidated within a select few. In such instances, a cabal of media magnates holds the ability to shape the public agenda, suppressing dissenting viewpoints that run counter to their own political and economic interests. The undue centralization of media power further enables collusion between media tycoons and other influential figures, including political factions, individual policymakers, and corporate titans.

The implications of such undue influence extend to media diversity and pluralism, two fundamental tenets crucial to the functioning of the media in a democratic society (Raeijmaekers & Maeseele, 2015).

The excessive consolidation of media power, wherein media owners wield near-monopolistic control over the media ecosystem, presents a raft of grave threats to democracy. This concentration of media power is inherently undemocratic as it bestows authority upon unelected organizations and "undermines the ability of citizens to acquire and exchange the information and ideas necessary to make informed decisions about public life" (Freedman, 2014: 12). Moreover, the consolidation of media power undermines the integrity of the media market by enabling media corporations to amass substantial resources that can be leveraged to manipulate competition within the industry (Winseck, 2008).

Nevertheless, the economic power alone is not sufficient to explain the impact of concentrated media power. Some scholars argue that the influence of media companies has been disrupted by the emergence of powerful digital players. Other scholars suggest that media power should not solely be viewed through an economic lens, but as a complex interplay of "symbolic power of 'constructing reality' (both factual representations and credible fictions)" (Couldry, 2000: 4). This perspective highlights that media power is not a concrete entity controlled by institutions and imposed on audiences but rather a social process within the media landscape that produces content for consumption by nonmedia individuals (Freedman, 2014). Couldry emphasizes that media power is a multifaceted phenomenon, encompassing both cultural and economic dimensions. Corner further adds that media power consists of both structural and discursive elements, media power finding itself often in conflict with other forms of power (Corner, 2011).

The study of media power has therefore revealed the complexity beyond the conventional perception of media power as merely a manifestation of political influence wielded by a media tycoon or interest group, or the cultural influence of emerging technologies. According to Freedman (2014), media power in neoliberal Western societies defies simplistic explanations or attribution to a singular origin. A nuanced understanding of the intricate interplay between media entities and diverse institutions is essential in explaining how individuals receive information, acquire knowledge, and how their ability to engage in democratic processes is shaped and altered.

One key component of media power is the concentration of ownership (Noam, 2009). The strategic control over a growing array of media platforms enables owners to wield significant influence. Through concentrated ownership, media proprietors can expand their reach, enhancing their societal impact and financial standing. The allure of these outlets is heightened for those who hold political power who are drawn to the potential leverage such media power can provide.

As media owners align themselves with the ruling elite, we are witnessing a troubling trend of instrumentalization, wherein media organizations are compromising their editorial autonomy by bending their coverage in line with directions from governmental entities or corporate interests, or both (Mancini, 2012). This phenomenon poses a significant obstacle to journalistic integrity, as reporters are compelled to prioritize the financial or political agendas of their proprietors and superiors instead of serving their public.

Over the recent decades, heightened instrumentalization has led to a much harsher form of media control known as media capture. This phenomenon has been observed in numerous countries where influential figures in positions of political authority establish a framework of dominance over the media through mechanisms such as regulation, financial backing, and ownership (Schiffrin, 2021).

Media capture primarily relies on economic tactics, such as the use of public funds to support media outlets and the acquisition of media ownership, but this form of control also encompasses a cultural aspect evident in the shaping of editorial content to align with the agendas of the captors (government entities and affiliated businesses) while also catering to the preferences and requirements of the populace.

Four Main Elements of Media Capture

The emergence of media capture in a growing body of nations has been facilitated by a combination of factors, most notably the waning viability of the media industry as a result of economic downturns and the significant transformations in technology, which have had a profound impact on the operational frameworks of privately owned, commercially supported media outlets (Dragomir, 2019).

The term 'media capture' was initially introduced in academic discourse by economists drawing upon the concept of regulatory capture, a phenomenon in which regulators develop a bias toward the entities they are tasked with overseeing (Stigler, 1971). Economists have used the concept of capture to examine the political manipulation of the media within contexts of press freedom (Besley & Prat, 2006), the resulting political consequences of such manipulation (Corneo, 2006), and the deleterious effects of media capture on societal inequality (Petrova, 2008).

In recent decades, the phenomenon of media capture has garnered increasing attention from scholars in the fields of media studies and political science, leading to a more comprehensive examination of the concept. Political scientist Alina Mungiu-Pippidi has defined media capture as a condition in which the media lack autonomy to express independent viewpoints and fulfill their primary function of disseminating information to the public, remaining instead in a state of limbo, influenced by vested interests beyond just the government, thereby serving alternative agendas (Mungiu-Pippidi, 2013). Schiffrin has underscored a crucial aspect that sets media capture apart from other forms of governmental control and traditional instances of media ownership concentration: the involvement of both private entities and the government (Schiffrin, 2017).

In an effort to understand the phenomenon of media capture on a national scale, the author of this chapter has designed a media capture matrix based on empirical data gathered from a slew of countries (Dragomir & Söderström, 2022) grappling with various forms of control mechanisms. According to this matrix, media capture is a combination of four fundamental elements: control of regulatory bodies (regulatory capture), dominance over public/state media, discriminatory allocation of state financial resources, and acquisition of substantial portions of the private media industry.

These four developments must be present to lead to a situation of media capture by a select group of politicians and business magnates who wield unchecked influence over shaping the media narrative to suit their own interests (Dragomir, 2019).

The first element, regulatory capture emerges as a concerning issue, where government entities exert their influence to shape regulatory processes in favor of politically aligned individuals. Various regulatory bodies such as broadcast regulators, print media watchdogs, data regulators, and competition authorities hold decision-making powers that impact the licensing and operations of media channels (Dragomir, 2019). This phenomenon of regulatory capture is not novel, as governments worldwide have historically sought to manipulate regulatory processes to benefit their allies or media entities with ties to influential businessmen (Irion et al., 2019). However, in the context of media capture environments, the control exerted over media regulators is particularly strict, given their leading role as gatekeepers with the ability to significantly impact the operations of numerous media enterprises.

Furthermore, a crucial aspect of media capture lies in the control exerted over state and public service media. These institutions, akin to regulatory bodies, heavily rely on government funding for their operations and have governance structures often influenced by government-appointed officials (Benson & Powers, 2011). Efforts to revamp state media into public service entities have been undertaken in various regions over the last 30 years, spanning Eastern Europe, Latin America, Africa, and select Asian nations. Nevertheless, endeavors to establish contemporary, editorially autonomous public service platforms have largely faltered due to the reluctance of the political elite to relinquish control over these entities (Dragomir & Söderström, 2023).

In addition to regulatory authorities and public media, control of privately owned media is imperative for achieving capture. Two main mechanisms employed to attain a high degree of control over private media include the allocation of state funds to private media, particularly through state advertising, and the acquisition of private media ownership.

State funding serves as a potent tool in controlling privately owned media, particularly in the aftermath of prolonged economic downturns that have undermined the financial viability of the media industry. State advertising contracts, for instance, are strategically deployed to incentivize compliance with governmental directives by rewarding compliant media outlets with financial support, while simultaneously penalizing dissenting media entities by withholding state funds (Bátorfy & Urbán, 2020). The strategic manipulation of public funds to consolidate control over the media landscape carries significant implications for smaller media organizations, which, deprived of access to public funding, often find themselves grappling with severe financial hardships that ultimately force them into closure (Dragomir, 2018).

The acquisition of privately owned media outlets plays a crucial role in the architecture of media capture, facilitating extensive reach and market influence. As evidenced by instances of media capture, governments employ state-controlled entities or businesses affiliated with politically aligned individuals to procure these media assets. Often using state resources, these companies may disguise their acquisitions as loans, obtained from government or state-owned financial institutions, to finalize such transactions (Burazer, 2021).

The Impact of Capture

A group of scholars contend that the impact of media power is often exaggerated. As argued by Schudson, the news media has the ability to magnify certain viewpoints and bestow credibility upon individuals and organizations; however, the extent of its impact is not as profound as commonly believed (Schudson, 1982). Therefore, the argument goes, media power is limited, with consumers of news playing a crucial role in allowing this power to shape society. This is particularly evident in the current digital news landscape, characterized by a decentralized and fragmented structure, where the concentration of media power has reached its limitations (Jarvis, 2009).

A separate cohort of academics on the other hand have cautioned against underestimating the influence of media, viewing it as either a fundamental component of modern existence (Kittler, 1999) or as a disruptive force driven by technology (Downes, 2009). Freedman (2014) instead advocates for a more nuanced perspective on media power, acknowledging its potential to shape society and impact individuals and institutions, albeit within the broader context of competing forces vying for resources (Corner, 2011).

The concept of media capture takes the discourse surrounding media influence to a more complex level, more aligned with the assertions of scholars cautioning against the underestimation of media power. The immediate repercussions of media capture encompass the heightened barriers to entry, as new players, particularly smaller entities, are impeded from obtaining broadcast licenses or other regulatory advantages due to governmental control over regulatory bodies. Furthermore, in contexts characterized by capture, the government obstructs access to public funds for media outlets with independent editorial coverage, while ensuring that governance bodies of public and state media are filled with individuals closely aligned with the authorities to uphold governmental interests. Additionally, a significant portion of private media operators are coerced by their owner to adhere to the official agenda.

A plethora of scholarly investigations studying the concept of media capture have surfaced; however, a more comprehensive analysis of its repercussions is imperative to grasp the varied transformations it instigates across multiple spheres. Empirical evidence suggests that capture has a highly detrimental effect on journalism and market and influences to a high degree the audiences during key democratic events, particularly elections (Dragomir, 2024).

When it comes to journalism, the effects of media capture are vast and enduring. In environments where a substantial portion of the media industry is under government control, the opportunities for unbiased journalism are significantly diminished. This ultimately results in a decline in professional standards, increased polarization, and a weakened presence of the media sector as a whole.

In countries struggling with media capture, swathes of media entities have been acquired by oligarchic entities with ties to governmental authorities, these outlets being repurposed as propaganda platforms to serve the interests of both the ruling business elite and the government. In environments heavily influenced by such capture, pro-government forces collaborate to synchronize their editorial strategies, effectively operating as cogs in a centralized propaganda machine. A prime example of this trend can be observed in Hungary, where a concerted effort to consolidate media control has culminated in the establishment of the Central European Press and Media Foundation (KESMA). This foundation, spearheaded by loyalists aligned with Prime Minister Orbán's administration, brought under its control a total of 476 media outlets, all of which were transferred to the foundation by their pro-government owners (Griffen, 2020).

The exponential growth of propaganda media has also resulted in a degradation of professionalism. The media ecosystem in captured environments is characterized by a stark contrast between a dominant sector that thrives on substantial public backing and a vulnerable, diminishing cluster of independent media that relies on meager financial resources, predominantly from philanthropic contributions or audience support. In such a milieu, ethical norms and standards are disregarded, with journalists in state-controlled media willingly serving as purveyors of government-approved messaging. In countries like Zimbabwe, government officials aligned with the ruling party Zanu-PF employ significant influence over the editorial direction of the nation's public media outlets (Mabweazara et al., 2020).

In captured environments, government control over the editorial agenda also has pernicious effects on the quality of news content. Within media-captured systems, the public narrative is largely shaped by the government propaganda machine, which disseminates messages aligned with the authorities' interests. This erosion of journalistic standards not only undermines the professional reputation of journalists but also exacerbates political polarization, with adverse implications for the quality of democracy.

In parallel with this development, media capture also leads to "structural polarization of the news environment" (Klimkiewicz, 2021), a phenomenon that turns the media landscape into a battleground between outlets aligned with the government and those scrutinizing the governing bodies. In such a context, impartial reporting on contemporary events becomes increasingly scarce.

De-professionalization, structural polarization, and escalating instability together have a profound impact on the journalistic profession within captured environments, where adherence to journalistic standards and norms is becoming increasingly challenging amid the dominance of well-funded propaganda channels.

The phenomenon of media capture exerts a significantly disruptive influence on media markets, too, particularly impacting their level of competitiveness. Within captured media environments, dominant government-controlled media entities benefit from preferential regulations and financial backing from the state, thereby gaining a substantial competitive edge over independent media organizations. Market distortion emerges as a prominent consequence of capture in many highly affected media systems, with clear manifestations of this trend evident in regions such as Central and Eastern Europe (Dragomir, 2024).

State advertising serves as a potent instrument used to manipulate the market in favor of state-affiliated media entities. In countries like Serbia, where the authorities and their affiliated enterprises exert significant control over a string of media platforms, this phenomenon presents a formidable obstacle to the sustainability of independent journalism. Government-backed outlets, operating at both the national and local levels, enjoy a considerable competitive advantage, largely due to the substantial financial support they regularly receive from the state (Burazer, 2021).

Across Latin America, where media ownership concentration ranks among the highest globally, dominant players in the industry command substantial market power. In this context, governments, often engaged in contentious relationships with major media corporations, leverage state advertising as a means to garner support from these influential entities. Argentina exemplifies this dynamic, with state advertising playing a crucial role in the operations of media conglomerates. During the tenure of Alberto Fernández, for example, the government allocated approximately US$180 million in advertising expenditures between December 2019 and August 2022, with a significant portion directed toward the country's leading media groups (Mastrini et al., 2023). In Africa, national governments emerge as the primary patrons of the news media landscape. In Rwanda, for instance, industry insiders estimate that up to 90% of advertising expenditure originates from state coffers (Ogola, 2017).

Media capture also significantly impacts the advertising landscape, reshaping the strategies and flow of commercial advertisements. Governmental influence permeates key sectors, whether through corporate entities aligned with the ruling regime or via state bodies and politically affiliated regulators whose mandates hold sway over businesses. Consequently, many enterprises opt to steer clear of independent media platforms, apprehensive of potential repercussions stemming from official quarters.

In Czechia, a formerly robust media landscape has been significantly altered by the involvement of Andrej Babiš, a wealthy oligarch with control over a major industrial conglomerate, in the leadership of Mafra, a prominent publishing entity. This development had a profound effect on advertising practices, with numerous businesses opting to withdraw their advertisements from independent media outlets out of concern for potential repercussions from the Babiš-affiliated authorities (Klima, 2022).

Media capture also poses a significant challenge to the sustainability of media outlets, as the overwhelming influence of government-aligned media skews the competitive landscape. This phenomenon allows businesses with close ties to the government to amass considerable market dominance, further exacerbated by preferential access to state resources. Consequently, independent media organizations are left financially vulnerable, lacking financial support from the state and facing dwindling advertising revenues. This financial strain often leads to a reduction in operational capacity. Additionally, media capture stifles innovation and investment in the industry, as the presence of government-controlled giants deters potential investors. The saturation of state-funded content in captured media environments hinders the introduction of alternative business models, such as subscription services, further entrenching the status quo (Nussipov, 2019).

Finally, the impact of capture on audiences, whether they be engaged citizens in a democratic society or consumers of media content influencing their political and consumer choices, holds significant weight. Nevertheless, the examination of this facet of capture remains limited, particularly in terms of data that can explain the extent to which people's decision-making is influenced by exposure to captured media.

Recent research has shed some light on the intricate relationship between media capture and the distortion of collective decision-making processes, particularly within the realm of politics. The concentration of wealth at high levels has been identified as a key factor contributing to increased corruption within the media landscape, enabling affluent individuals to acquire media entities for the purpose of influencing public opinion (Corneo, 2006).

The outcomes of elections serve as a telling barometer of the extent to which captured media can influence the choices of the populace. A relevant case study can be found in Hungary, where the right-wing party Fidesz has maintained a firm grip on power since 2010, largely due to an extensive propaganda apparatus consisting of numerous media platforms controlled by its oligarchs. An exposé detailing the encroachment of capture in Hungary reveals that, as of 2017, the majority of the country's 18 local newspapers have fallen under the ownership of allies of Prime Minister Orbán, resulting in a noticeable homogenization of their editorial content (Nolan, 2019).

Government manipulation of the news agenda has been shown to have a significant impact on the political landscape, as indicated by research examining the relationship between media capture and political outcomes (Besley & Prat, 2006). A study conducted as part of Illiberal Turn, a research project conducted by the Loughborough University in the United Kingdom, revealed a clear inverse relationship between individuals' views on immigration and their consumption of public service media in nations where the media is under government control, such as Hungary and Poland (Kondor et al., 2022).

However, in certain media environments where information dissemination is heavily influenced, the effectiveness of propaganda is lower (Enikolopov & Petrova, 2015). For example, transparency regarding the origins of media content enables individuals to discern the controllers of the information they consume, leading some to occasionally question the credibility of such sources (Jie et al., 2014). In some instances, propaganda runs the risk of backfiring if the narrative presented starkly contrasts or directly contradicts the beliefs held by the audience (Maja et al., 2015).

CONCLUSION

Media capture as a novel power-related phenomenon has become increasingly prevalent over the past decade in a variety of countries spanning from Hungary and Poland in Eastern Europe to Turkey, Nicaragua in Central America, Egypt in the Middle East and North Africa (MENA) region, and Cambodia in Southeast Asia, among many others.

Anchored in the collusion between influential, often autocratic, governments and corporate interests in seizing and manipulating media platforms to advance a narrative that promotes the government's agenda and protects the privileged access of a political and business elite to public assets, media capture has serious consequences for democracy.

Ushering in a novel paradigm of power, media capture has an enduring and damaging impact on the integrity and autonomy of journalism, as well as the competitiveness of the media market, ultimately posing grave repercussions for societies at large, engendering substantial disparities in the dissemination of information and engagement in democratic processes.

REFERENCES

Bátorfy, A., & Urbán, Á. (2020). State advertising as an instrument of transformation of the media market in Hungary. *East European Politics, 36*(1), 44–65. https://doi.org/10.1080/21599165.2019.1662398

Benson, R., & Powers, M. (2011). *Public media and political independence. Lessons for the future of journalism from around the world.* New York University.

Besley, T., & Prat, A. (2006). Handcuffs for the grabbing hand? Media capture and government accountability. *American Economic Review, 96*(3), 720–736. https://doi.org/10.1257/aer.96.3.720

Burazer, N. (2021). Media capture – An increasing threat to Serbian Democracy. *Südosteuropa Mitteilungen, 2–3*, 29–38.

Corneo, G. (2006). Media capture in a democracy: The role of wealth concentration. *Journal of Public Economics, 90*(1–2), 37–58. https://doi.org/10.1016/j.jpubeco.2005.08.002

Corner, J. (2011). *Theorising media: Power, form and subjectivity.* Manchester University Press.

Couldry, N. (2000). *The place of media power: Pilgrims and witnesses of the media age*. Routledge.
De Tocqueville, A. (1838/2003). *Democracy in America*. Lawbook Exchange.
Downes, L. (2009). *The laws of disruption: Harnessing the new forces that govern life and business in the digital age*. Basic Books.
Dragomir, M. (2018). Control the money, control the media: How government uses funding to keep media in line. *Journalism, 19*(8), 1131–1148. https://doi.org/10.1177/1464884917724621
Dragomir, M. (2019). *Media capture in Europe*. Media Development Investment Fund (MDIF). https://www.mdif.org/wp-content/uploads/2023/10/MDIF-Report-Media-Capture-in-Europe.pdf
Dragomir, M. (2024). The capture effect. How media capture affects journalists, markets and audiences. *Central European Journal of Communication*.
Dragomir, M., & Söderström, A. (2022). *The State of State Media. A global analysis of the editorial independence of state media based on the state media matrix* (2022 ed.). Media and Journalism Research Center. https://journalismresearch.org/wp-content/uploads/2022/10/State-Media-2022.pdf
Dragomir, M., & Söderström, A. (2023). *From puppet to powerhouse: A global study of the independence of state and public media*. Media and Journalism Research Center. https://journalismresearch.org/wp-content/uploads/2023/12/State-Media-2023.pdf
Enikolopov, R., & Petrova, M. (2015). Chapter 17: Media capture: Empirical evidence. In S. P. Anderson, J. Waldfogel, & D. Strömberg (Eds.), *Handbook of media economics* (Vol. 1, pp. 687–700). North-Holland. https://doi.org/10.1016/B978-0-444-63685-0.00017-6
Freedman, D. (2014). *The contradictions of media power*. Bloomsbury Publishing.
Griffen, S. (2020). Hungary: A lesson in media control. *British Journalism Review, 31*(1), 57–62. https://doi.org/10.1177/0956474820910071
Irion, K., Delinavelli, G., Coutinho, M. F., Fathaigh, R. Ó., Jusić, T., Klimkiewicz, B., et al. (2019). *The independence of media regulatory authorities in Europe*. European Audiovisual Observatory. https://rm.coe.int/the-independence-of-media-regulatory-authorities-in-europe/168097e504
Jarvis, J. (2009). *What would Google do?* Collins Business.
Jie, B., Golosov, M., Qian, N., & Kai, Y. (2014). *Understanding the influence of government controlled media: Evidence from air pollution in China*. Working Paper.
Kittler, F. (1999). *Gramophone, film, typewriter*. Stanford University Press.
Klima, M. (2022). *Media capture in the Czech Republic: Lessons learnt from the Babiš era and how to rebuild defences against media capture*. IPI. https://ipi.media/wp-content/uploads/2022/03/Media-Capture-in-the-czech-Republic.pdf

Klimkiewicz, B. (2021). The public sphere and the changing news media environment in Poland: Towards structural polarisation. *Javnost – The Public, 28*(1), 53–74. https://doi.org/10.1080/13183222.2021.1861408

Knee, J. A., Greenwald, B. C., & Seave, A. (2009). *The curse of the mogul: What's wrong with the world's leading media companies.* Penguin.

Kondor, K., Mihelj, S., Štětka, V., & Tóth, F. (2022). News consumption and immigration attitudes: A mixed methods approach. *Journal of Ethnic and Migration Studies, 48*(17), 4129–4148. https://doi.org/10.1080/1369183X.2022.2054786

Mabweazara, H. M., Muneri, C. T., & Ndlovu, F. (2020). News "media capture", relations of patronage and clientelist practices in Sub-Saharan Africa: An interpretive qualitative analysis. *Journalism Studies, 21*(15), 2154–2175. https://doi.org/10.1080/1461670X.2020.1816489

Maja, A., Enikolopov, R., Petrova, M., Santarosa, V., & Zhuravskaya, E. (2015). Radio and the rise of the Nazis in prewar Germany. *Quarterly Journal of Economics, 130*(4), 1885–1939. https://www.jstor.org/stable/26372641

Mancini, P. (2012). Instrumentalization of the media vs. political parallelism. *Chinese Journal of Communication, 5*(3), 262–280. https://doi.org/10.1080/17544750.2012.701415

Mastrini, G. N., Repetto, C. B., Espada, A., & Razzeto, M. (2023). *Media and journalism in Argentina: Politics, money and technology.* Media and Journalism Research Center. https://journalismresearch.org/wp-content/uploads/2023/10/Argentina-COMPLETE-MIM-2023.pdf

Mungiu-Pippidi, A. (2013). Freedom without impartiality. The vicious circle of media capture. In P. Gross & K. Jakubowicz (Eds.), *Media transformations in the post-Communist world* (pp. 33–47). Lexington Books.

Noam, E. (2009). *Media ownership and concentration in America.* Oxford University Press.

Noam, E. (2018). Beyond the mogul: From media conglomerates to portfolio media. *Journalism, 19*(8), 1096–1130. https://doi.org/10.1177/1464884917725941

Nolan, D. (2019). Remote controller: What happens when all major media, state and private, is controlled by Hungary's government and all the front pages start looking the same. *Index on Censorship, 48*(1), 54–56. https://doi.org/10.1177/0306422019842100

Nussipov, A. (2019). *Media influence matrix: Kazakhstan. Funding journalism.* Center for Media, Data and Society.

Ogola, G. (2017, April 18). How African governments use advertising as a weapon against media freedom. *The Conversation.* https://theconversation.com/how-african-governments-use-advertising-as-a-weapon-against-media-freedom-75702

Petrova, M. (2008). Inequality and media capture. *Journal of Public Economics*, 92(1–2), 183–212. https://doi.org/10.1016/j.jpubeco.2007.04.004

Raeijmaekers, D., & Maeseele, P. (2015). Media, pluralism and democracy: What's in a name? *Media, Culture and Society*, 37(7), 1042–1059. https://doi.org/10.1177/0163443715591670

Schiffrin, A. (Ed.). (2017). *In the service of power: Media capture and the threat to democracy*. National Endowment for Democracy. https://www.cima.ned.org/resource/service-power-media-capture-threat-democracy/

Schiffrin, A. (Ed.). (2021). *Media capture: How money, digital platforms, and governments control the news*. Columbia University Press.

Schudson, M. (1982). *The power of news*. Harvard University Press.

Starr, P. (2004). *The creation of the media: Political origins of modern communications*. Basic Books.

Stigler, G. (1971). The theory of economic regulation. *The Bell Journal of Economics and Management Science*, 2(1), 3. https://doi.org/10.2307/3003160

Street, J. (2001). Conglomerate control: Media moguls and media power. In J. Street (Ed.), *Mass media, politics and democracy* (pp. 124–144). Springer.

Tarde, G. (2010). *On communication and social influence: Selected papers*. University of Chicago Press.

Winseck, D. (2008). The state of media ownership and media markets: Competition or concentration and why should we care? *Sociology Compass*, 2(1), 34–47. https://doi.org/10.1111/j.1751-9020.2007.00061.x

CHAPTER 3

Misinformation Campaigns, Populism, and the Role of Journalism

Michael Hameleers ⓘ

INTRODUCTION

Citizens are increasingly concerned about encountering false information and 'fake news' in their newsfeeds. About 50% of all news users across different regions in the world indicate that they find it difficult to discern between true and fake news (Newman et al., 2023). A similar proportion of news users is more likely to distrust than to trust the media. These severe epistemic issues may be explained against the backdrop of the fast-paced diffusion of misinformation and accusations of false information targeted at the media and journalists. Indeed, 'misinformation'—here defined as an umbrella term for either intentionally false (disinformation) or unintentionally false (misinformation) (also, see e.g., Wardle & Derakhshan, 2017)—has been regarded as an undermining or disruptive force for democracy (e.g., Bennett & Livingston, 2018). Misinformation may result in confusion about which sources, media channels, or

M. Hameleers (✉)
University of Amsterdam, Amsterdam, Netherlands
e-mail: M.Hameleers@uva.nl

© The Author(s), under exclusive license to Springer Nature Switzerland AG 2024
M. Goyanes, A. Cañedo (eds.), *Media Influence on Opinion Change and Democracy*, https://doi.org/10.1007/978-3-031-70231-0_3

statements to trust, and cause cynicism related to established institutions, such as the media or science.

In this chapter, we consider the challenges of misinformation embedded in a wider context of distrust, delegitimizing attacks on journalism, and the prevalence of populist beliefs that emphasize a central boundary between 'honest' people and 'deceptive' others, including widespread attacks on the media considered as an enemy of the people. Crucially, we regard misinformation as a three-faced problem throughout this chapter: it exists as a perception related to the honesty and accuracy of information, a (populist) accusation targeted at the mainstream media or other knowledge disseminators, and an information-based threat related to the dissemination of information that is inaccurate and/or not based on relevant expert knowledge (Vraga & Bode, 2020). Together, these three elements of misinformation may contribute to increasing relativism toward factual information, distrust in established information, and polarization related to alternative versions of reality and the truth surrounding key events, such as immigration, climate change, and health-related issues.

The chapter will proceed in the following ways. First of all, an overview of the democratic consequences and persuasiveness of the three different aspects of misinformation will be presented. After this, the integration of the three elements or faces of the misinformation disorder will be discussed. Here, the chapter will forward a theoretical account of how misinformation perceptions, accusations of fake news and exposure to falsehoods may together contribute to the erosion of agreement on basic facts, and an epistemic democracy where truths are subject to polarization. By delving deeper into the overtime processes responsible for these developments, the chapter offers a starting point for interventions and new research lines on the downward spiral of misinformation.

The Three Faces of Misinformation: Exposure to Falsehoods, Perceived Misinformation, and Fake News Accusations

Exposure to False Information

Most research to date has looked at misinformation from the perspective of disseminators or recipients of false information. In this case, misinformation is seen as information that is false or inaccurate, and not in line with relevant expert knowledge (Vraga & Bode, 2020). A distinction between misinformation and disinformation is often made in the literature. Misinformation refers to unmotivated errors, or false information that is not created or disseminated with the intention to deceive recipients (Wardle & Derakhshan, 2017). Disinformation, in contrast, refers to intentionally false information that may be created or spread to fuel cynicism, amplify political divides, delegitimize political actors or issue positions, and sow confusion in domestic and foreign settings (e.g., Bennett & Livingston, 2018; Chadwick & Stanyer, 2022; Freelon & Wells, 2020). Often, disinformation is associated with the radical right wing or the strategic delegitimizing communication of populist actors (e.g., Marwick & Lewis, 2017). Resonating with populism's binary outlook on reality and politics, disinformation may emphasize a distinction between social groups, and create a delegitimizing narrative that attacks the out-group, such as immigrants, ethnic minorities, scientists, and journalists.

Although some literature has indicated that disinformation or misinformation may be easy to distinguish from true content (e.g., Damstra et al., 2021), this position has been challenged in more recent studies. Crucially, to come across as a legitimate alternative narrative to conventional knowledge, disinformation often (strategically) mimics the styles and claims of established information (Hameleers & Yekta, 2023). To offer an example, disinformation may rely on alternative (fake) experts, decontextualized statistical information, or visual content taken out of the context to offer seemingly authentic proof for misleading statements (Brennen et al., 2021). Thus, although disinformation could rely on emotions, a circumvention of experts and an appeal to the sentiments of ordinary people, it may also rely on more conventional and accepted modes of truth-telling that are traditionally deemed as trustworthy arguments. This may explain disinformation's persuasiveness: by offering seemingly authentic and legitimate proof for deceptive claims, it may be accepted as truthful information by recipients. Especially in a context where multiple truth claims on the same issues are in constant competition for acceptance and legitimacy (Waisbord, 2018), people who are uncertain about what to believe may be drawn to disinformation narratives that resonate and respond to their distrust in established institutions. Why would people believe established truth claims on COVID-19, climate change or immigration when the alternative narrative spread by disinformation actors is also substantiated by expert knowledge, visual proof, and statistical evidence?

This question does raise the issue of the conditionality of disinformation's persuasiveness. Not all citizens are attracted to disinformation, and not all recipients may be persuaded by the arguments that are presented. In this setting, extant literature suggests that disinformation may mostly appeal to people with similar beliefs as expressed in the false information, which means that the effects of disinformation follow a confirmation bias (e.g., Hameleers et al., 2020). As a specific example of this bias, Zimmermann and Kohring (2020) found that disinformation had the strongest effects for people distrusting the media.

This can partially be explained as a result of the congruence between disinformation's statements and people's existing beliefs related to the conventional information disseminated by the established press. In other words: counterfactual claims may be most persuasive among people who perceive that established accounts of reality are dishonest or inaccurate. On a societal level, this may indicate that disinformation has a polarizing effect on issue attitudes: people distrusting established institutions and mainstream media may select disinformation's alternative narrative. The delegitimizing claims they encounter may reinforce their distrust in the established institutions, and make the selection of more disinformation likely. On the other end of the divide, in contrast, more trusting citizens who are not cynical toward the mainstream media and knowledge disseminators may not select disinformation, or actively seek information that disproves disinformation's delegitimizing narrative (i.e., through fact-checks). The poles of society that either cling on to established facts or alternative facts disseminated through disinformation may therefore become further apart over time.

Despite this potential disruptive consequence, we should relativize and contextualize the threats of disinformation in the wider information ecosystem. Despite popular concerns that misinformation and fake news are all around, recent empirical evidence shows that disinformation may be a relatively marginal phenomenon. Specifically, less than 1% of people's general media diet may consist of false information (e.g., Acerbi et al., 2022). This means that the great majority of all information that people come across is factually accurate. Although some contexts may be less resilient to disinformation than others—such as visual communication on Facebook (Yang et al., 2023)—people are much more likely to encounter trustworthy or honest information than information that intends to mislead them. This also places the polarizing potential of disinformation into perspective: although distrusting or uncertain citizens may be drawn to disinformation, the large majority of citizens may mostly be exposed to information that is trustworthy. Disinformation may stand out more, and may spread quickly among certain network when it contains a shocking, disruptive, and negative appeal, but we should not overestimate its potential to directly persuade the majority of citizens in the current information landscape.

Perceived Misinformation

Despite the observation that misinformation may not permeate the information ecosystem, people are very concerned about false information and their ability to distinguish it from reliable content. As exemplified by the Reuters Digital News Report, about half of all participants across dispersed regions in the world is very concerned about misinformation online (Newman et al., 2023). In light of this, there may be a discrepancy between the risk perceptions related to encountering and recognizing false information and the actual scope of misinformation as an informational disorder. Hence, although misinformation may be relatively likely in some high-risk settings—such as hyper-partisan alternative media (e.g., Hameleers & Yekta, 2023; Heft et al., 2019)—people encounter it far less than they think (e.g., Acerbi et al., 2022). But what are the consequences of perceiving that information is false and what happens when this risk perception is blown out of proportion?

Beliefs related to the lack of facticity and unmotivated errors (misinformation perceptions) have different consequences than beliefs related to goal-directed and intentional falsehoods (disinformation beliefs) (Hameleers et al., 2020). Misinformation beliefs, at least to a moderate extent, correspond more to the democratic ideal of a critical citizenry that possess the motivation and ability to verify information, and to doubt content that is suspicious and different from familiar or existing cognitions related to persons, situations, or beliefs. People who perceive that actors unwillingly disseminate false information in some conditions may be better able to hold untrustworthy sources accountable and may actively approach alternative sources of information to compensate for the lack of facticity in previously encountered information (Hameleers et al., 2020).

This is different for disinformation beliefs. Disinformation beliefs correspond to systematic levels of cynicism related to the intentions of communicators, and thus extend the scope of facticity ratings. As disinformation beliefs deny the honesty and well-intended nature of information sources, they may not invite the approach of novel information or the careful processing of (faulty) message arguments (Hameleers et al., 2020). More specifically, if people perceive that the media or other knowledge disseminators are lying to them motivated by the intention to gain profit or harm opponents (Hameleers et al., 2021), they may selectively avoid all established information sources. Such more cynical beliefs correspond to the widespread belief among (right-wing) populist voters that the media are an enemy of the people that spread fake news (e.g., Schulz et al., 2020). In the context of disinformation beliefs, empirical evidence around the COVID-19 pandemic reveals that beliefs related to the intended manipulation, fabrication, or dissemination of falsehoods lower compliance with official guidelines, correspond to the rejection of established information sources, and overall result in nondemocratic tendencies (Hameleers et al., 2020).

Taken together, it is important to approach mis- or disinformation as wider issues that also involve people's beliefs related to false or deceptive information, which is especially relevant to consider in a context of mounting distrust in knowledge dissemination, polarization around factual information, and the weaponization of misinformation by radical (populist) actors. As we know little about how risk perceptions or concerns related to misinformation correspond with the scope of mis- and disinformation across various communication contexts, focusing on perceptions is also relevant in the context of actual exposure to misinformation. In an ideal world, people's perceptions about the risks and resilience to misinformation should correspond with the likelihood of encountering actual misinformation. When they under- or overestimate misinformation's scope and influence, negative democratic perceptions of disproportionate risk perceptions may be observed—such as (systematic) media avoidance or the approach of alternative factual claims driven by cynicism. More generally, focusing on the connection between misinformation as an information threat and a perceptual threat, an important hypothesis that warrants testing across contexts is that inflated concerns about intentionally false information motivate the selection of actual disinformation that resonates with people's perceptions about the untrustworthiness of conventional information sources.

Disinformation as a Label: Fake News as a Weaponized Term

In a context where perceptions of falsehoods are omnipresent, it may be highly effective to accuse others and opposed constructions of reality of being fake news. Hence, more than half of the world population distrusts the news, and is (very) concerned about recognizing false information and distinguishing it from the truth (Newman et al., 2023). Amid such a crisis of trust, facts and truths have become relative, partisan, and competitive (Van Aelst et al., 2017). Facts are dismissed as opinions or even lies in a context where all information may be doubted or seen as potentially fabricated. Thus, the widespread discussions and concerns about the problems surrounding mis- and disinformation may have created the perfect storm for a delegitimizing fake news discourse (e.g., Waisbord, 2018).

In this setting, the distinction between fake news as a label versus genre has been particularly relevant (Egelhofer & Lecheler, 2019). Hence, fake news is not just false and deceptive information (a genre of information that is untrue) but also something that is used as a blame-shifting tool, often used in right-wing populism to blame the elites or mainstream media for spreading disinformation and untruths. This blame-shifting discourse strongly resonates with the core ideas of populism, as it emphasizes a moral and causal divide between the honest ordinary people and the corrupt and lying others that do not represent the people in an accurate and honest manner. Not surprisingly, fake news as a label is a communication strategy found to be prominent among right-wing populist politicians in Western democracies (Farhall et al., 2019). But why would politicians or other actors accuse the media or opposed political elites of spreading disinformation?

One of the central aims of populist rhetoric—and disinformation—is to enhance cynicism toward the established order, sow discord, and polarize societies (e.g., Bennett & Livingston, 2018). Disinformation accusations may be useful in this regard as they delegitimize the establishment and enhance (deep) factual disagreements between camps in society that may not cling on to a shared factual reality (Van Aelst et al., 2017). Importantly, extant research has found that disinformation accusations have real consequences that may be in line with the intended goal: Exposure to accusations of disinformation lowers news trust, and may contribute to the belief that established institutions are dishonest (e.g., Egelhofer et al., 2022; Van Duyn & Collier, 2019). Just like actual disinformation, then, blaming other actors of spreading false information intentionally may cause epistemic confusion and distrust, which may pave the way for the anti-establishment narratives of populist contenders.

The weaponization of fake news and disinformation, or related terms that are used to blame opposed actors for deceiving the people, does not stand in isolation of other aspects of the disinformation order. Hence, in a context of high trust in the media and low populist success, fake news accusations may have a small impact, and may be much less prevalent. The context of distrust in established institutions combined with relativism or uncertainty about facts and disinformation may offer a discursive opportunity structure that can be exploited by malicious actors to attack and erode the fabric of democracy. This brings us to the core argument of this chapter that is developed further in the next section: disinformation as an informational, perceptual, and discursive threat is a part of the same epistemic crisis fueled by contextual factors that may have been neglected in current approaches and counterstrategies.

Fueling a Spiral of Distrust? Disinformation as an Epistemic Disorder

The three faces of disinformation come together in a context of an epistemic crisis. As it is difficult to establish a fixed causal order between disinformation as informational genre, a delegitimizing label, and a perception of citizens, we postulate that disinformation is part of a reinforcing downward spiral of distrust. In other words, by means of example, disinformation perceptions may be both cause and consequence of the weaponized use of fake news and exposure to actual disinformation. In a similar vein, disinformation as a genre may have a wider impact on society because of its political use in right-wing populism that creates a discursive opportunity structure for the spread of disinformation. To disentangle the spiral for conceptual purposes, we can distinguish between disinformation's causes and contexts, exposure and selection, and consequences.

The Causes and Context of Disinformation

The widespread belief that disinformation is omnipresent, and increasing levels of skepticism toward truth claims of the established order, can be regarded as the context that shapes the pervasiveness of disinformation. Arguably, today's fragmented digital landscape can be regarded as consisting of multiple epistemic communities (Waisbord, 2018). Here, multiple claims on reality compete for the audience's attention, whereas various modes of truth-telling are exploited to make competing claims seem legitimate (Hameleers & Yekta, 2023). This may cause confusion among citizens, who either may lose trust in all information or selectively pick a fitting version of reality to reaffirm their identity. Either way, trust in established claims on reality may be eroding due to the constant attack on the narratives disseminated by the mainstream, which connect to the 'fake news' label also involved in the spiral of distrust and epistemic polarization surrounding disinformation. Concretely, both the abundance of legitimized counterfactual narratives and the delegitimization of established truths may erode trust and create an appeal for disinformation narratives that share this delegitimizing perspective on sociopolitical reality. The three aspects of disinformation thus come together in shaping a context of distrust, factual relativism, uncertainty, and epistemic communities. This context may be exploited by malicious actors to raise cynicism, push alternative narratives, or divide the electorate.

Exposure and Selection of Disinformation

Literature on confirmation-biased selective exposure predicts that people have a tendency to expose themselves to information that reassures their prior beliefs (e.g., Knobloch-Westerwick et al., 2020). Due to such cognitive processes influencing selection of information in an overburdened information setting, disinformation may be most influential for people with higher perceptions of disinformation. Hence, people with low trust in established disseminators of knowledge, such as the mainstream media and journalists, may selectively avoid the media they deem to be peddlers of fake news. To get informed about political issues and other important topics, they may shut themselves off in online epistemic communities that recognize, acknowledge, and amplify their distrust, offering counterfactual disinformation narratives as an alternative. These online communities have been associated with populist constructions of knowledge and reality (e.g., Hameleers & Yekta, 2023; Müller & Schulz, 2021). Hence, they cultivate a binary worldview in which the honest people are contrasted to lying and corrupt elites, including the mass media. Over time, as a consequence of the reinforcement of distrust, people may shut themselves off in communities that are completely detached from established truth claims. This fuels selective exposure to fake news accusations and disinformation on the one hand and the avoidance of established truth claims on the other hand.

Crucially, the selection biases leading to disinformation exposure are partially beyond the control or awareness of citizens. Due to the affordances of social media, people's media choices may be curated by their prior selection, search history, or other factors tracked by platforms. Based on this, people not only may select the information that best fits their beliefs but are already presented with a predetermined selection of media choices based on their digital traces and history. This creates an uneven playing field that is curated to reinforce existing beliefs and create an image of like-mindedness. Over time, algorithms may also lead to more restricted, one-sided, and extremer options. For example, people may use some search terms on YouTube that indicate their uncertainty related to the established claims that COVID-19 is a virus originating from Wuhan. They may click on a video that summarizes doubts, and find more related content that casts doubt on established claims. Over time, however, the algorithm may feed these doubting and critical citizens with extremer content also containing conspiracies related to the topic they were interested in. Thus, over time, entering the curated flows of information with (healthy) doubt and skepticism may evolve into a system-level rejection of established truth claims due to the amplification of distrust.

Consequences: Epistemic Polarization in a Post-truth World

The interconnectedness between disinformation's three aspects may eventually cause polarization along epistemic lines. Not only do people disagree on how certain issues should be solved, such as climate change or international involvement in armed conflicts; they also come to disagree on the factual foundations of disagreement. This means that the core principles of truth that are the basis of a deliberative democracy are at stake (also see Arendt, 1967): When people disagree on some basic facts that can be deemed true or false, how can we ever solve pressing societal issues that require factual consensus? Although the disconnect between politics and truth has always plagued politics and society, the challenges become more pronounced than ever in the current context of the digital society, the weaponization and discourse around disinformation, and people's growing uncertainty and skepticism related to factual knowledge and expert interpretations. Here, we postulate that epistemic polarization is the main consequence to worry about: the growing cleavages between groups in society that do not share the same understanding of basic facts on core issues that divide the electorate, such as climate change or immigration. Over time, caused by the three faces of disinformation, deep factual disagreements between groups in society are consolidated, meaning that finding common ground has become nearly impossible. Thus, in light of this worrisome development, people belong to different epistemic communities that feed them with congruent claims on the truth, which are irreconcilable to the claims on truth on the same issue held by opposed epistemic communities.

Epistemic polarization goes beyond the well-documented concept of (affective) polarization mostly attached to the bipartisan system in the US (e.g., Iyengar et al., 2012). This concept seems to assume that people disagree on policies and ideological positions (i.e., pro-guns, anti-immigration, or pro-life). Despite the fierce and often identity-driven and emotional oppositions, people may still agree on some basic facts that underlie their opposition (i.e., the number of immigrants or the amount of guns in the US). Epistemic polarization goes further and assumes that there is even no agreement on the basic facts that drive different ideological or policy perspectives. For example, fueled by fake news accusations targeted at scientists, established media, or other institutions, people in opposed epistemic communities select different truth claims on the number of guns or deaths caused by guns, or expose themselves to different sources of competing (fake) experts that offer different claims to legitimize basic facts.

This is alarming for different reasons. First, to make well-informed political decisions, people should base themselves on accurate factual information. When such information is consciously and unconsciously undermined, attacked, and delegitimized, people can no longer make well-informed decisions. Second, urgent problems in society—such as climate change—require collective action and coordinated efforts of people crossing ideological differences or partisan divides. Although one can disagree and debate on how human-induced global warning should be dealt with, disagreeing on whether the issue actually exists makes it impossible to even discuss solutions and interventions. Third, the wide availability of seemingly legitimate and authentic claims on reality that are competing may lead to a citizenry that withdraws from politics due to uncertainty and distrust. When the perception that everything can be fake gets widespread, and when (populist) actors are attacking the truth claims they disagree with, people may no longer believe that there is a truth they can believe in, and shut themselves off from political information altogether. Thus, participation in the democratic process is at stake when relativism toward the truth is cultivated.

Conclusion

Disinformation has often been regarded as an undermining force for democracies across the globe. It may polarize audiences, fuel cynical beliefs related to politics, or amplify support for radical right-wing movements (e.g., Bennett & Livingston, 2018; Marwick & Lewis, 2017). Despite the growing scholarly attention to concepts such as fake news, disinformation, misinformation, and their link to populist attitudes, extant research has by and large failed to regard disinformation as part of a wider epistemic crisis that goes beyond the dissemination of false information. Indeed, the salience of disinformation in public opinion, media discourse, and politicians' communication may have the intended or unintended consequence that people loose trust in all information, become uncertain about what to believe, or resort to counterfactual narratives that resonate with amplified beliefs of factual relativism. In this setting, we believe that it is crucial to focus on the connection between three core aspect of the disinformation order: the perceived risk perceptions and disinformation beliefs surrounding weaponized falsehoods, labeling information as fake news, and the actual dissemination and selection of counterfactual disinformation narratives aligning with distrust and cynicism.

These three aspects are likely to be connected in a spiral of cynicism and disinformation, with the consequence of growing epistemic cleavages in society. Hence, perceiving that disinformation is omnipresent may contribute to higher levels of vulnerability to accusations of disinformation and deceptive or false information. More specifically, when people believe that disinformation is present across all sources, including established media, expert knowledge, and political institutions, they may not select or trust established claims on the truth. Instead, they may approach (hyperpartisan) alternative media that share a similar cynical outlook on established institutions of knowledge. The approach of these media and their often delegitimizing disinformation narratives (Hameleers & Yekta, 2023), in turn, may enhance already-existing perceptions about disinformation and the prevalence of false information in the digital media society. Against this backdrop, the causes, content, and effects of disinformation are connected in a downward spiral of factual relativism: exposure to actual disinformation, accusations of disinformation, and risk perceptions related to disinformation may engender deep factual disagreements in society and contribute to increasing relativism toward facts and truth claims (Van Aelst et al., 2017). Because of disinformation's undermining influence on the truth, people may become more uncertain or driven by partisan and identity-driven considerations in choosing between competing versions of truth presented to them.

This connection has important ramifications for both interventions and future research in disinformation. In this chapter, we urge future research to more comprehensively investigate how different aspects of the disinformation order are connected to each other, and how they together may have longer-term effects on how reality is perceived. To understand the dynamics of the disinformation spiral, research needs to go beyond a focus on disinformation as either a genre or a label (Egelhofer & Lecheler, 2019) or a perception of the news audience (Hameleers et al., 2020). Longitudinal surveys, diary studies, or linkages between panel survey data and content analyses may be used to better understand how perceived, discursive, and actual disinformation influence each other over time, and whether this leads to increasing cleavages in society that no longer agree on the same basic truths.

Future research may also be designed to offer more insights into the extent whether risk perception related to disinformation are proportional to its threat across various contexts. Although research to date suggests that people may overestimate the risks of disinformation (e.g., Acerbi et al., 2022), with negative ramifications for overall news trust (e.g., van der Meer et al., 2023), we currently lack insights on whether this discrepancy holds across contexts that are more or less resilient to disinformation (Humprecht et al., 2020). We therefore are in dire need of comparative approaches that explore the dynamics of disinformation across higher- and low-risk settings. Beyond country-level comparisons, this context-sensitive endeavor would include being sensitive to polarized versus nonpolarized issues, visual versus textual modes of presentation, and alternative versus legacy media formats.

The connection between different elements of the disinformation order also has ramifications for interventions and responses to disinformation. Crucially, as (disproportional) risk perceptions related to disinformation may have negative ramifications for news trust, it is important that perceptions of disinformation and trust in real information are also integrated at targeted outcome of interventions and policy responses. Hence, we should acknowledge that media trust is low across different settings, with roughly 50% of the population distrusting the news most of the time whilst being unsure on how to determine whether information is fake or real (Newman et al., 2023). As disinformation is far less salient than honest information, even in high-risk visual social media settings (Yang et al., 2023), enhancing news trust through transparency in information gathering procedures may at least be as important as fighting or preventing disinformation. In conclusion, resilience to disinformation may not only comprise of interventions targeted at disinformation or individual-level fact-checking or media literacy. Resilience may be achieved by a reinforcement of structural factors related to trust and access to high-quality information, and a more profound understanding of the dynamics and uncertainty related to fact-based information. Here, perceptions of distrust and disinformation may be remedied by revealing how knowledge disseminators can make mistakes in the process of covering (fast-paced) events and situations, explicating that such mistakes are honest and not driven by intentions to deceive or misinform the public.

As a concluding remark, we hope that this chapter inspires research and practitioners to view disinformation as more than false information, and acknowledge how it is part of and cause of a wider epistemic crisis related to distrust and factual uncertainty. We should also acknowledge that the disinformation order entails the strategic weaponization of fake news to divide the electorate and to attack inconvenient truths. When we acknowledge how perceptions and discursive uses of fake news and related terms are causing and amplifying factual disagreements and cleavages in society, we may start to repair the crisis of trust or induce resilience to false information through the reinforcement of honest information.

References

Acerbi, A., Altay, S., & Mercier, H. (2022). Research note: Fighting misinformation or fighting for information? *Harvard Kennedy School Misinformation Review.* https://doi.org/10.37016/mr-2020-87

Arendt, H. (1967, February 25). Truth and politics. *The New Yorker.*

Bennett, L. W., & Livingston, S. (2018). The disinformation order: Disruptive communication and the decline of democratic institutions. *European Journal of Communication, 33*(2). https://doi.org/10.1177/0267323118760317

Brennen, J. S., Simon, F. M., & Nielsen, R. K. (2021). Beyond (mis)representation: Visuals in COVID-19 misinformation. *The International Journal of Press/Politics, 26*(1), 277–299. https://doi.org/10.1177/1940161220964780

Chadwick, A., & Stanyer, J. (2022). Deception as a bridging concept in the study of disinformation, misinformation, and misperceptions: Toward a holistic framework. *Communication Theory, 32*(1), 1–24. https://doi.org/10.1093/ct/qtab019

Damstra, A., Boomgaarden, H. G., Broda, E., Lindgren, E., Strömbäck, J., Tsfati, Y., & Vliegenthart, R. (2021). What does fake look like? A review of the literature on intentional deception in the news and on social media. *Journalism Studies, 22*(14), 1947–1963. https://doi.org/10.1080/1461670X.2021.1979423

Egelhofer, J. L., Boyer, M., Lecheler, S., & Aaldering, L. (2022). Populist attitudes and politicians' disinformation accusations: Effects on perceptions of media and politicians. *Journal of Communication, 72*(6), 619–632. https://doi.org/10.1093/joc/jqac031

Egelhofer, J. L., & Lecheler, S. (2019). Fake news as a two-dimensional phenomenon: A framework and research agenda. *Annals of the International Communication Association, 43*, 97–116. https://doi.org/10.1080/23808985.2019.1602782

Farhall, K., Carson, A., Wright, S., Gibbons, A., & Lukamto, W. (2019). Political elites' use of fake news discourse across communications platforms. *International Journal of Communication, 13.* https://ijoc.org/index.php/ijoc/article/view/10677/2787

Freelon, D., & Wells, C. (2020). Disinformation as political communication. *Political Communication, 37*, 145–156. https://doi.org/10.1080/10584609.2020.1723755

Hameleers, M., Brosius, A., & de Vreese, C. H. (2021). Where's the fake news at? European news consumers' perceptions of misinformation across information sources and topics. *Harvard Kennedy School Misinformation Review.* https://doi.org/10.37016/mr-2020-70

Hameleers, M., van der Meer, G. L. A., & Brosius, A. (2020). Feeling "disinformed" lowers compliance with COVID-19 guidelines: Evidence from the US, UK, Netherlands and Germany. *Harvard Kennedy School Misinformation Review, 1.* Special issue on COVID-19 and misinformation. https://doi.org/10.37016/mr-2020-023

Hameleers, M., & Yekta, N. (2023). Entering an information era of parallel truths? A qualitative analysis of legitimizing and de-legitimizing truth claims in established versus alternative media outlets. *Communication Research.* https://doi.org/10.1177/00936502231189685

Heft, A., Mayerhöffer, E., Reinhardt, S., & Knüpfer, C. (2019). Beyond Breitbart: Comparing right-wing digital news infrastructures in six Western democracies. *Policy & Internet, 12*(1), 20–45. https://doi.org/10.1002/poi3.219

Humprecht, E., Esser, F., & Van Aelst, P. (2020). Resilience to online disinformation: A framework for crossnationalcomparative research. *The International Journal of Press/Politics, 25*(3), 493–516.

Iyengar, S., Sood, G., & Lelkes, Y. (2012). Affect, not ideology: A social identity perspective on polarization. *Public Opinion Quarterly, 76*(3), 405–431. https://doi.org/10.1093/poq/nfs038

Knobloch-Westerwick, S., Mothes, C., & Polavin, N. (2020). Confirmation bias, ingroup bias, and negativity bias in selective exposure to political information. *Communication Research, 47*(1), 104–124. https://doi.org/10.1177/0093650217719596

Marwick, A., & Lewis, R. (2017, May 15). *Media manipulation and disinformation online*. Data & Society Research Institute. https://datasociety.net/library/media-manipulation-and-disinfo-online/

Müller, P., & Schulz, A. (2021). Alternative media for a populist audience? Exploring political and media use predictors of exposure to Breitbart, Sputnik, and Co. *Information, Communication & Society, 24*(2), 277–293. https://doi.org/10.1080/1369118X.2019.1646778

Newman, N., Fletcher, R., Eddy, K., Robertson, C. T., & Nielsen, R. K. (2023). *Digital news report 2023*. Reuters Institute for the Study of Journalism. https://reutersinstitute.politics.ox.ac.uk/sites/default/files/2023-06/Digital_News_Report_2023.pdf

Schulz, A., Wirth, W., & Müller, P. (2020). We are the people and you are fake news: A social identity approach to populist citizens' false consensus and hostile media perceptions. *Communication Research, 47*(2), 201–226. https://doi.org/10.1177/0093650218794854

Van Aelst, P., Strömbäck, J., Aalberg, T., de Esser, F., Vreese, C. H., Matthes, J., et al. (2017). Political communication in a high-choice media environment: A challenge for democracy? *Annals of the International Communication Association, 4*, 3–27. https://doi.org/10.1080/23808985.2017.1288551

Van der Meer, T. G., Hameleers, M., & Ohme, J. (2023). Can fighting misinformation have a negative spillover effect? How warnings for the threat of misinformation can decrease general news credibility. *Journalism Studies*. https://doi.org/10.1080/1461670X.2023.2187652

Van Duyn, E., & Collier, J. (2019). Priming and fake news: The effects of elite discourse on evaluations of news media. *Mass Communication and Society, 22*(1), 29–48. https://doi.org/10.1080/15205436.2018.1511807

Vraga, E. K., & Bode, L. (2020). Defining misinformation and understanding its bounded nature: Using expertise and evidence for describing misinformation.

Political Communication, 37(1), 136–144. https://doi.org/10.1080/ 10584609.2020.1716500

Waisbord, S. (2018). Truth is what happens to news: On journalism, fake news, and post-truth. *Journalism Studies, 19*(13), 1866–1878. https://doi.org/1 0.1080/1461670X.2018.1492881

Wardle, C., & Derakhshan, H. (2017). *Information disorder: Toward an interdisciplinary framework for research and policymaking.* Council of Europe. http://tverezo.info/wp-content/uploads/2017/11/PREMS-162317-GBR-2018-Report-desinformation-A4-BAT.pdf

Yang, Y., Davis, T., & Hindman, M. (2023). Visual misinformation on Facebook. *Journal of Communication.* https://doi.org/10.1093/joc/jqac051

Zimmermann, F., & Kohring, M. (2020). Mistrust, disinforming news, and vote choice: A panel survey on the origins and consequences of believing disinformation in the 2017 German parliamentary election. *Political Communication, 37*(2), 215–237. https://doi.org/10.1080/10584609.2019.1686095

CHAPTER 4

Journalistic Role Performance and Its Effects

María Luisa Humanes

INTRODUCTION

Journalism studies have traditionally paid little attention to the audience (Costera Meijer & Kormelink, 2019) even though there can be no journalism without audiences (Masip, 2016). In their proposed hierarchy of influences analysis, Shoemaker and Reese (2014) introduce the audience as one of the elements related to professional routines that influences journalistic practice given that considerations of audience interests are incorporated into these routines. The essence of journalism is to fulfill certain functions—to provide reliable and truthful information, to watch out for abuses by the powerful or to serve as a platform for civic demands—which

---

This chapter is part of the research project Journalism Models in the Multiplatform Context (CSO2017-82816-P), which is in turn part of the international project Journalistic Role Performance (www.journalisticperformance.org).

M. L. Humanes (✉)
Universidad Rey Juan Carlos, Madrid, Spain
e-mail: marialuisa.humanes@urjc.es

© The Author(s), under exclusive license to Springer Nature Switzerland AG 2024
M. Goyanes, A. Cañedo (eds.), *Media Influence on Opinion Change and Democracy*, https://doi.org/10.1007/978-3-031-70231-0_4

citizens have internalized as normative ideals, and whose fulfillment they perceive and evaluate through news content.

Changes in the media and journalistic ecosystem have placed audiences in a more active position not only in terms of media and content selection but also with respect to their own participation in the creation of this content. In regard to the changes taking place in the industrial model of journalism, Reese and Shoemaker (2016) state, "News was what news organizations produced, and journalists were the professionals who worked for them. How does our model fit with the new media world where the lines are not as tidy?" (p. 391). As such, audiences are increasingly influential in the newsmaking process, and it is essential to understand what they expect from the media and whether these expectations match those of journalists and the media (Tandoc Jr & Duffy, 2016).

In this chapter, we will reflect on the effects that the materialization of journalistic roles has on audience members' perception and expectations. Thus far, the literature that explains the decline of trust in and the credibility of journalistic information has focused on factors such as biases, misinformation and fake news (see Ksiazek et al., 2023). However, it is less common to relate the implementation and fulfillment of certain media functions with phenomena that alienate audience members from the news media. Moreover, as Swart et al. (2022) have pointed out, our proposal focuses on "pushing audience studies forward beyond industry concerns and starting from the perspective of audiences themselves instead" (p. 8).

JOURNALISTIC ROLES: CONCEPTION, PERCEPTION AND PERFORMANCE

Research on professional roles in journalism dates back to the late 1960s. It was initially focused on the analysis of role conceptions and perceptions following the functionalist tradition of role theory (Humanes, 2003). This tradition gave rise to the different types of functions that can be performed by the news media.

In addition to extracting typologies related to different journalistic models, several authors have pointed out various dimensions into which these roles can be grouped. Donsbach (2012) points out three interrelated dimensions: the first (*participant-observational*) places the journalist on an axis in which they can be an impartial actor, offering information or playing an active role to influence the political process; the second (*advocacy-neutral*) shows two poles ranging from the journalist who offers their values and beliefs to the neutral journalist who does not take sides; and the third dimension (*commercial-educational*) shows the journalist oriented toward the search for audience by adjusting to their tastes versus the journalist who seeks to serve the public interest and a better functioning of democracy. Hanitzsch (2007) also proposes three theoretical dimensions in which the roles are grouped: the interventionist dimension, which reflects the dichotomy between the journalist who promotes their own values and the one who remains distanced and neutral; the distance from power dimension, which includes the adversarial journalist versus the journalist loyal to power; and the market-oriented dimension, which refers to the way in which the journalist conceives their audience as citizens or as consumers.

However, given that their research focuses on the conceptions and perceptions of the roles that are important for understanding journalism models, several authors have pointed out obvious inconsistencies between journalists' self-perceptions and what is reflected in the practice of journalism (Hallin & Mancini, 2004; Humanes, 2003). In recent years, there has been a shift in research on professional roles from perceptions (role conceptions) to the materialization of roles in news content (role performance). This perspective puts the focus of the study of professional roles on news content. Mellado, Hellmueller and Donsbach define the concept of role performance as "an outcome of dynamic negotiations influenced by different internal and external constraints that potentially inhibit but can also enable the practice of journalism" (Mellado et al., 2017, p. 8).

The most important element of the shift from the evaluative level of professional roles to the performative level (journalistic practice) is that it is understood that the news reflects the perceived functions or roles of journalists (the roles at the evaluative level) as well as influences derived from decisions made within the newsroom, from negotiations with different reference groups—information sources, for example—or from the processes of information verification (e.g., the presence of strategies related to objectivity). Based on this analytical perspective, scholars proposed that there may be a gap between the professional roles considered important by journalists and the professional roles perceived by the audience through the news.

The performance of professional roles is manifested in six different dimensions based on three axes (Mellado, 2015, 2021): the presence of the journalist's voice in the news, the relationship between journalism and power, and the way in which the audience is approached. Each of the six dimensions connects to indicators that can be measured in journalistic practice, that is, in news content.

The first axis emphasizes the presence or absence of the journalist as an actor in the news. The disseminator-interventionist model is measured using indicators of the degree to which the news item contains evidence of their presence, such as whether the news item contains the interpretation or opinion about the event. This dimension is related to the active or passive (neutral, distant) attitude of the journalist (Donsbach & Patterson, 2004). According to Mellado (2015), this model is particularly important because it measures how the news is narrated, meaning that it generally has a greater presence than the other roles. The two poles (disseminator-interventionist) form a unidimensional structure where the higher level of participation of the journalist's voice (e.g., value judgments, adjectives) implies a higher level of interventionism and vice versa.

The second dimension refers to the journalistic roles through which journalists and the media establish their relationship with the political and economic elites in a society. Two dimensions are identified: the watchdog, who proposes a relationship to power based on monitoring, questioning, criticism, reporting and even contesting power; and the loyal facilitator, which is more oriented toward either supporting power and maintaining the status quo or promoting national unity and patriotism.

The third domain involves how journalistic practices build the relationship with the audience, namely a commercial or public service relationship. In other words, it is about how audience members are viewed: as citizens, viewers or clients. Three roles are differentiated. The service role, which is linked to the provision of advice and guidance for audience members' daily lives, defines the viewer as a client. The info-entertainment role is based on sensationalism, emotions, morbidity and curiosity. Its purpose is to entertain and relax the audience-spectators. The civic role, meanwhile, deals with the provision of information and education related to demands, rights and duties and other issues related to the exercise of audience-citizenship and audience members' participation in social, political and cultural life (Mellado & van Dalen, 2014).

Citizen Expectations and Perceptions of Journalistic Roles

The literature on journalistic audiences is not conclusive about the relationship between the media and their audiences. On the one hand, work on the "news gap" shows that although normative theories suggest that the media play a series of roles that ensure that members of the public can exercise their rights, there is a gap between the supply of information and the demands of the audience (Boczkowski & Mitchelstein, 2013). Although Boczkowski and Mitchelstein limit this idea to the divergence between the media agenda and the topics of interest to the audience, it can be expanded to other topics in journalism studies and also to the study of professional roles. Therefore, it could be said that journalists and their audiences have different journalistic interests. This has been found in their study on journalist and audience preferences in Argentine digital newspapers (Mitchelstein et al., 2016). Also, Valenzuela et al. (2017) found discrepancies between the frames preferred by journalists and by the audience in their study on the effects of news characteristics on the dissemination of news by users on Facebook and Twitter in Chile.

From this perspective, these divergences may have important consequences for the functions of the media in the democratic system, such as providing contrasted and diverse information that allows for public debate and being vigilant in the face of power (Boczkowski & Mitchelstein, 2013, p. 141). These are consequences that affect trust in the media, as noted by Karlsson and Clerwall (2019): "viewed from an SCT perspective, the decrease in trust from the public can be interpreted as a mismatch between what the public expects from journalism and what journalism delivers, suggesting that the contractual ties are weakened or even dissolving" (p. 1184). Van Dalen (2019) notes that media and journalists must first have trust and legitimacy in order to play their roles. Thus, trust is related to the expectations that members of the public have that the media will fulfill its assigned social functions.

On the other hand, there is already abundant literature that suggests that journalists and the media are increasingly making journalistic decisions based on the tastes and demands of the audience, despite the possible reluctance of journalists to give up control (Anderson, 2011). Editorial decisions increasingly depend on audience metrics due to technological advances and economic pressures (see, for example, Welbers et al., 2016;

Tandoc Jr, 2014; Wendelin et al., 2017). This could lead to increased alignment of journalistic and audience interests.

In any case, few studies have linked these issues to research on journalistic roles. In this sense, Riedl and Eberl (2020) propose the need for a holistic understanding of roles that includes the point of view of journalistic audiences as a source of expectations.

However, so far little work has been done on audience attitudes toward journalistic roles. Most focus on the role expectations of the audience, the variables associated with them and the differences between audience and journalists with respect to what functions the media should fulfill.

From the perspective of uses and rewards, Burgoon et al. (1983) proposed determining whether the public recognizes multiple functions of the media in their pioneering study. One of the first conclusions of the research was the multidimensional nature of readers' expectations in relation to media functions, which results in four performances: (1) providing detailed and timely information about important events, (2) meeting audience members' need to relax, (3) facilitating knowledge and connection with one's local community and (4) serving as an extension of the individual's social world, the last two being the most valued. In addition, they confirmed discrepancies between the expectations of the audience and the interests of journalists, since the most important function for the latter is explaining important events followed by uncovering irregularities, that is, the function we call watchdog.

Also from the uses and gratifications perspective, Guo (2000) explored audience expectations of the media in an effort to determine whether these expectations differ according to media consumption habits, and their relationship to the political effects of the media during an election campaign in Hong Kong. Instead of using preestablished items and asking respondents to rate the importance of each one, she chose to ask an open-ended question. The answers were then coded and grouped into eight categories that reflect the informational demands that the audience placed on the news media: offering a more detailed number of issues in the elections, giving space to all voices, dedicating special sections to the election, refraining from taking biased positions, refraining from taking sides, being fair to the candidates, providing less negative coverage, eliminating personal attacks and refraining from digging through the trash. In a subsequent factor analysis, she arrived at three different expectations regarding the nature of election coverage: compressive coverage, objective coverage and positive coverage. She also found that expectations are associated with different media consumption habits and have consequences on the political effects of media as mediating elements.

Chung (2009) studied readers' perceptions of the roles of local online newspapers. She used a survey, asking respondents to rate the importance of the roles used in the Weaver et al. studies on a scale of 1 (not at all important) to 7 (extremely important). She identified a three-dimensional structure: (1) interpretive disseminator, (2) populist mobilizer and (3) adversary, the most important being the populist-mobilizer. The results were compared to those obtained by Weaver et al. (2007), and they found differences between the perceptions of citizens and journalists. While journalists consider the interpretive and adversarial roles to be the most important, the audience believes that they should exercise the populist mobilizing role and the civic role to a greater extent.

Nah and Chung (2012) started from the idea that readers of digital publications may perceive themselves as having closer relationships to journalists, which would lead to a better perception of the importance of the roles played by journalists in their local communities. They examine the extent to which social trust and credibility in the media predict audience perceptions of the various roles of both professional journalists and citizen journalists. The results showed that readers had a better perception of the roles exercised by professional journalists with the exception of the watchdog role. Respondents believe that both journalists should be more critical of the powerful. In addition, the authors were able to corroborate the importance of credibility and trust in the media as predictors of role perception.

In a comparison of the perceptions of journalists and the general public in Israel, Tsfati et al. (2006) found that journalists have a relatively more uniform perception of good journalism than the public, which is accompanied by differences between the two groups regarding the degree of importance of journalistic standards and practices: while journalists consider the interpretation of news more important than being objective, the public prefers objectivity and neutrality.

The work of Pointdexter, Heider and McCombs (2006) has addressed audience expectations of roles related directly to what is known as civic journalism. In their first study, they identify four different dimensions based on a factorial analysis of six roles and seven characteristics associated with traditional journalism and public journalism in local information (Heider et al., 2005). They are: (1) the good neighbor journalist, (2) the watchdog journalist, (3) the impartial and precise journalist and (4) the quick journalist. Most audience survey respondents stated that precision (94%) and impartial information (84%) are extremely important. However, two roles—monitoring the powerful and offering information quickly— did not receive strong support. This points to a gap between the survey respondents and the journalists in two elements that are an integral part of traditional journalism: the function of surveillance and the rapid dissemination of information. Using the typology that resulted from the previous study, Poindexter et al. (2006) decided to investigate the level of expectations regarding the role of the journalist as a good neighbor for different audience segments. Women, African Americans and Hispanics very positively evaluated this role, as did the segment of the public that expected the press to be concerned about crime and social issues, and they believe that television is the medium that can best address these concerns.

Riedl and Eberl (2020) addressed the expectations of the audience in Austria of journalistic roles and compared how they differ from journalists' understanding of roles. Using the concept developed by Hanitzsch et al. (2019), they determined that audiences highly value the roles of observer, analyst and informer, followed by those of mobilizer, watchdog and missionary. The role of host and salesperson and the role of collaborating with the powerful were less highly valued. When they compared the expectations of the public to the perceptions of journalists, they found a fair amount of alignment with regard to the greater importance given to the role of disseminator. They also both valued the entertainment role very little. The gap between the two groups is centered on the roles of activist, watchdog and collaborator with those in power. One important finding of this study is that the audience expects the media to play the role of watchdog over the elites and the role of the collaborator that supports these elites. The authors explain that this is due to the existence of different audiences with differing expectations. The study also connected these expectations with survey respondents' political attitudes and explored the degree to which these can explain the differing expectations. The authors found that political attitudes have an important explanatory capacity, as do other variables such as use of and trust in the media.

Tandoc Jr and Duffy (2016) analyzed the expectations of the role using a survey in Singapore. The most highly rated roles were allowing people to express themselves, promoting tolerance and diversity, and analyzing reality. The two lowest rated roles were influencing the political agenda and being an adversary of power. They also conducted a factorial analysis with 14 items that yielded three models of journalism: the audience-oriented journalist, the government-oriented journalist and the nation-oriented journalist. Finally, they found that media consumption and credibility do not explain expectations of certain roles, as occurs elsewhere. Rather, they found that age, sex, education and income are the variables with the highest explanatory capacity.

Van Der Wurff and Schoenbach (2014) also studied the expectations of roles in Holland. They used ten items grouped into two indexes (professional-oriented roles and user-oriented roles), which were rated by the survey respondents on a scale of 1 (not important at all) to 5 (very important). The most important roles were included in the professional dimension: offering information as quickly as possible, monitoring the government from a critical perspective, explaining social issues, training audience members to form their own opinions and engaging in critical monitoring of economic elites. The roles with the weakest ratings were allowing members of the public to express themselves, reporting on topics that are of interest to large audiences, encouraging people to participate in discussions, training people to contribute to the news and offering an opportunity to relax and be entertained.

Karlsson and Clerwall (2019) studied citizen expectations of good journalism in Sweden from a qualitative perspective. They determined that the audience expects good journalism to be objective and impartial and to be based on diverse and reliable sources. They also manifested support for the watchdog journalist role, which offers relevant information without being influenced by personal interests. Finally, members of the public also expect good journalism to tell news stories in an interesting, well-designed way and to do so accurately and in a way that can be easily read and that is adapted to their audiences.

Abdenour et al. (2021) analyzed audience perception of 20 professional roles and determined that the public valued journalistic roles that they call contextual much more. This refers to roles that inform the public of possible threats, precisely describe what is happening and report in a socially responsible manner. These roles are more important for citizens than the four traditional roles (disseminating, interpreting, populist mobilizer and adversarial). Survey respondents also rated providing information to the public quickly and avoiding unverified content highly, while seeking a broader audience and providing entertainment received little support. Together, the assessments of the interpretive role were slightly above average. The role of investigating the government was very important to members of the public, but they gave lower scores to adversarial roles.

When these perceptions are compared to those of journalists, the greatest gaps exist in regard to roles that emphasize a political agenda and an adversarial position with regard to business and the government.

Peifer (2018) has proposed a multidimensional scale for measuring the perceived importance of the news media (PINM), which is used to determine the degree to which audience values align with the regulatory roles of the media. Their study uses 35 items related to the various roles of the media that had already been theorized: informative, investigative, analytical, social empathy, mobilizing and public forum. The author validated the scale and confirmed that the perceived importance is related to news consumption and more concretely to the use of conventional media. This suggests that convincing people of the fundamental value of journalistic work could promote greater consumption of quality journalism.

Vos et al. (2019) found that news professionals and audiences have significantly different perceptions of 19 of the 20 journalistic roles. Journalists give more importance to the roles of reporting things as they are, educating the audience, providing the information that people need to make political decisions, monitoring and investigating leaders, and allowing people to express their points of view. The audience agreed with journalists in that they believe that reporting things as they are and educating the audience are the most important roles. However, they differ on the following: allowing people to express their points of view, providing the information that people need to make political decisions and serving as a neutral observer. They also analyzed explanatory factors of role perception and determined that age, political identity, media consumption habits and selective exposure cause differences in the importance given to different roles.

Following previous scholars, Willnat et al. (2019) proposed testing whether journalists believe the following roles to be very important: investigating the government, offering analyses of issues and discussing national and international politics. The audience believes the following roles to be more important: obtaining information quickly, avoiding unverified content and focusing on the broadest audiences. The results confirmed that journalists believe the interpretative role to be most important, while the public values the role of dissemination. Both groups share similar understandings of the roles of the press.

Loosen et al. (2020) compared public expectations to journalists' role approaches in Germany. For the audience—though with marked differences based on sociodemographic characteristics—the most important roles were serving as an independent observer, reporting objectively, providing an in-depth analysis of the news and criticizing the actions of those in power when necessary. When they compared the results of the audience to the journalists' approaches, they concluded that there is a high level of congruency regarding which journalistic tasks are considered most important.

Gil de Zúñiga and Hinsley (2013) move from role expectations to the perception of role performance. They start from the idea of the discrepancies between what journalists believe to be good journalism and audience perceptions, analyzing the gap between journalists' opinions of their work and those of audience members. They conducted two surveys with journalists and members of the public in which they asked them to rate the importance of eight items on a scale of 1 to 7 that correspond to both routines and roles: being objective, covering stories that should be covered, helping people, getting information to the public quickly, providing analyses and interpretations of complex problems, verifying facts, giving everyday people the opportunity to express their opinions and serving as a watchdog. The most important roles of good journalism in journalists' opinion are covering stories that should be covered, being objective and getting information to the public quickly. The highest rated aspects for members of the public were getting information to the public quickly and covering stories that should be covered. However, being objective placed last in public perception. The public does not believe that journalists are doing good work, which points to the industry's apparent inability to respond in a way that strengthens news consumers' perception. Finally, they also concluded that there is a relationship between consumption of traditional news and a better perception of journalistic work.

Fawzi and Mothes (2020) analyzed the expectations and assessment of the German audience of journalistic role performance, finding discrepancies between the roles that the audience expects the media to play and their evaluation of the roles performed in the news. They also determined that this misalignment is related to low levels of trust in the media and with populist attitudes.

Truyens and Picone (2021) have linked public expectations of journalistic norms to different types of audiences based on their news consumption patterns, identifying differences between the assessments of different groups of consumers. Traditional media outlets' audiences trust more in watchdog journalism, while individuals who consume news only incidentally value the role of offering reliable information more.

Journalistic Roles Research Agenda: From Media-centric Approach to Audience Expectations

The literature review presented above suggests that there is a need to expand on the effects (mainly avoiding the news and losing confidence in the media) that this gap could have between the roles sustained and materialized by the media and news professionals and audience expectations regarding said functions. Members of the public perceive, identify and use journalistic roles based on the information published by the media. As such, analyzing their expectations and perceptions of these roles allows us to learn about the model—or models—of journalism that audience members expect to find in the media and the degree to which there is a mismatch (or not) between their expectations and perception and the performance of journalistic roles.

To conclude this chapter, we propose the following roadmap, which empirically addresses the following topics:

1. Learning about audience expectations of the journalistic roles that the media should perform. At this level, audience role expectations correspond to orientations (concepts) of the roles by journalists at the normative level. The main goal would be to discover the latent functions that the audience expects the media to play. A second issue, which is related to the first, addresses the need to determine whether or not there is a gap between audience role expectations and those of journalists.
2. Second, scholars must analyze whether there is a gap between the audience perception of journalistic role performance and perceived role enactment on the part of journalists.
3. Audience perceptions of the performance of journalistic roles must also be addressed. There is a need to uncover the latent functions that the audience perceives in role performance and to determine whether there is a gap between audience perception of the performance of journalistic roles and the manifestation of said roles in news content.
4. It is also necessary to identify the factors that explain both audience role expectations and their perception of role performance and the gap between expectations and perceptions of role performance. This will allow scholars to expand their knowledge of the causes that

determine the distance between the journalistic models demanded by audiences and the journalistic culture promoted by journalistic companies and journalists.
5. Finally, one necessary task involves relating this "conflict" between journalistic models to intentional avoidance of the news, understanding that this emerges as a reaction to journalism's failure to meet audience expectations. In this sense, Skovsgaard and Anderson (2020) refer to two types of causes of news avoidance: intentional and unintentional. Intentional avoidance is based on the dislike that some people develop of the news due to their belief that news coverage is too pessimistic and negatively affects their emotional state or based on skepticism or distrust toward the news media, or a sense of news overload. However, the question of whether the gap between role expectations and the perception of their implementation can explain this phenomenon of avoidance has not been addressed.

In addition, the gap between expectations and perceptions of role performance should also be related to distrust of the media and how it impacts civic engagement and the legitimacy of journalism. As we noted in the literature review, various studies have related role expectations to confidence in the media (Nah & Chung, 2012; Riedl & Eberl, 2020) and with external legitimacy of the profession (Vos et al., 2019).

These lines of work also involve a methodological challenge. Previous studies mainly used a deductive approach through a survey of both citizens and journalists. There are very few inductive studies that utilize quantitative techniques (e.g., Karlsson & Clerwall, 2019).

The research strategy has mainly been based on asking survey respondents to assess the importance that they give to a set of items that measure different journalistic roles using different scales. These items have mainly been used in surveys of journalists in the past to measure their understandings and perceptions of professional roles. In particular, the scales developed by Weaver et al. (2007) and by Hanitzsch et al. (2011, 2019) have been used.

There are, however, critiques of this methodological approach. For Karlsson and Clerwall (2019), surveys start from a predefined understanding of journalistic roles and of "good journalism" that can lead survey respondents (journalists or audience members) to consider certain roles to be important only because they have been proposed in the survey questions. Similarly, Martínez-Nicolás (2015) also questions whether the results are not merely a methodological effect derived from an aprioristic decision and proposes introducing observational and conversational-type strategies in studies on professional roles.

Jane Singer (2017) argues that the combination of quantitative and qualitative techniques is rare in research on professional roles. Standaert et al. (2021) argue that the items used to investigate roles cannot capture the full range of journalistic roles. In an effort to address this issue, their questionnaire for journalists includes an open question in which they ask journalists to identify the three most important roles at the regulatory level. Therefore, we propose here a combination of quantitative and qualitative techniques: survey and focus groups.

It is not a question of rejecting the application of the questionnaire, which we propose to use to measure both the audience's role expectations and their perception of the implementation of journalistic roles. Two dependent variables are proposed based on the operationalization of the roles. The dependent variable, audience role expectations, will be addressed through the following question in the questionnaire: What importance do you attach to each of these functions performed by journalists and the media? The dependent variable, audience perception of role performance, will be addressed through the following question: How often do you think journalists and the media perform each of these functions in practice? A set of indicators (sociodemographic, ideological orientation, media consumption, news consumption through different types of media, main means of getting information, interest in different news topics, and trust in the media and in journalists) will be used as explanatory variables of the audience's role expectations, their perception of role performance and the gap between expectations and perceptions of role performance.

As indicated above, the qualitative approach to journalistic roles is very limited (see, for example, Ranji, 2022). This is also true for work on audience role expectations. As Loosen et al. (2020) have noted: "we know nothing about how the role items, which were all developed for the survey of journalists, are interpreted by the citizens we surveyed" (p. 1761). More specifically, Vos et al. (2019) believe that "qualitative studies, such as focus groups and in-depth interviews, could provide insight on how individuals view the journalistic field and the public's roles in it" in future research on audience role expectations.

Conducting focus groups with members of the audience will allow us to delve deeper into the expectations of citizens regarding journalistic roles and how they evaluate their implementation: What meaning do audiences give to the different roles that they understand correspond to good journalism? It is also interesting to know what the implications are for citizens if the media does not meet their expectations when they consume news.

References

Abdenour, J., McIntyre, K., & Smith Dahmen, N. (2021). Seeing eye to eye: A comparison of audiences' and journalists' perceptions of professional roles and how they relate to trust. *Journalism Practice, 15*(3), 329–347. https://www.tandfonline.com/doi/abs/10.1080/17512786.2020.1716828

Anderson, C. W. (2011). Between creative and quantified audiences: Web metrics and changing patterns of newswork in local US newsrooms. *Journalism, 12*(5), 550–566. https://doi.org/10.1177/1464884911402451

Boczkowski, P. J., & Mitchelstein, E. (2013). *The news gap: When the information preferences of the media and the public diverge*. MIT Press.

Burgoon, J. K., Bernstein, J. M., & Burgoon, M. (1983). Public and journalist perceptions of newspaper functions. *Newspaper Research Journal, 5*(1), 77–89. https://doi.org/10.1177/073953298300500108

Chung, D. S. (2009). How readers perceive journalists' functions at online community newspapers. *Newspaper Research Journal, 30*(1), 72–80. https://doi.org/10.1177/073953290903000108

Costera Meijer, I., & Kormelink, T. G. (2019). Audiences for journalism. *The International Encyclopedia of Journalism Studies*, 1–7.

Donsbach, W. (2012). Journalists' role perception. In W. Donsbach (Ed.), *The international encyclopedia of communication*. Blackwell.

Donsbach, W., & Patterson, T. E. (2004). Political news journalists. In F. Esser & B. Pfetsch (Eds.), *Comparing political communication: Theories, cases, and challenges* (pp. 251–270). Cambridge University Press.

Fawzi, N., & Mothes, C. (2020). Perceptions of media performance: Expectation-evaluation discrepancies and their relationship with media-related and populist attitudes. *Media and Communication, 8*(3), 335–347. https://doi.org/10.17645/mac.v8i3.3142

Gil de Zúñiga, H., & Hinsley, A. (2013). The press versus the public. What is "good journalism?". *Journalism Studies, 14*(6), 926–942. https://doi.org/10.1080/1461670X.2012.744551

Guo, Z. (2000). Media use habits, audience expectations and media effects in Hong Kong's first legislative council election. *Gazette, 62*(2), 133–151. https://doi.org/10.1177/0016549200062002004

Hallin, D., & Mancini, P. (2004). *Comparing media systems: Three models of media and politics*. Cambridge University Press.

Hanitzsch, T. (2007). Deconstructing journalism culture: Toward a universal theory. *Communication Theory*, *17*(4), 367–385. https://doi.org/10.1111/j.1468-2885.2007.00303.x

Hanitzsch, T., Hanusch, F., Mellado, C., Anikina, M., Berganza, R., Cangoz, I., et al. (2011). Mapping journalism cultures across nations: A comparative study of 18 countries. *Journalism Studies*, *12*(3), 273–293. https://doi.org/10.1080/1461670X.2010.512502

Hanitzsch, T., Hanusch, F., Ramaprasad, J., & De Beer, A. S. (Eds.). (2019). *Worlds of journalism: Journalistic cultures around the globe*. Columbia University Press.

Heider, D., McCombs, M., & Poindexter, P. M. (2005). What the public expects of local news: Views on public and traditional journalism. *Journalism and Mass Communication Quarterly*, *82*(4), 952–967. https://doi.org/10.1177/107769900508200412

Humanes, M. L. (2003). Evolución de roles y actitudes. Cultura y modelos profesionales del periodismo. *Telos*, *54*. https://telos.fundaciontelefonica.com/archivo/numero054/cultura-y-modelos-profesionales-del-periodismo/?output=pdf

Karlsson, M., & Clerwall, C. (2019). Cornerstones in journalism: According to citizens. *Journalism Studies*, *20*(8), 1184–1199. https://doi.org/10.1080/1461670X.2018.1499436

Ksiazek, T. B., Kim, S. J., Nelson, J. L., Park, A., Patankar, S., Sabalaskey, O., & Taneja, H. (2023). Distrust profiles: Identifying the factors that shape journalism's credibility crisis. *Media and Communication*, *11*(4), 308–319. https://doi.org/10.17645/mac.v11i4.7071

Loosen, W., Reimer, J., & Hölig, S. (2020). What journalists want and what they ought to do (in) congruences between journalists' role conceptions and audiences' expectations. *Journalism Studies*, *21*(12), 1744–1774. https://doi.org/10.1080/1461670X.2020.1790026

Martínez-Nicolás, M. (2015). Investigar las culturas periodísticas. Propuesta teórica y aplicación al estudio del periodismo político en España. *Revista Internacional de Comunicación y Desarrollo (RICD)*, *1*(1), 127–137. https://revistas.usc.gal/index.php/ricd/article/view/2177

Masip, P. (2016). Investigar el periodismo desde la perspectiva de las audiencias. *Profesional de la Información*, *25*(3), 323–330. https://doi.org/10.3145/epi.2016.may.01

Mellado, C. (2015). Professional roles in news content: Six dimensions of journalistic role performance. *Journalism Studies*, *16*(4), 596–614. https://doi.org/10.1080/1461670X.2014.922276

Mellado, C. (2021). Theorizing journalistic roles. In C. Mellado (Ed.), *Beyond journalistic norms* (pp. 22–45). Routledge.

Mellado, C., Hellmueller, L., & Donsbach, W. (2017). Journalistic role performance: A new research agenda in a digital and global media environment. In C. Mellado, L. Hellmueller, & W. Donsbach (Eds.), *Journalistic role performance: Concepts, contexts, and methods* (pp. 1–19). Routledge.

Mellado, C., & Van Dalen, A. (2014). Between rhetoric and practice: Explaining the gap between role conception and performance in journalism. *Journalism Studies*, 15(6), 859–878. https://doi.org/10.1080/1461670X.2013.838046

Mitchelstein, E., Boczkowski, P. J., Wagner, C., & Leiva, S. (2016). The news gap in Argentina: Contextual factors and preferences of journalists and the audience. *Palabra Clave*, 19(4), 1027–1047. https://doi.org/10.5294/pacla.2016.19.4.4

Nah, S., & Chung, D. S. (2012). When citizens meet both professional and citizen journalists: Social trust, media credibility, and perceived journalistic roles among online community news readers. *Journalism*, 13(6), 714–730. https://doi.org/10.1177/1464884911431381

Peifer, J. (2018). Perceived news media importance: Developing and validating a measure for personal valuations of normative journalistic functions. *Communication Methods and Measures*, 12(1), 55–79. https://doi.org/10.1080/19312458.2017.1416342

Poindexter, P. M., Heider, D., & McCombs, M. (2006). Watchdog or good neighbor? The public's expectations of local news. *Harvard International Journal of Press/Politics*, 11(1), 77–88. https://doi.org/10.1177/1081180X05283795

Ranji, B. (2022). Journalistic illusio in a restrictive context: Role conceptions and perceptions of role enactment among Iranian journalists. *Journalism*, 23(2), 517–532. https://doi.org/10.1177/1464884920922026

Reese, S. D., & Shoemaker, P. J. (2016). A media sociology for the networked public sphere: The hierarchy of influences model. *Mass Communication and Society*, 19(4), 389–410. https://doi.org/10.1080/15205436.2016.1174268

Riedl, A., & Eberl, J. M. (2020). Audience expectations of journalism: What's politics got to do with it? *Journalism*, 23(8), 1682–1699. https://doi.org/10.1177/1464884920976422

Shoemaker, P., & Reese, S. (2014). *Mediating the message in the 21st century. A media sociology perspective*. Routledge.

Singer, J. (2017). Triangulating methods in the study of journalistic role performance. In C. Mellado, L. Hellmueller, & W. Donsbach (Eds.), *Journalistic role performance: Concepts, contexts, and methods* (pp. 224–238). Routledge.

Skovsgaard, M., & Anderson, K. (2020). Conceptualizing News Avoidance: Towards a Shared Understanding of Different Causes and Potential Solutions. *Journalism Studies*, 21(4), 459–476. https://doi.org/10.1080/1461670X.2019.1686410

Standaert, O., Hanitzsch, T., & Dedonder, J. (2021). In their own words: A normative-empirical approach to journalistic roles around the world. *Journalism, 22*(4), 919–936. https://doi.org/10.1177/1464884919853183

Swart, J., Groot Kormelink, T., Costera Meijer, I., & Broersma, M. (2022). Advancing a radical audience turn in journalism. Fundamental dilemmas for journalism studies. *Digital Journalism, 10*(1), 8–22. https://doi.org/10.1080/21670811.2021.2024764

Tandoc, E. C., Jr. (2014). Journalism is twerking? How web analytics is changing the process of gatekeeping. *New Media & Society, 16*(4), 559–575. https://doi.org/10.1177/1461444814530541

Tandoc, E. C., Jr., & Duffy, A. (2016). Keeping up with the audiences: Journalistic role expectations in Singapore. *International Journal of Communication, 10*, 3338–3358. https://ijoc.org/index.php/ijoc/article/view/4565/1714

Truyens, P., & Picone, I. (2021). Audience views on professional norms of journalism. A media repertoire approach. *Journalism and Media, 2*(2), 258–274. https://doi.org/10.3390/journalmedia2020015

Tsfati, Y., Meyers, O., & Peri, Y. (2006). What is good journalism? Comparing Israeli public and journalists' perspectives. *Journalism, 7*(2), 152–173. https://doi.org/10.1177/1464884906062603

Valenzuela, S., Piña, M., & Ramírez, J. (2017). Behavioral effects of framing on social media users: How conflict, economic, human interest, and morality frames drive news sharing. *Journal of Communication, 67*(5), 803–826. https://psycnet.apa.org/doi/10.1111/jcom.12325

Van Dalen, A. (2019). Journalism, trust, and credibility. In K. Wahl-Jorgensen & T. Hanitzsch (Eds.), *The handbook of journalism studies* (pp. 356–371). Routledge.

Van Der Wurff, R., & Schoenbach, K. (2014). Civic and citizen demands of news media and journalists: What does the audience expect from good journalism? *Journalism and Mass Communication Quarterly, 91*(3), 433–451. https://doi.org/10.1177/1077699014538974

Vos, T., Eichholz, M., & Karaliova, T. (2019). Audiences and journalistic capital. *Journalism Studies, 20*(7), 1009–1027. https://doi.org/10.1080/1461670X.2018.1477551

Weaver, D., Beam, R. A., Brownlee, B. J., Voakes, P. S. & Wilhoit, G. C. (2007). *The American journalist in the 21st century: U.S. news people at the dawn of a new millennium.* .

Welbers, K., Van Atteveldt, W., Kleinnijenhuis, J., Ruigrok, N., & Schaper, J. (2016). News selection criteria in the digital age: Professional norms versus online audience metrics. *Journalism, 17*(8), 1037–1053. https://doi.org/10.1177/1464884915595474

Wendelin, M., Engelmann, I., & Neubarth, J. (2017). User rankings and journalistic news selection: Comparing news values and topics. *Journalism Studies*, *18*(2), 135–153. https://doi.org/10.1080/1461670X.2015.1040892

Willnat, L., Weaver, D. H., & Wilhoit, G. C. (2019). The American journalist in the digital age. *Journalism Studies*, *20*(3), 423–441. https://doi.org/10.1080/1461670X.2017.1387071

CHAPTER 5

Big Data, Artificial Intelligence and Their Effects: The Birth of an Alert Society

João Canavilhas

INTRODUCTION

Public opinion has been a fundamental element in democracies. It conditions government initiatives, shapes the strategy of the opposition and limits political discussion to certain issues.

Despite this importance, the concept is not easy to define (Steinberg, 1972), and throughout history it has undergone changes, many of which have been motivated by the way in which communication between people has changed. At a certain point in history, especially in the eighteenth century, public opinion was linked to public spaces—cafés and clubs—where the most prominent members of society expressed their opinions (Sena, 2007). At a later stage, newspapers began to mediate reality, becoming the "contemporary stage for public debate" (Pena, 2005, p.29).

These two moments illustrate in a simplified way, the difficulties in defining the concept since it is strongly dependent on the spaces where the discussion takes place and who has access to those same spaces. This is why

J. Canavilhas (✉)
Universidade da Beira Interior – Labcom, Covilhã, Portugal
e-mail: jc@ubi.pt

© The Author(s), under exclusive license to Springer Nature Switzerland AG 2024
M. Goyanes, A. Cañedo (eds.), *Media Influence on Opinion Change and Democracy*, https://doi.org/10.1007/978-3-031-70231-0_5

public opinion is often confused with published opinion (in the media), something that has changed with the media fragmentation caused by the new media.

Although authors such as Arendt (1995) maintain that public opinion is the information that individuals share with each other involuntarily, it is indisputable that this exchange of information is strongly influenced by the media. For this reason, classic studies in the field of journalism have developed various theories that have sought to study the effects of the media on society. Agenda-Setting (McCombs & Shaw, 1972), for example, argues that it is the media that dictates the topics that citizens discuss. Framing (Goffman, 1974/1986), on the other hand, argues that the media decide how events are framed, thus conditioning discussion and influencing public opinion.

With the expansion of the Internet and Web 2.0, the situation has changed. The traditional media have lost their centrality in the ecosystem and, as a result, their exclusive power to define and frame the issues under discussion. Blogs and social networks, new actors located on the periphery of journalism (Tandoc, 2019), began to compete for consumers' attention, and even managed to impose the agenda on traditional media.

In addition to the emergence of these competitors, a global economic crisis began in 2008, which, together with an accelerated process of technological evolution, gave rise to a "perfect storm" (Jukes, 2013). The traditional media were thus left in a fragile situation just when they needed to compete for users' attention with these new media adapted to the network society (Nossek & Adoni, 2017).

With a weakened traditional media system and new discussion stages emerging on the web, it has become necessary to rethink the public sphere (Bennett & Pfetsch, 2018). The fragmentation of information into information units distributed on social networks has facilitated readers' choices, making it easier to select what interests them and get rid of what doesn't (Boczkowski & Mitchelstein, 2015), something that wasn't so simple in traditional media. If the traditional media facilitated the process of forming public opinion by providing space for public debate (Curran, 1991), the new media have multiplied the number of spaces and freed up access to these stages of debate. Considering that the public sphere is the "communicative space that is constituted by the processes of public discursive interaction and the formation of public opinion" (Borges, 2014, p. 99), it can be said that the new media have considerably increased the size of this sphere.

With the massification of smartphones, the ways of accessing content and spaces for debate have changed (Westlund & Färdigh, 2015), creating more channels and new possibilities. According to Canavilhas et al. (2023, p. 135), "globally, the public sphere has been going through information chaos, where traditional intermediaries such as the media have seen their primary function of ordering and organizing information transmission and acting as watchdogs of political activity disrupted."

With readers dispersed across thousands of online spaces, accessing information via smartphones (Walker, 2019) and using the most diverse social networks to inform themselves (Westerman et al., 2014), public discussions have taken place on the most diverse stages, making it difficult to follow the debates.

This new form of information consumption—involving digital networks and smartphones—generates millions of pieces of data about users, which has become a new raw material for personalizing information. This offer is chosen by algorithms that process the data and, depending on how they have been programmed, create information bubbles (Pariser, 2011) that condition users. Not all users are aware of this action by the algorithms, so the public sphere is once again conditioned by a system capable of imposing agendas and frameworks, but now in a way that is invisible to society, since digital social networks and smartphones are spaces for individual consumption. Perhaps this is why the growing influence of the new media on public opinion is only visible during elections, with a growing gap between what appears to be public opinion and what citizens' real choices are.

The Rise of Big Data and Artificial Intelligence

Data is the oil of the twenty-first century (The Economist, 2017). Such a peremptory statement runs the risk of being strongly contested because different products are being compared. What is the relationship between a fuel that is a tangible good (oil) and a set of information that is an intangible good?

In fact, what is at issue is not their purpose, but the nature of each one, or rather their role in society. Just as oil (still) underpins the fuels used in almost every sector of the economy, data now powers an important part of emerging technologies.

Industry replaced coal with oil in the middle of the twentieth century. Coal, which had been the dominant fuel in industry since the start of the

Industrial Revolution, was overtaken by the efficiency, versatility, and availability of oil, with an impact on the technologies used in production and transportation.

Data was a neglected asset for many years. The advent of digitalization, the expansion of the Internet and the massification of social networks and smartphones has turned it into an essential asset, especially as society has started to generate more data and technological advances in computerization have made it possible to store and process it.

With these advances, data has gained a prominent role in decision-making. In science, business and politics, data-driven trends have become the basis for health diagnoses, business strategies and public policies, improving efficiency, identifying opportunities, and optimizing processes.

The continuous advance of online technologies, mobile communications and artificial intelligence has added value to data as it is the fuel for some of these technologies. In the case of Artificial Intelligence (AI), data is fundamental to its performance and so the quality of databases is the element that determines the quality of algorithms (FRA, 2019), just as raw materials determine the quality of consumer products.

Artificial intelligence gained great visibility at the end of 2022 with the launch of ChatGPT by openAI, but its development began in the 1950s. It was its generative facet that aroused the interest of public opinion and brought the subject to the front pages, above all because it put its power within the reach of any citizen.

In previous years, AI had already been at the center of public discussion, and precisely because of its connection to politics. In 2018, the world learned that Cambridge Analytica, a political consulting firm, used data collected from Facebook without users' permission to target personalized political messages (Fornasier & Beck, 2020). Perhaps this was the first moment when the public realized the importance of data and how they were voluntarily making it available for third parties to manipulate. Until then, the public knew that the data provided to companies to issue customer cards was used to personalize advertising, but this case has shown the other side of the use of databases: their use in politics.

The Cambridge Analytica case showed that apparently benign actions, such as publishing posts on a social network, could in fact be fuel for building not just consumer profiles, but psychological profiles. While in the first case it is a mere commercial marketing tool to direct personalized offers to the consumer, in the second case we are faced with a potential for manipulation with an impact on the quality of democracies since it sought to condition political choices (Christiano, 2022).

Thus, the power of data was joined by the power of artificial intelligence in transforming this data into actions aimed at conditioning electoral results, giving rise to disinformation phenomena (García-Marín et al., 2022), another hot topic, especially after the results of the 2016 US and 2018 Brazilian elections.

These cases were fundamental for public opinion to understand the link between social media and democracy, things that until then seemed to have little, if any, connection. An innocent post about attending the concert of a band you like could, in the end, serve to profile you and, later, send you manipulated messages about the band's political positions, trying to shape your opinion.

Analyzing Public Opinion Through Big Data Using AI

The concept of public opinion has evolved depending on the spaces where discussions between citizens take place. From the Greek Agora to bourgeois salons, from newspapers to the new media, the concept has changed depending on the participants and the spaces in which the issues are discussed.

Today, the media ecosystem has changed profoundly, with the new media playing a central role in society. From a mediacentric system (Motta, 2005), in which the traditional media were the only senders and therefore had some control over the message, we have moved to an Icentric system, in which each user has the power to send messages. In this way, control of the flow of information has been lost and the public's attention has been dispersed among a multitude of sources. First with blogs, then with so-called citizen journalism (Rosen, 2008) and later with digital social networks, "the people formerly known as the audience" (Rosen, 2012) took center stage in the ecosystem. Traditional media are now forced to fight for their social relevance, vying for the attention of public opinion that has migrated to digital media (Boczkowski, 2004).

The audience, which previously only consumed information, has also started producing it with their smartphones and distributing it on social networks. Along with content, users of the new media end up providing their own data, thus generating huge amounts of information with great potential for use. Two concepts have thus emerged: big data and artificial intelligence.

To talk about big data, it is necessary to address four fundamental elements: information, technology, methods, and impacts (De Mauro et al., 2016). Although the term refers to the processing and analysis of large amounts of data, it is commonly used to identify large amounts of data (structured or not) generated by the most varied types of actions carried out by users. In the case of humans, this could be the way they browse the web, use their smartphones, or make card payments, for example. All these actions generate data about their behavior and make it possible to draw up a profile of everyone. But there are many other sources: natural phenomena generate data that allows weather forecasts to be made, traffic generates data that allows apps to be fed, etc., etc. So, you could say that big data is, after all, the universe at work.

In the case of AI, we're talking about "systems that display intelligent behaviour by analysing their environment and taking actions – with some degree of autonomy – to achieve specific goals" (EU, 2018). Despite its limitations when it comes to interpreting certain phenomena (Sandoval-Martín & La-Rosa Barrolleta, 2023), AI is showing trends towards solutions and is being used in fields as diverse as image recognition or natural language processing, which is the basis of the chatbots, its most visible face today.

Thus, analyzing public opinion in today's fragmented ecosystem is only possible with the help of artificial intelligence technologies, since its size and dispersion generates millions of pieces of data that are humanly impossible to process.

Perhaps for this reason, the development of systems that seek to analyze the feelings of social media users in real time is one of the fastest growing areas of AI. The reason for this interest is the centrality that social networks have gained in societies, being spaces where it has become necessary to create alerts to identify extremist phenomena that may represent threats to society (Becker et al., 2011).

Curiously, these alerts that powers seek to implement to detect dangerous phenomena for countries are a hallmark of today's society, which has entered a new era following the massification of mobile devices with Internet access and the implementation of push systems.

From the Network Society to the Alert Society

The expansion of the Internet led Castells (1996) to talk about a new society characterized by the mediation of digital networks, the so-called network society. In this new scenario, organizations and individuals have changed the way they act and interact, which has had an impact on social organization.

ICT, particularly technologies associated with the Internet, have become "the technological basis of the network society" (Castells, 1996, p. 469), allowing individuals to communicate instantaneously at a distance, work collaboratively without simultaneous physical presence and build virtual networks that constitute a new power capable of challenging the vertical hierarchy characteristic of traditional societies. Movements such as the Arab Spring have shown the power of social networks to challenge traditional forms of power, thus illustrating some of the virtues of this new network society in the field of political action.

New technologies are also at the origin of what Bauman (2000) calls the "liquid society." The metaphor of liquidity has been used by the author in various works to describe the instability and fluidity of institutional and personal relationships today. In contrast to the solid societies of the past, where there were very clear hierarchies, long-term employment relationships and stable personal relationships, the liquid society is marked by ephemerality, volatility, speed, and fragmentation, with a direct impact on relationships between individuals and between individuals and institutions. Traditional powers, including the media, are losing importance and societies are constantly being reconfigured.

One of the characteristics of this society is unbridled consumption, which is linked to happiness (Bauman, 2000). Purchasing goods and services and advertising them on digital social networks is the new form of happiness, but it can quickly turn into dissatisfaction due to a lack of approval from followers (likes and positive emoticons) or because others are showing off something that is even more socially valued. According to the author, this constant search for happiness through the admiration of others leads to a liquidation of one's own identity as the individual adapts to the approval of others, losing their identity.

Unbridled consumption has been facilitated by a globalized offer and the emergence of electronic systems that facilitate the process. Platformization (Van Dijk et al., 2018) and the massification of mobile devices are two elements that facilitate and encourage consumption by allowing access to a global market and increasingly simplified and time-sensitive forms of payment. In the specific case of the smartphone, its role is twofold because as well as being a privileged channel for this type of action, it is also the preferred interface for publicizing these acts on social networks because it makes it easier to capture images and publish them immediately on the move.

Initially, the success of mobile phones lay in the fact that they offered their owners a permanent connection, conveying a sense of personal security (Dimmick et al., 1994). With the emergence of smartphones, another important feature was accentuated: communication/group integration (Quinn & Oldmeadow, 2013), thus becoming an aggregator of communities. In its smart version, the smartphone has become a personal, ubiquitous, and permanently connected meta device (Aguado & Martínez, 2006), becoming the preferred means of accessing the Internet (Westlund, 2012).

As well as making it possible to consume in all contexts (Peters, 2012), smartphones also incorporate a range of technologies that make it possible to read timetables, location (GPS), movement (accelerometer) and even some biometric data. These technological capabilities are also sources of millions of pieces of data, which, together with the information available on social networks, provide institutions and companies with a perfect portrait of each consumer.

The fact that smartphones allow direct access to everyone makes it possible to personalize the information directed at them, both in terms of personal preferences and behavior. It has therefore become a highly customizable channel, with alerts being one of its emblematic uses.

Today, most countries have warning systems through multiple channels that allow them to reach populations to inform them of imminent risks (Adam et al., 2012). Until now, these warnings were issued by the traditional media, with age or geographic segmentation, for example. A storm in a certain region could be announced on the local radio or TV, but this method did not guarantee that tourists passing through the region would have contact with the message.

Smartphones have made it possible for these alerts to be personalized, which is why tsunami alerts in the Pacific, tropical storms in the Caribbean or high temperatures in Portugal use these devices as a channel to reach the population, and all kinds of segmentation is possible.

This potential has spread to all areas and, today, alerts exist in every activity we carry out. The media themselves are exploiting this possibility by offering alerts on certain topics or breaking news stories. Google, for example, has its own alert system which users can activate by choosing words or topics of interest. The same goes for some of the best-known social networks, which allow alerts for hashtags, people, or groups, sending these alerts via push notifications.

Nowadays, it's safe to say that any extraordinary phenomenon can be immediately communicated to the target audience, be it an entire country or a very specific group. This means that we have moved from a pull system, in which people sought information, to a push system, in which information seeks people (Fidalgo & Canavilhas, 2009). What is new is not the reversal of direction in the distribution of information, because that was already happening on the web with alerts and feed readers: what is new is that this push nature has become personalized and transversal to the whole of society. The media, government organizations, health entities and companies, for example, have started using alerts to reach each citizen with a personalized message.

This situation makes it possible to say that we currently live in an alert society, in which our actions are increasingly conditioned by the personalized messages we receive. The greater the degree of personalization, the greater the familiarity we feel with the senders, since they show that they know us. The consequence is that they gain our trust, which causes us to lower our privacy defenses, exposing ourselves more and more and, therefore, becoming more and more transparent.

Transparent and Alert Society: Risks and Opportunities for Democracies

Traditionally, the media had the responsibility of providing citizens with the essential information to decode their social context and make the best political choices (Schudson, 1978). With the implosion of the traditional ecosystem, everything has changed: the success of mobile technologies, the massification of online platforms, the abundance of data and the emergence of artificial intelligence have dispersed this role among a wide range of entities, making the system completely uncontrollable and unpredictable.

In this set of changes, the two novelties are big data and artificial intelligence, since the personal channel—smartphones—already existed beforehand. But it is the combination of the three that puts society on its guard against a series of opportunities and risks.

In the field of opportunities, the processing of the abundance of data by artificial intelligence allows solutions to be found that are better adapted to each problem. The data generated by citizens' consumption, for example, allows us to get to know territories in detail, making it possible to manage more efficiently and adapt public policies to the real needs of citizens in each community. Instead of national policies that are applied across the board, public authorities could get to know the wishes and desires of citizens in their real context and to develop policies adapted to that reality.

Instead of multiplying structures, it becomes possible to optimize those that exist and invest in the gaps that this community has, seeking to mitigate them with proximity offers and developing transport infrastructure that facilitates this. The so-called smart territories (Gracias et al., 2023) are the result of using the data generated by the systems to improve people's lives. Whether in health, education, culture, the environment or transport, there are many opportunities to use data and AI to improve the public social system and thus make the benefits of democracies clearer.

Another interesting aspect, which also contributes to bringing citizens closer to the defense of public affairs, is the possibility of improving their civic participation. Over the last few decades, the image of democracies has suffered a profound deterioration (Dogan, 1997; Howe, 2017) due to their distance from the real needs of the population. As is often heard at election time, politicians only remember voters during campaign periods, so it is essential to tell citizens that their voice is heard, and their opinions are taken into account. This is possible by creating automatic channels that receive information and process it using artificial intelligence to return solutions adapted to each situation.

And even though they are often problems that are difficult to solve, it is always possible to reduce their impact on the community or, at the very least, to give an answer that shows that it is impossible to solve the problem at that time.

However, the circulation of data also carries risks, as we have seen in some cases in the recent past. First, because a large part of the population does not even realize how much data they provide to systems, particularly on social networks, putting their privacy at risk. Publishing or redistributing political messages exposes users to hate messages, for example (Di Fátima, 2023). The publication of a photo and all the metadata associated with it, the expression of a preference about an attitude or a simple like on a post by a third party generates information that can be used to make that person a target for messages that reinforce their position or try to persuade them to change their position.

The risk of these systems is that they make people's lives increasingly transparent, making them targets for campaigns, which can be both commercial and political. The crowd effect does the rest of the work: fearing being excluded from groups, citizens tend to join causes with large public support, often ignoring the fact that digital networks do not mirror society. If this was already a reality in the traditional media, the problem is even more visible in these networks, especially since the networks themselves enclose users in information bubbles (Pariser, 2011), favoring disinformation processes by removing the possibility of contrasting sources, as journalism does.

This new reality contains an antagonism that is difficult to understand: "in a global society where freedom of choice is at its highest, users are confined to platforms whose algorithms isolate part of the audience in decontextualized information niches" (Canavilhas, 2023, p. 84). This problem poses a risk to democracies because it is the trigger for the growth of extremism in society. Enclosed in a digital information bubble, and living in a society in which physical contacts lose relevance, the ideas transmitted by the networks seem to be the dominant currents in society, which rarely corresponds to reality, but tends to be the case if this action is continued.

Social media algorithms, fed by user-generated data, do an invisible job of shaping opinions. The longer the cycles, the greater the amount of data and the stronger the influence of these mechanisms in changing users' opinions.

Aware of this reality, governments around the world have put pressure on social networks to make their algorithms more transparent and to implement measures to prevent hate messages and extremism, thus seeking to mitigate their dark side (Piyajanaka, 2023). But governments are also under pressure due to the growing use of AI in making important decisions, especially due to the opacity of systems that are veritable black boxes (Fink, 2017). It is true that in recent years there has been a lot of legislation on transparency in the use of AI, but its effectiveness is limited because the digital world is constantly changing, making it impossible or impossible to implement it successfully.

Society is increasingly dependent on digital networks, a situation that has liquidated personal and institutional relationships, making it difficult to decode social phenomena. The ephemeral and the opinions of others have become increasingly important, forcing individuals to be permanently attentive to change to stay on trend and thus win the approval of their relational geography.

Thanks to their features, smartphones allow their owners to be always-on, with alerts acting as an alarm clock for permanent connection to the news. The reception and reaction data provided by each individual and the intelligent systems do the rest, processing the information and issuing alerts so that the consumer feels that nothing of interest is happening without their knowledge.

In this situation, the individual feels they have total control of their sphere of interest, freeing themselves from the public sphere that the traditional media imposed on them and which, curiously, sought to function "like an alarm system" in detecting social problems (Borges, 2014, p.100). In the new ecosystem, this alarm loses intensity in the face of new personalized digital alerts, making society more unpredictable because it is more permeable to invisible phenomena.

In an alert society, individuals are influenced by invisible microspheres (family or friends) that operate on social networks and are accessed through apps installed on smartphones. Opinions are shaped by algorithms that process personal data and transform it into targeted messages to achieve certain objectives. The success or failure of these actions only gains visibility when they are transformed into votes, personal actions, or social movements. Only then is it possible to analyze and react, but sometimes it is too late to correct, especially when it comes to extremist movements and actions.

References

Adam, A., Eledath, J., Mehrotra, S., & Venkatasubramanian, N. (2012). Social media alert and response to threats to citizens (SMART-C). *International Conference on Collaborative Computing.* https://doi.org/10.4108/ICST.COLLABORATECOM.2012.250713

Aguado, J. M., & Martínez, I. (2006). El proceso de mediatización de la telefonía móvil: de la interacción al consumo cultural. *Revista Zer, 11*(20), 319–343. https://doi.org/10.1387/zer.3770

Arendt, H. (1995). *Qu'est-ce que la politique?* Édition du Seuil.

Bauman, Z. (2000). *Liquid modernity.* Polity Press.

Becker, H., Naaman, M., & Gravano, L. (2011). Selecting quality Twitter content for events. *Proceedings of the International AAAI Conference on Web and Social Media, 5*(1), 442–445. https://doi.org/10.1609/icwsm.v5i1.14145

Bennett, W. L., & Pfetsch, B. (2018). Rethinking political communication in a time of disrupted public spheres. *Journal of Communication, 68*(2), 243–253. https://doi.org/10.1093/joc/jqx017

Boczkowski, P. J. (2004). *Digitizing the news. Innovation in online newspapers.* The MIT Press.

Boczkowski, P. J., & Mitchelstein, E. (2015). *La brecha de las noticias: La divergencia entre las preferencias informativas de los medios y el público.* Ediciones Manantial.

Borges, S. (2014). Opinião Pública: história, crítica e desafios na era transnacional. *Exedra, 9.*

Canavilhas, J. (2023). *Manual de jornalismo na Web.* Livros Labcom.

Canavilhas, J., Campos Domínguez, E., & García Orosa, B. (2023). Journalism, crisis and politics: A communications approach in times of change. In M. C. Negreira-Rey, J. Vázquez-Herrero, J. Sixto-García, & X. López-García (Eds.), *Blurring boundaries of journalism in digital media* (Studies in Big Data) (Vol. 140, pp. 135–149). Springer. https://doi.org/10.1007/978-3-031-43926-1_10

Castells, M. (1996). *A Sociedade em Rede.* Paz e Terra.

Christiano, T. (2022). Algorithms, manipulation, and democracy. *Canadian Journal of Philosophy, 52*(1), 109–124. https://doi.org/10.1017/can.2021.29

Curran, J. (1991). Rethinking the media as a public sphere. In P. Dahlgren & C. Sparks (Eds.), *Communication and citizenship – Journalism and the public sphere* (pp. 27–57). Routledge.

De Mauro, A., Greco, M., & Grimaldi, M. (2016). A formal definition of Big Data based on its essential features. *Library Review, 65*(3), 122–135. https://doi.org/10.1108/LR-06-2015-0061

Di Fátima, B. (2023). Preface. In B. di Fátima (Ed.), *A global approach to hate speech on social media* (pp. 11–15). Labcom Books.

Dimmick, J. W., Sikand, J., & Patterson, S. J. (1994). The gratifications of the household telephone: Sociability, instrumentality and ressurance. *Communication Research, 21*(5), 643–663. https://psycnet.apa.org/doi/10.1177/009365094021005005

Dogan, M. (1997). Erosion of confidence in advanced democracies. *Studies in Comparative International Development, 32,* 3–29. https://doi.org/10.1007/BF02687328

EU. (2018). *Communication from the Commission to the European Parliament, The European Council, The Council, The European Economic and Social Committee and the Committee of the Regions on Artificial Intelligence for Europe.* https://eur-lex.europa.eu/legal-content/EN/TXT/PDF/?uri=CELEX:52018DC0237&from=EN

Fidalgo, A., & Canavilhas, J. (2009). Todos os jornais no bolso: Pensando o jornalismo na era do celular. Em C. Rodrigues (Org.). Jornalismo On-Line: modos de fazer (pp. 96–146). PUC Rio.

Fink, K. (2017). Opening the government's black boxes: Freedom of information and algorithmic accountability. *Information, Communication & Society, 21*(10), 1453–1471. https://doi.org/10.1080/1369118X.2017.1330418

Fornasier, M. O., & Beck, C. (2020). Cambridge Analytica: Escândalo, Legado e Possíveis Futuros para a Democracia. *Direito em debate, 53*, 182–195. https://doi.org/10.21527/2176-6622.2020.53.182-195

FRA-European Union for Fundamental Rights. (2019). *Agency data quality and artificial intelligence – mitigating bias and error to protect fundamental rights.* https://fra.europa.eu/sites/default/files/fra_uploads/fra-2019-data-quality-and-ai_en.pdf

García-Marín, D., Elías, C., & Soengas-Pérez, X. (2022). Big Data and disinformation: Algorithm mapping for fact checking and artificial intelligence. In J. Vázquez-Herrero, A. Silva-Rodríguez, M. C. Negreira-Rey, C. Toural-Bran, & X. López-García (Eds.), *Total journalism* (Studies in Big Data) (Vol. 97, pp. 123–135). Springer. https://doi.org/10.1007/978-3-030-88028-6_10

Goffman, E. (1974/1986). *Frame analysis: An essay on the organization of experience.* Harvard University Press.

Gracias, J. S., Parnell, G. S., Specking, E., Pohl, E. A., & Buchanan, R. (2023). Smart cities—A structured literature review. *Smart Cities, 6*, 1719–1743. https://doi.org/10.3390/smartcities6040080

Howe, P. (2017). Eroding norms and democratic deconsolidation. *Journal of Democracy, 28*(4), 15–29. https://doi.org/10.1353/jod.2017.0061

Jukes, S. (2013). A perfect storm. In K. Fowler-Watt & S. Allan (Eds.), *Journalism: New challenges* (pp. 1–18). Centre for Journalism, and Communication Research, Bournemouth University.

McCombs, M., & Shaw, D. (1972). The agenda setting function of mass media. *Public Opinion Quaterly, 36*(2), 176–187. https://www.jstor.org/stable/2747787

Motta, L. M. (2005). The opposition between mediacentric and socieocentric paradigms. *Brazilian Journalism Research, 1*(1), 10.25200/BJR.v1n1.2005.34.

Nossek, H., & Adoni, H. (2017). Coexistence of "old" and "new" news media in a transitional media system: News repertories in Israel. *Participations, 14*(2), 399–415.

Pariser, E. (2011). *The filter bubble: What the Internet is hiding from you.* Penguin Press.

Pena, F. (2005). *Teoria do jornalismo.* Editora Contexto.

Peters, C. (2012). Journalism to go: The changing spaces of news consumption. *Journalism Studies, 13*(5–6), 695–705. https://doi.org/10.1080/1461670X.2012.662405

Piyajanaka, A. (2023, August 3). The dark side of artificial intelligence in social media security. *Medium.* https://medium.com/@asiripiyajanaka/the-dark-side-of-artificial-intelligence-in-social-media-security-7da2edaf6925

Quinn, S., & Oldmeadow, J. (2013). The martini effect and social networking sites: Early adolescents, mobile social networking and connectedness to friends. *Mobile Media & Communication, 1*(2), 237–247. https://doi.org/10.1177/2050157912474812

Rosen, J. (2008). A most useful definition of citizen journalism. http://archive.pressthink.org/2008/07/14/a_most_useful_d.html

Rosen, J. (2012). The people formerly known as the audience. In M. Mandiberg (Ed.), *The social media reader* (pp. 13–16). New York University Press. https://doi.org/10.18574/nyu/9780814763025.003.0005

Sandoval-Martín, T., & La-Rosa Barrolleta, L. (2023). Investigación sobre la calidad de las noticias automatizadas en la producción científica internacional: metodologías y resultados. *Cuadernos.Info, 55,* 114–136. https://doi.org/10.7764/cdi.55.54705

Schudson, M. (1978). *Discovering the news. A social history of American newspapers.* Wiley.

Sena, N. M. (2007). Espaço público, opinião e democracia. *Estudos em Comunicação, 1,* 270–304.

Steinberg, C. S. (1972). *Meios de Comunicação de Massa.* Cultrix.

Tandoc, E. C. (2019). Journalism at the periphery. *Media and Communication, 7*(4), 138–143. https://doi.org/10.17645/mac.v7i4.2626

The Economist. (2017, 6 May). The world's most valuable resource is no longer oil, but data. https://www.economist.com/leaders/2017/05/06/the-worlds-most-valuable-resource-is-no-longer-oil-but-data

Van Dijk, J., Poell, T., & De Waal, M. (2018). *The platform society: Public values in a connective world.* Oxford University Press.

Walker, M. (2019). *Americans favor mobile devices over desktops and laptops for getting news.* Pew Research Center. https://pewrsr.ch/3qsBtF7

Westerman, D., Spence, P. R., & Van Der Heide, B. (2014). Social media as information source: Recency of updates and credibility of information. *Journal of Computer-Mediated Communication, 19,* 171–183. https://doi.org/10.1111/jcc4.12041

Westlund, O. (2012). Producer-centric versus participation-centric: On the shaping of mobile media. *Northern Lights, 10,* 107–121.

Westlund, O., & Färdigh, M. A. (2015). Accessing the news in an age of mobile media: Tracing displacing and complementary effects of mobile news on newspapers and online news. *Mobile Media & Communication, 3*(1), 53–74. https://doi.org/10.1177/2050157914549039

PART II

Opinion Change and Democracy in Public Service Media

CHAPTER 6

Public Value and Liberal Democracies: The Potential of Public Service Media as Islands of Trust in the Digital Public Sphere

Marta Rodríguez-Castro

INTRODUCTION

On April 24, 2024, Spain's Prime Minister Pedro Sánchez posted on his X account a letter to the public in which he cancelled his public agenda for five days to reflect on his continuity in office. The reason behind this unprecedented decision stemmed from news received that same morning:

This chapter is part of the activities of the research project "Public Service Media in the face of the platform ecosystem: public value management and evaluation models relevant for Spain" (PID2021-122386OB-I00), funded by the Spanish Ministry of Science and Innovation, the State Research Agency and the European Regional Development Fund.

M. Rodríguez-Castro (✉)
Universidade de Santiago de Compostela, Santiago de Compostela, Spain
e-mail: m.rodriguez.castro@usc.gal

© The Author(s), under exclusive license to Springer Nature Switzerland AG 2024
M. Goyanes, A. Cañedo (eds.), *Media Influence on Opinion Change and Democracy*, https://doi.org/10.1007/978-3-031-70231-0_6

a court had initiated proceedings against Begoña Gómez, the president's wife, following a complaint filed by the far-right union Manos Limpias, accusing her of influence peddling based on unverified information published in minor digital media.[1] Five days later, Pedro Sánchez announced that he would stay on as Prime Minister, while lighting the spark of a national debate on disinformation and fake news, on the need to develop policies to fight against defamation campaigns that influence the political debate and the public sphere, and what is even more interesting, on the very definition of what a news media outlet is.

Many reflections can be drawn from this exceptional event—such as the responsibility associated with a high-level public office or the expression of emotions and vulnerability by political representatives. However, one of the most pertinent debates regarding this episode, also emphasized in the Prime Minister's speech, is the challenges posed by today's fragmented and increasingly polarized digital public sphere, and how these pose a threat to the sustainability of healthy and robust democracies. In times when disinformation spreads in social media and in disputable news media outlets, it becomes increasingly difficult to find and identify reliable news and, thus, separate the wheat from the chaff.

Against this backdrop, in this chapter it is argued that Public Service Media (PSM) should pursue their recognition as *islands of trust* (Bardoel & d'Haenens, 2008; Nissen, 2006; Sørensen et al., 2020; Urbániková & Smejkal, 2023), that is, a key source of information for all citizens, a lighthouse that could help the public navigate the news environment and empower citizens in the digital public sphere. To this end, the ideal of public service media should be materialized both in theory and in practice, ensuring the functioning of these public entities is guided towards the creation of public value, rather than moved by political capture.

First, the problems that have been part of the discussion on the public sphere are presented and transposed to the digital realm. Second, it is argued how the ideal of PSM can contribute to reinforcing the public sphere by adopting a public value strategy. It is concluded that for the ideal of PSM to materialize, greater external consensus and internal efforts have to be addressed.

---

[1] For more information on this event, see Ramírez (2024) in *The Guardian*.

The Digital Public Sphere: Old Problems, New Challenges

The public sphere is one of the most contested and tricky concepts in social sciences (Rauchfleisch, 2017). Departing from Habermas' (1962) conceptualization and drawing from later theoretical developments of the concept, Fuchs defines the public sphere as "a realm of society that stands in-between, mediates, and interfaces the economy, politics, and culture" (Fuchs, 2021a, p. 211). Thus, the public sphere provides a space for human communication "about matters that are of public relevance – that is, concern the many" (Fuchs, 2021a, p. 211). This definition integrates the sociological approach started by Habermas, who revolutionized the notion of the public sphere by contextualizing it within a wider political, cultural, and social context and advancing previous theories that only dealt with the public sphere in relation to public opinion (Habermas, 2023).

The approach outlined by Habermas is of particular interest when studying the relationship between media systems and deliberative politics, the foundation of liberal democracies. The communicative spaces that structure the public sphere mediate political communication and shape the opinions of citizens, who participate in these spaces and gather information about political, economic, and social issues that affect them (Fuchs, 2021b). The digital public sphere, understood not as "a separate sphere of society but a dimension and aspect of the public sphere in societies where digital information and digital communication are prevalent" (Fuchs, 2021b, p. 13), still faces the same problems as the traditional notion of the public sphere when it comes to materializing its ideal version.

The issues that hamper the perfect functioning of the public sphere have been narrowed down by Price (1992) to five major constraints of the public: (1) lack of competence, (2) lack of resources, (3) the tyranny of the majority, (4) susceptibility to persuasion, and (5) the dominance of elites. Next, we will delve into each of these questions, updating them to the dynamics of the digital environment.

The lack of competence of the public refers to the idea that it cannot be expected that citizens are politically active and involved in all public issues that affect them, either because there is a lack of interest or a lack of energy. Under this presumption—which could be interpreted as quite condescending and paternalistic—democratic theory would ask citizens for more than they are able and willing to give, resulting in partial or inaccurate information shaping the public opinion. This rooted understanding of citizens' lack of competence and interest in public issues is reflected nowadays in the trend towards intentional news avoidance, that is, "low news consumption over a continuous period of time caused by a dislike for news" (Skovsgaard & Andersen, 2020, p. 463). Along with the dislike for news, intentional news avoidance has also been linked to news reporting being too negative, to low trust in news and to news overload (Goyanes et al., 2023; Skovsgaard & Andersen, 2020). The latter being a consequence of the increased media offer available in the digital realm and incidental news exposure (Schäfer, 2023), as citizens might encounter news when using social media or being online for other reason. The intertwine of these intrinsic features of the digital public sphere (incidental news exposure, news overload and intentional news avoidance) hamper its realization, thus eroding the function of liberal democracies.

A second problem pointed by Price (1992) refers to the lack of resources, as in the public lacking the knowledge and literacy required to understand, analyze, and interpret the topics that affect them. The adaptation of this problematic to the digital public sphere adds another level of complexity: the lack of resources to distinguish which sources of information to trust. The aforementioned expansion of the media offer implies that news media now share space and compete with other sources of information that operate under logics different from journalistic ethics as well as with direct sources of disinformation. As Serrano-Puche et al. (2023) argue, trust in digital media is now mediated by the blurring of the traditional boundaries of journalism, the hybridization of classical and digital logics, and, again, the broadening of the media offer that leads to increasing competition among digital agents for the public's online attention. In addition to the threats of disinformation streams, misinformation practices undertaken by individuals who share false or inaccurate information without being aware also contribute to this low-trust atmosphere in the digital realm. As trust in news is deemed "a requirement for any democracy to function properly" (Holtrup et al., 2024, p. 159), the lack of resources of the public to navigate the information environment becomes a major threat for a correct functioning of the public sphere.

Third, Price (1992) mentions the tyranny of the majority, that is, the risk of silencing minority opinions that might not be as popular as mainstream perspectives or tastes, in line with the spiral of science theory (Noelle-Neumann, 1974). Even though the spread of social media was initially seen as a new means for individual and collective expression in digital public forums (Benkler, 2006), the intertwine of the logics of digital capitalism and algorithmic recommendation led to a different scenario. In the digital public sphere, the automation of content suggestions and recommendations strengthen the dynamics of the spiral of silence and lead to the increase of self-censorship (Cheong et al., 2022; Hoffmann & Lutz, 2017). Moreover, the rise of cyber-aggressions in general (DeMarsico et al., 2022), and online harassment to journalists in particular (Holton et al., 2023) add to the factors that erode a plural and diverse public sphere where different approaches and perspectives can be freely debated.

In strong connection with this, algorithmic recommendation and personalization in digital media, along with increasing political and social polarization (Yarchi et al., 2021) exacerbates the public's susceptibility to persuasion, the fourth concern listed by Price (1992). Such vulnerability, as argued by Price, is especially strong when persuasive communication is emotional and not rational. In the digital realm, the formation of echo chambers and filter bubbles through news personalization and selective exposure has led to dissonant public spheres and, as stated by Gil De Zúñiga et al. (2023) the polarization of the public prompts greater resistance to political persuasion and changes of opinion. Therefore, while the public becomes more influenceable by information that confirms their own perspective, their resistance to new or different approaches hampers the ideal notion for the public sphere, for which openness to contrasting diverse viewpoints is crucial.

The final problem identified in the literature by Price (1992) is the dominance of elites, who control the dynamics of the public sphere and influence democratic debate. In the digital public sphere this problem is accentuated by intensified media concentration levels and platform dominance (Knoche, 2021). As tech giants expanded globally and diversified their business areas—social media, news outlets, entertainment—their market power became undisputable and their control over the public debate intensified. The role of digital platforms in the digital public sphere and their influence in liberal democracies requires new regulation that is adapted to platform logics, such as the European Union's Digital Markets Act (European Union, 2022a) and Digital Service Act (European Union, 2022b). As proven by extensive research (Badr, 2021; Hendrickx & Van Remoortere, 2024; Masduki & D'Haenens, 2022), media concentration hampers diversity and pluralism, thus once again constraining the public debate within the public sphere.

Public Service Media as *Islands of Trust* in the Digital Public Sphere: A Public Value-Based Approach

Public service broadcasters are key agents within national media systems and thus have traditionally played an important role in shaping the dynamics of the public sphere. After their transition to public service media organizations and the legitimization of the expansion of their public service remit to the digital realm (D'Arma et al., 2021; Donders, 2019; Lowe & Bardoel, 2007), PSM organizations are struggling to retain their long-standing relevance in the digital public sphere, where global online platforms owned by powerful tech companies concentrate most market power (Martin, 2021), both in terms of revenues and, what matters most for public service media, in terms of audience reach.

However, considering the problematics that characterize the digital public sphere, the strong presence of an agent that treasures and promotes democratic and civil values, rather than commercial interests, is key to sustaining a balanced and fair public debate and, thus, healthy liberal democracies. In line with other authors, such as Fuchs (2021b), we will argue that Public Service Media should reinforce their compromise with a public value strategy so that they become *islands of trust* in the digital public sphere: a recognizable, independent, and public interest resource that citizens can rely on. The theoretical proposal that will be described in this section departs from the ideal conception of public service media. It should be noted that, in practice, these media organizations operate under diverse sources of pressure, such as political capture (Media and Journalism Research Center, n.d.), budget constraints (EBU-MIS, 2024) or attacks from far-right agents (Holtz-Bacha, 2021), among others, that hamper the realization of this PSM ideal.

This ideal version of Public Service Media has been shaped lately by the goal of public value creation. Public value has its roots in the management theory that was first developed by Moore (1995) with the aim to renovate public sector management and promote innovation and collaboration within public administration. Since then, this approach has permeated to the field of European PSM, where the notion of public value was used to legitimize the expansion of public service broadcasters' activities beyond traditional broadcasting and into digital services. Although there is not just a single definition of what public value is, as public managers should develop their own according to the needs of the stakeholders and the organization's operational capabilities, this approach has been useful in the delineation of the values that public service media should adhere to in order to fulfill their public service remit in the digital environment.

Thus, recent approaches led by the European Broadcasting Union (EBU, 2012), but also by PSM organizations individually (like the ARD in Germany, the Austrian ORF, the BBC in the United Kingdom or the VRT in Belgium) and scholars (Chivers & Allan, 2022; Gransow, 2018) have attempted to conceptualize the public value of public service media. For the purpose of the argument that is being developed in this chapter, we will depart from the adaptable conceptualization of public value undertaken by Cañedo et al. (2022), where the authors identified twelve public value dimensions for public service media: social engagement, diversity, innovation, independence, excellence, universality, citizen participation, media literacy, accountability, territorial cohesion, social justice, and cooperation.

Through the reinforcement of these public value dimensions, public service media could become *islands of trust* and contribute to strengthening a healthy public sphere, as specific strategies linked to these principles can partially counterbalance the problems that had been explained in the previous section. Table 6.1 illustrates the main points of this argument,

Table 6.1 Theoretical approach to PSM's contribution to strengthening the digital public sphere

Problems in the materialization of the public sphere	Complications from the digital public sphere	Public value-based solution
Lack of competence	Incidental news consumption, news overload, intentional news avoidance	Excellence, universality
Lack of resources	Disinformation and misinformation, low trust in news	Media literacy, excellence, cooperation
Tyranny of the majority	Algorithmic recommendations, self-censorship, online harassment	Diversity, independence
Susceptibility to persuasion	Polarization, echo chambers, selective exposure	Independence, territorial cohesion, social engagement
Dominance of elites	Market concentration and platform dominance	Citizen participation, social justice

Note: Processed by the author

summarizing how the traditional problems of the public sphere, along with the new layer of casuistic that is brought to the table by digitization and platformization, could be approached by public value-based solutions undertaken by PSM.

The lack of competence of the public exacerbated by news overload, incidental news consumption and intentional news avoidance could be soothed by reinforcing excellence and universality within PSM. Excellence is here understood as the aggregation of quality, professionalism, and leadership. Only by providing high-quality content—specially news—and by sticking to the highest professional standards in journalistic practice can PSM content be relevant for their public. Moreover, PSM are in a good position to innovate in their journalistic practices and formats such as constructive journalism, that has been identified as a good means to fight against news fatigue produced by the excess of *bad news* (Skovsgaard & Andersen, 2020). The Swedish public television SVT, for instance, has been working with constructive journalism since 2009 (McIntyre & Gyldensted, 2017) and considers part of its public service remit to provide information that is encouraging and solution-based, while still reporting on hard news.

Universality, on the other hand, refers to the obligation for public service media to provide a service that is accessible for everyone, regardless of their location, their media competences, their abilities, and their media consumption preferences. Due to their public funding, public service broadcasters have always had to provide a universal service, but in times of media change, universal access also translates as being able to provide media content through different platforms. This means that PSM organizations should rethink their distribution strategies in order to be able to provide quality content in their own platforms, but also through third-party platforms. While this entails greater risk for brand erosion and implies giving away part of the control over the content monitorization and monetization, PSM have to be present in those platforms where the public is, ensuring that public value content is also part of the digital diets of their audiences—even if it is *incidentally*. Some PSM organizations are already exploring this strategy. For instance, the Flemish VRT distributes informative content adapted to young audiences with their brand *nws*, that not only relies on its own website, but also—and mostly—on its Instagram and TikTok accounts (Hendrickx, 2023).

To tackle the lack of resources of the public, considering the waves of disinformation and misinformation and the declining levels of trust in news,

PSM should endeavor to promote media and digital literacy, cooperation, and, again, excellence. Excellence because the first step in the process of regaining the public's trust in the news is to strengthen the informative mission of PSM by safeguarding the provision of high-quality, plural, critical, and independent information (Rodríguez-Castro & Pérez-Seijo, 2024).

Media literacy, along with digital literacy, have become key public value dimensions. Public service media should "facilitate the understanding of citizens concerning essential issues for social coexistence" (Cañedo et al., 2022, p. 594) and embrace a counselling function that would imply sharing knowledge, advising citizens on public issues, and empowering the public so that they have the tools and the competences to navigate the current media and digital environments. If effective, media and digital literacy strategies could contribute to lessen the spread of misinformation and to develop greater public resistance to disinformation.

Moreover, cooperation, understood as the development of coordinated strategies involving institutions and/or other media outlets, becomes a transversal requirement in the current media environment, that demands coordinated and supranational actions that tackle global needs. In this regard, PSM organizations have traditionally been keen in the development of coordinated strategies and the creation of networks that operate under shared values. One recent example is the EBU's initiative *A European Perspective*, a project based in the cooperation among the digital newsrooms of public service broadcasters that promotes the exchange of national news that are then featured in each outlet's news services websites (Rodríguez-Castro & Arriaza-Ibarra, 2023). With this collaboration, not only a European public sphere is promoted, but also disinformation on what happens in neighboring countries is undercut with the distribution of trustworthy, reliable news.

Third, the tyranny of the majority, propelled in the digital environment by algorithmic recommendations, self-censorship, and online harassment, could be mitigated by strengthening two core values of PSM: diversity and independence. Diversity and pluralism entail the integration of different perspectives and giving voice to minorities, that might find it harder to have their viewpoints included in other mainstream media. By providing a safe space for the expression of different perspectives and compromising with plural newsmaking, public service media could offer content that would make every citizen feel represented. In the digital realm, some PSM organizations have adapted the diversity principle to their algorithmic recommendations, that are designed to provide a diverse media diet, rather than a personalized experience based on reinforcing user preferences (Helberger, 2015). In addition to this, as public service broadcasters are expected to be independent from political and commercial pressures, they are the most suited media actors for embracing internal pluralism, as no bias should affect the selection of journalists and media professionals.

In connection to this, the public's susceptibility to persuasion, intensified by polarization, echo chambers and selective exposure, could also be subdued by ensuring diversity and independence in public service media, as well as territorial cohesion and social engagement. If PSM organizations regain the trust of the public with reinforced independence, thus becoming *islands of trust* that all segments of audience find trustworthy, polarization could be tackled. Previous research has pointed out that public service media news consumption reduces political selective exposure, which leads to greater cohesion in fragmented public spheres (Bos et al., 2016). To this aim, PSM should operate under the value of social engagement, that is understood as their mission to put citizens at the center of their actions and satisfy the public's information, entertainment and education needs. This would be a prerequisite for them to become *islands of trust* and should penetrate all other public value dimensions.

Lastly, the elites' dominance of the public sphere, exacerbated by increasing levels of concentration in the media market and platform dominance could be counterbalanced by reinforcing citizen participation and social justice within stronger public service media. Citizen participation entails both participation in content production and in governance practices and decision-making. As public value management relies on the participation of stakeholders, namely, citizens, PSM should aspire to become open and participatory media organizations, thus enhancing their democratic contribution to the public sphere (Grünangerl et al., 2012). Some PSM organizations have already embraced this principle and engage in public debates about their role with the public. That is the case, for instance, of the Austrian ORF that regularly organizes *DialogForums*, open forums for citizens and other stakeholders to express their viewpoints on different aspects affecting the public service broadcaster. If the insights from the public are included in the PSM organization's decision-making, this would result in more democratic and citizen-oriented media services.

In the same vein, operating under the principle of social justice, which entails the traditional defense of human rights, but also emerging values such as the right to privacy in the digital environment, is crucial in the process of public service media becoming *islands of trust*. In times where digital platforms sustain their businesses with the commercialization of users' data, PSM should provide a safe space for citizens to move online with the guarantee that their data will be handled according to ethical values (Sørensen et al., 2020).

CONCLUSIONS

In this chapter, we have argued that the materialization of the ideal conceptualization of public service media, operating under public value logics, could contribute to the revitalization of the public sphere by addressing the problematics associated with its fulfillment and the difficulties added by digitization and platformization. This argumentation is in line with previous studies that point to the potential of strong public media in sustaining a bolder, more democratic, and healthier public sphere (Fuchs, 2021b; Fuchs & Unterberger, 2021; Nikunen & Hokka, 2020; Thomass et al., 2022). It is not the purpose of this chapter to argue that public service media are the only agents that could approach this mission, nor that they should do it on their own. In this sense, it is also important to note that the ideal of PSM does not always materialize, as even the BBC, traditionally considered the paradigm of public service broadcasting, operates with imperfections (Freedman, 2019).

Instead, it is argued that these organizations should lead the way in public value creation and thus become *islands of trust*, so that citizens know that they rely on them for the fulfillment of their communication needs. To enable the realization of this ideal version of public service media, external and internal action are required. Externally, greater efforts must be made in order to safeguard PSM's independence. The European Media Freedom Act (European Union, 2024) has made some advances in this regard by establishing guidelines aimed at reducing political interference in PSM's editorial decisions, but it is still too soon to assess the impact that this new regulatory framework has had.

On the other side, public service media should embrace public value strategies and act under the principles that have been discussed in this chapter. To do so, public service media organizations should benefit from the implementation of innovative practices—such as advancing in the use of Artificial Intelligence in the public interest—as well as from cooperation with other media agents and institutions that share the same values and purposes. By promoting stronger and more accountable public service media, a healthier and more robust public sphere is encouraged as well.

References

Badr, Z. (2021). More or more of the same: Ownership concentration and media diversity in Egypt. *The International Journal of Press/Politics*, *26*(4), 774–796. https://doi.org/10.1177/19401612211025164

Bardoel, J., & d'Haenens, L. (2008). Reinventing public service broadcasting in Europe: Prospects, promises and problems. *Media, Culture and Society*, *30*(3), 337–355. https://doi.org/10.1177/0163443708088791

Benkler, Y. (2006). *The wealth of networks: How social production transforms markets and freedom*. Yale University Press.

Bos, L., Kruikemeier, S., & De Vreese, C. (2016). Nation binding: How public service broadcasting mitigates political selective exposure. *PLoS One*, *11*(5). https://doi.org/10.1371/journal.pone.0155112

Cañedo, A., Rodríguez-Castro, M., & López-Cepeda, A. M. (2022). Distilling the value of public service media: Towards a tenable onceptualization in the European framework. *European Journal of Communication*, *37*(6), 586–605. https://doi.org/10.1177/02673231221090777

Cheong, H. J., Baksh, S. M., & Ju, I. (2022). Spiral of silence in an algorithm-driven social media content environment: Conceptual framework and research propositions. *KOME*, *10*(1), 32–46. https://doi.org/10.17646/KOME.75672.86

Chivers, T., & Allan, S. (2022). *What is the public value of public service broadcasting? Exploring challenges and opportunities in evolving media contexts. Discussion Paper 2022/01*. Creative Industries Policy and Evidence Centre (PEC). Retrieved from https://orca.cardiff.ac.uk/146569/

D'Arma, A., Raats, T., & Steemers, J. (2021). Public service media in the age of SvoDs: A comparative study of PSM strategic responses in Flanders, Italy and the UK. *Media, Culture and Society*, *43*(4), 682–700. https://doi.org/10.1177/0163443720972909

DeMarsico, D., Bounoua, N., Miglin, R., & Sadeh, N. (2022). Aggression in the digital era: Assessing the validity of the cyber motivations for aggression and deviance scale. *Assessment*, *29*(4), 764–781. https://doi.org/10.1177/1073191121990088

Donders, K. (2019). Public service media beyond the digital hype: Distribution strategies in a platform era. *Media, Culture and Society*, *41*(7), 1011–1028. https://doi.org/10.1177/0163443719857616

EBU. (2012). *Empowering society. A declaration on the core values of public service media*. https://www.ebu.ch/files/live/sites/ebu/files/Publications/EBU-Empowering-Society_EN.pdf

EBU-MIS. (2024). *Funding of public service media*. EBU.

European Union. (2022a). Regulation (EU) 2022/1925 of the European Parliament and of the Council of 14 September 2022 on contestable and fair markets in the digital sector and amending Directives (EU) 2019/1937 and

(EU) 2020/1828 (Digital Markets Act). https://eur-lex.europa.eu/legal-content/EN/TXT/?uri=uriserv%3AOJ.L_.2022a.265.01.0001.01.ENG&toc=OJ%3AL%3A2022%3A265%3ATOC

European Union. (2022b). Regulation (EU) 2022/2065 of the European Parliament and of the Council of 19 October 2022 on a single market for digital services and amending Directive 2000/31/EC (Digital Services Act). https://eur-lex.europa.eu/legal-content/EN/TXT/?uri=celex%3A32022bR2065

European Union. (2024). Regulation (EU) 2024/1083 of the European Parliament and of the Council of 11 April 2024 establishing a common framework for media services in the internal market and amending Directive 2010/13/EU (European Media Freedom Act). https://eur-lex.europa.eu/legal-content/EN/TXT/?uri=CELEX%3A32024R1083

Freedman, D. (2019). "Public Service" and the journalism crisis: Is the BBC the answer? *Television and New Media*, *20*(3), 203–218. https://doi.org/10.1177/1527476418760985

Fuchs, C. (2021a). *Foundations of critical theory media, communication and society volume two* (Vol. 2). Routledge.

Fuchs, C. (2021b). The digital commons and the digital public sphere how to advance digital democracy today. *Westminster Papers in Communication and Culture*, *16*(1). https://doi.org/10.16997/wpcc.917

Fuchs, C., & Unterberger, K. (2021). *The public service media and public service Internet manifesto*. University of Westminster Press. https://doi.org/10.16997/book60.e

Gil De Zúñiga, H., Marné, H. M., & Carty, E. (2023). Abating dissonant public spheres: Exploring the effects of affective, ideological and perceived societal political polarization on social media political persuasion. *Political Communication*, *40*(3), 327–345. https://doi.org/10.1080/10584609.2022.2139310

Goyanes, M., Ardèvol-Abreu, A., & Gil de Zúñiga, H. (2023). Antecedents of news avoidance: Competing effects of political interest, news overload, trust in news media, and "News Finds Me" perception. *Digital Journalism*, *11*(1), 1–18. https://doi.org/10.1080/21670811.2021.1990097

Gransow, C. (2018). *Public Value-Konzepte im öffentlichen Rundfunk*. Springer Fachmedien Wiesbaden. https://doi.org/10.1007/978-3-658-19360-7

Grünangerl, M., Trappel, J., & Gerard-Wenzel, C. (2012). Public value and participation of civil society – A case for public service or community media? *kommunikation.medien*.

Habermas, J. (1962). *Strukturwandel der Öffentlichkeit. Untersuchungen zu einer Kategorie der bürgerlichen Gesellschaft*.

Habermas, J. (2023). *A new structural transformation of the public sphere and deliberative politics*. Polity Press.

Helberger, N. (2015). Merely facilitating or actively stimulating diverse media choices? Public service media at the crossroad. *International Journal of Communication*, 9, 1324–1340. https://ijoc.org/index.php/ijoc/article/view/2875/1374

Hendrickx, J. (2023). The rise of social journalism: An explorative case study of a youth-oriented Instagram news account. *Journalism Practice*, 17(8), 1810–1825. https://doi.org/10.1080/17512786.2021.2012500

Hendrickx, J., & Van Remoortere, A. (2024). Exploring the link between media concentration and news content diversity using automated text analysis. *Journalism*, 25(2), 353–371. https://doi.org/10.1177/14648849221136946

Hoffmann, C. P., & Lutz, C. (2017). Spiral of silence 2.0: Political self-censorship among young facebook users. *ACM International Conference Proceeding Series, Part F129683*. https://doi.org/10.1145/3097286.3097296

Holton, A. E., Bélair-Gagnon, V., Bossio, D., & Molyneux, L. (2023). "Not Their Fault, but Their Problem": Organizational responses to the online harassment of journalists. *Journalism Practice*, 17(4), 859–874. https://doi.org/10.1080/17512786.2021.1946417

Holtrup, S., Henke, J., Steffan, D., & Möhring, W. (2024). The reciprocal effects of perceived accuracy and trust in news media: A two-wave online panel study in the context of the 2021 German federal election. *Journalism and Mass Communication Quarterly*, 101(1), 156–177. https://doi.org/10.1177/10776990231202692

Holtz-Bacha, C. (2021). The kiss of death. Public service media under right-wing populist attack. *European Journal of Communication*, 36(3), 221–237. https://doi.org/10.1177/0267323121991334

Knoche, M. (2021). Media concentration: A critical political economy perspective. *TripleC*, 19(2), 371–391. https://doi.org/10.31269/TRIPLEC.V19I2.1298

Lowe, G. F., & Bardoel, J. (Eds.). (2007). *From public service broadcasting to public service media*. Nordicom.

Martin, E. N. (2021). Can public service broadcasting survive Silicon Valley? Synthesizing leadership perspectives at the BBC, PBS, NPR, CPB and local U.S. stations. *Technology in Society*, 64, 101451. https://doi.org/10.1016/j.techsoc.2020.101451

Masduki, & D'Haenens, L. (2022). Concentration of media ownership in Indonesia: A setback for viewpoint diversity. *International Journal of Communication*, 16, 2239–2259. https://ijoc.org/index.php/ijoc/article/view/17769/3759

McIntyre, K., & Gyldensted, C. (2017). Constructive journalism: An introduction and practical guide for applying positive psychology techniques to news production. *The Journal of Media Innovations*, 4(2), 20–34. https://doi.org/10.5617/jomi.v4i2.2403

Media and Journalism Research Center. (n.d.). *State Media Monitor*. Retrieved from https://statemediamonitor.com/
Moore, M. (1995). *Creating public value: Strategic management in government*. Harvard University Press. https://doi.org/10.1177/027507409702700305
Nikunen, K., & Hokka, J. (2020). Welfare state values and public service media in the era of datafication. *Global Perspectives, 1*(1). https://doi.org/10.1525/gp.2020.12906
Nissen, C. (2006). *Public service media in the information society*. Council of Europe. https://rm.coe.int/1680483b2f
Noelle-Neumann, E. (1974). The spiral of silence a theory of public opinion. *Journal of Communication, 24*(2), 43–51. https://doi.org/10.1111/j.1460-2466.1974.tb00367.x
Price, V. (1992). *Public opinion*. Sage.
Ramírez, M. (2024, April 30). The Pedro Sánchez crisis makes it clear: Spain's politicians are playing with fire. *The Guardian*. https://www.theguardian.com/commentisfree/2024/apr/30/pedro-sanchez-spain-crisis-prime-minister
Rauchfleisch, A. (2017). The public sphere as an essentially contested concept: A co-citation analysis of the last 20 years of public sphere research. *Communication and the Public, 2*(1), 3–18. https://doi.org/10.1177/2057047317691054
Rodríguez-Castro, M., & Arriaza-Ibarra, K. (2023). La construcción de una esfera pública europea a través de la colaboración y la innovación: A European Perspective, la redacción más grande de Europa. *Espejo de Monografías de Comunicación Social, 21*, 219–231. https://doi.org/10.52495/c14.emcs.21.p107
Rodríguez-Castro, M., & Pérez-Seijo, S. (2024). El combate de la desinformación como valor de los medios de comunicación de servicio público. In J. R. Araújo, L. A. Muñoz, & F. J. P. Rojano (Eds.), *El impacto de la desinformación en el ámbito local* (pp. 37–53). Editorial Fragua.
Schäfer, S. (2023). Incidental news exposure in a digital media environment: A scoping review of recent research. *Annals of the International Communication Association, 47*(2), 242–260. https://doi.org/10.1080/23808985.2023.2169953
Serrano-Puche, J., Rodríguez-Salcedo, N., & Martínez-Costa, M. P. (2023). Trust, disinformation, and digital media: Perceptions and expectations about news in a polarized environment. *Profesional de La Información, 32*(5). https://doi.org/10.3145/epi.2023.sep.18
Skovsgaard, M., & Andersen, K. (2020). Conceptualizing news avoidance: Towards a shared understanding of different causes and potential solutions. *Journalism Studies, 21*(4), 459–476. https://doi.org/10.1080/1461670X.2019.1686410

Sørensen, J. K., van den Bulck, H., & Kosta, S. (2020). Stop spreading the data: PSM, trust and third-party services. *Journal of Information Policy, 10*, 474–513. https://doi.org/10.5325/jinfopoli.10.2020.0474

Thomass, B., Fidalgo, J., Grönvall, J., Karadimitriou, A., & Nord, L. (2022). Public service media: Exploring the influence of strong public service media on democracy. In J. Trappel & T. Tomaz (Eds.), *Success and failure in news media performance: Comparative analysis in the Media for Democracy Monitor 2021* (pp. 187–209). Nordicom. https://doi.org/10.48335/9789188855589-9

Urbániková, M., & Smejkal, K. (2023). Trust and distrust in public service media: A case study from the Czech Republic. *Media and Communication, 11*(4), 297–307. https://doi.org/10.17645/mac.v11i4.7053

Yarchi, M., Baden, C., & Kligler-Vilenchik, N. (2021). Political polarization on the digital sphere: A cross-platform, over-time analysis of interactional, positional, and affective polarization on social media. *Political Communication, 38*(1–2), 98–139. https://doi.org/10.1080/10584609.2020.1785067

CHAPTER 7

Public Service Media and National Resilience in the Age of Information Disorders: A Two-Dimensional Conceptualization for Policy-Making

Auksė Balčytienė ⓘ *and Minna Aslama Horowitz* ⓘ

RESILIENCE AS A NEW POLICY PRINCIPLE

Public Service Broadcasting (PSB) has traditionally been integral to the European media landscape. It continues to be viewed as a crucial stakeholder in safeguarding freedom of expression and ensuring access to information. In the European Union (EU) and numerous Member States, PSB has played a central role in fostering 'cultural citizenship' (e.g., Jauert & Lowe, 2005). Additionally, the past few decades have witnessed the

---

A. Balčytienė
Vytautas Magnus University, Kaunas, Lithuania
e-mail: aukse.balcytiene@vdu.lt

M. A. Horowitz (✉)
University of Helsinki, Helsinki, Finland
e-mail: minna.aslama@helsinki.fi

© The Author(s), under exclusive license to Springer Nature Switzerland AG 2024
M. Goyanes, A. Cañedo (eds.), *Media Influence on Opinion Change and Democracy*, https://doi.org/10.1007/978-3-031-70231-0_7

emergence of 'public service broadcasting beyond broadcasting', where PSBs provide contents and services in the multi-media environment, now often labeled as public service media (PSM) (Lowe & Bardoel, 2008). Still, the market-driven narrative surrounding public service media has persistently posed challenges to public service remits in Europe and elsewhere, further exacerbated in recent years: the challenges faced by commercial legacy media in the digital economy have raised concerns regarding the perceived unfair advantages PSM enjoy and their entitlement to operate on commercial platforms (Van Dijck & Poell, 2014).

In the 2020s, the EU has embraced a new narrative and related policy measures. The European Democracy Action Plan (EDAP, see: European Commission, 2020) is an overarching plan to strengthen the *resilience* of democracies across the EU. The 2030 Digital Compass: The European Way for the Digital Decade, setting the pathway for EDAP, further notes that Europe's approach to the digital economy includes ensuring the security and resilience of its digital ecosystem and supply chains (European Commission, 2021). The Compass is openly a response to platform power and related challenges, as amplified during the pandemic. It mentions a variety of policy initiatives, from data regulation to the Digital Services Act (DSA) package, and envisions many innovative digital projects and developments by 2030 to ensure European economic success and overall regional resilience. Unsurprisingly, this new resilience narrative also underpins the European debates on disinformation and other related challenges, including various strategies against online harms and the new legacy media-focused proposal, the European Media Freedom Act (EMFA).

The focus on national resilience is not unsurprising in the context of the so-called information disorders such as disinformation and hate speech (Wardle & Derakshan, 2017) that distort the veracity and reliability of public information available for citizens' opinion formation. Many problems with public communication have been attributed to the so-called platformization (Poell et al., 2019; Van Dijck et al., 2019), and the EU's policy efforts, such as the DSA package, are geared to curb global platform power. Still, recent studies indicate that resilience against online disinformation is built on various national structural characteristics. Factors such as political context, economic elements, and aspects related to media consumption contribute to resilience—and a robust PSM seems to be one of the concrete structural aspects that define highly resilient societies (Humprecht et al., 2020, 2021).

In this light, PSM is arguably a key element in a national policy-making toolkit to ensure universal availability of quality, vetted content and a variety of views—aspects that most definitions of public media adhere to (e.g., EBU, 2014; UNESCO, 2001)—these aspects could be seen as central to public opinion-formation and fostering informed citizenship. However, while resilience is often used as a policy buzzword (see, e.g., Miyamoto, 2021), no comprehensive definition for its applicability exists, and no conceptual framework defines the specific ways in which PSM, as a media institution with an exceptional set of functions, can be positioned to support national resilience.

In this chapter, we seek to define national resilience insofar as it applies to public communication and specifically to PSM as a national media institution in the age of rampant disinformation and other 'information disorders' (Wardle & Derakshan, 2017). We propose a dual concept: it entails structural considerations ('information resilience') and an individual's communicative, knowledge-related capacities and capabilities to participate in society ('epistemic resilience', see Fig. 7.1).

This structure allows us to discuss national resilience as a part of PSM remit and its role in society. Finally, we call for a discursive policy shift that will position PSM at the heart of democracy in a national context.

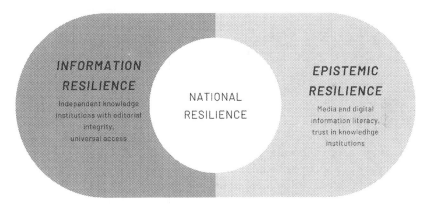

Fig. 7.1 Two dimensions of national resilience. Note: processed by the author

Resilience Against Information Disorders: A Concept of Two Dimensions

In the past decade, resilience as a social scientific concept (Buzzanell, 2010) has become popular for understanding complex systems' challenges, often referring to an individual and a community's 'psycho-social' ability to respond to change (e.g., Welsh, 2014). While resilience is arguably a relatively current policy concept regarding communication, its current use is associated with strength in the face of adversity, such as different online harms and other threats to democratic communication environments (Amazeen & Bucy, 2019; Golob et al., 2021; Juurvee & Arold, 2021; Manwaring & Holloway, 2023). It has been argued that a nation's resilience to address disinformation and other information harms resides in the connection between the 'microsphere' of those involved in creating harms and the 'macrosphere' of decision-making (Bjola & Papadakis, 2020; see also Chohan & Hu, 2022; Miyamoto, 2021; Shackelford et al., 2020).

Various conceptual frameworks have been designed to grasp related complex challenges. For example, in 2017, the Council of Europe published a framework for 'information disorders' (Wardle & Derakshan, 2017) for journalists, political decision-makers, and researchers. The framework distinguishes between different types of content based on their purpose. Misinformation refers to misleading content, which can also be unintentional. Disinformation, on the other hand, is intentionally produced false content, including conspiracy theories. Malinformation means using content, factual or not, to harm individuals or groups. While it is essential to understand different forms of harm, increasing focus on academic and applied analyses has in the past years been the question of media trust as a multidimensional, many-sided experience (e.g., Horowitz et al., 2021; Jakobsson & Stiernstedt, 2023; Rodríguez-Pérez & Canel, 2023; Jerónimo & Esparza, 2022; Kõuts-Klemm et al., 2022)—a conceptualization that can help to understand the impact of information disorders.

Still, resilience is about robust trust and *individual-* and *system-level* capacities to minimize the impact of information disorders (Boulianne et al., 2022). It has been argued that resilience specifically relies on national systems and actors (Frischlich & Humprecht, 2021; Kõuts-Klemm et al., 2022): it arises from society members' trust in the fundamental structures and functionality of society, trust in various information organizations such as national media, and individuals' trust in each other. This definition also focuses on public communication as a prerequisite for forming opinions about what and whom to trust. Namely, information is central to national resilience and the construction of trust—its quality and the flow of information among key players.

In democratic societies, national media has traditionally played a crucial role as a conveyor of information and a trust builder (Christians & Nordenstreng, 2004). Since the last decades of the last century, with global economic expansion and intensified digitalization, national media's role has transformed. For example, news is increasingly consumed on the Internet through global online platforms and social media. Similarly, communication has been marked by internationalization trends and, in recent years, a continuous state of so-called multi-crises. At the same time, competition for audiences and advertising revenue has intensified, and access to information—both knowledge and entertainment—has become commercialized. From an individual perspective, all of this has led to inequality and the fragmentation of civil society, whether it concerns news sources or technological skills (Nieminen, 2019).

This observation about the changed communications environment and the meanings attached to media and communication is particularly significant for the role of PSM. The current context challenges the still-popular approach found in dominant thinking about the technologically determined effects of disruptive communication. Instead, when referring to dysfunctional communication, it seems plausible that the formation of conflicting views is influenced by enduring and unresolved controversies and local societal struggles revolving around developmental histories, social upheavals, individual losses, and cultural traditions specific to each geographic, cultural, and socio-psychological context (see, e.g., Bennett & Livingston, 2018; Kreiss, 2021).

Hence, the analysis of responsiveness strategies applied against disinformation must be nuanced and sensitive to the specificities of both individual and situational conditions. While 'national resilience' appears to be a desirable state to be attained for democratic sustainability, its specificities and characteristics, such as principles in policies and programs, must be assessed concerning the sociocultural values and traditions of the general informational context. Among these cultural characteristics are the dominating principles within the political culture and media functioning environment. Even so, individual factors, such as media significance and digital skills, socio-psychological aspects, such as awareness of various (cognitive) biases, and moral reasoning capacities in decision-making and information processing matter equally much (Balčytienė, 2023).

All these observations and calls for greater attention to contextually shaped capacities resonate with further challenges for democratic opinion-making and impact democratic sustainability in contemporary societies. For example, trust, according to several studies (e.g., Edelman, 2023; Newman et al., 2022), has significantly eroded globally, towards both the structures of society and the media, over the years. Rebuilding information resilience and the included trust is not straightforward, as numerous factors, including the media landscape, influence the trust experience. On the one hand, trust in society's information institutions as a whole, but also specific platforms, media, and sources, such as journalists, plays a role. The topic can influence trust and the information recipient's background factors and personal experiences.

All these trends have led to weakening of what could be called *information resilience*. In this context, information resilience refers to reliable, contextually sensitive information that supports society's structures and individuals' well-being, conveyed by a functional and diverse media system. Thus, information resilience means the ability of society, the national media landscape, and individuals to resist information disorders. Consequently, information resilience can highlight structural factors supporting a robust national media system and democracy.

Still, no structural factors can alone protect democratic communication. Information needs to be used for debates and other forms of civic participation that are essential features of opinion formation, further professionalization of media, and the development of democratic civics (Dahlgren, 2006, 2018). What is needed is also *epistemic resilience*, that is, the ability and willingness of individuals to engage with public communication as knowledge that has meaning for the said individual and society. This 'human factor' provides a significant challenge today: trust in society and official, professional entities producing information is declining, leading to a multiplication of societal and individual problems caused by information disorders.

Society finds it increasingly challenging to function in an environment of continuous mistrust. Individuals face greater difficulty navigating an information landscape with numerous actors where information disorders occur daily. Rebuilding lost trust is challenging, as numerous factors influence trust. In this sense, epistemic resilience signifies that an individual is capable and willing to understand the role of communication as an essential aspect of democracy, both in terms of an individual's ability to understand and relate oneself to the surrounding society and the functioning of the entire society (Balčytienė & Horowitz, 2023).

In other words, resilience against information disorders can be seen as an interplay between structural conditions as manifested in a robust media system and epistemic awareness and capabilities of citizens to actively participate in critical inquiry coupled with willingness for trust-building regarding institutions and other individuals. In this sense, the national resilience of public communication is 'psycho-social' and needs special cultivation by national knowledge institutions.

From this perspective, national countries' responses to the influx of disinformation and dysfunctional communication should be examined not only through structural measures such as available policy initiatives and governance decisions made or the number of education programs applied. Instead, developing strategies to combat disinformation should be treated as a sociopolitical and sociocultural process involving the development of required awareness of emerging (dis)information vulnerabilities. Due to their remit and ascribed values, PSM organizations can be seen as key actors in cultivating democratic resilience and opinion formation.

Resilience, PSM, and Public Opinion Formation: Structural Considerations for Policy

From a classical point of view, the role of news media is essential for opinion formation (Christians & Nordenstreng, 2004). However, today, journalists and journalism are facing serious professional challenges (Carlson & Lewis, 2015): from the point of view of democratic and deliberative communication, it is journalists who must define the societal significance of news and what issues and whose voices will be heard.

But certain contextual conditions must be met for these ideals of inclusive, participatory, and deliberative communication to happen and become effective. First, citizens must access information sources from news media channels. Also, citizens must rely on trustworthy sources to form opinions.

However, such idealized hopes and practices are a sign from the past. With accelerating communication and expanding digital content offers, professional journalism is gradually losing its previously dominant role as a meaningful agenda-setter. Traditional news media is no longer the only news provider for many groups (Altay et al., 2023). In addition, people in

Europe frequently indicate that their first source of daily news is often derived from social media sites and feeds.

This kind of 'structural transformation'—of sources for public opinion formation to global arenas opaquely governed by the principles of 'surveillance capitalism' (Zuboff, 2019)—is fundamentally worrisome for the ideals and practices of national democracies. Building and defending information resilience means, on the one hand, combating the impact of global entities in national contexts and, on the other hand, strengthening forms of trusted information dissemination nationally, responding to contextual needs. To be sure, while many disinformation challenges are global, they also take specific regional and national forms.

Predominantly, the national aspect appears to be of critical significance, as well as the role of PSM. As already noted, disinformation vulnerability is nationally shaped and is defined within the perspective of national sociostructural inequalities, among which media use, and media trust are defining features. Likewise, it is no wonder that the search for solutions to information disorders has shifted attention to national media systems and facilitated the independence, diversity, and sustainability of those media outlets—and PSM as one key institution to strengthen structural resilience. This approach has already been recognized in the EU's European Media Freedom Act, which seeks to ensure the role of PSM as independent media outlets. Similarly, the Rule of Law Report of the European Commission of 2022 included, for the first time, a section on PSM that states the importance of their existence as independent parts of the media sector. Indeed, the basic remit of PSM, formed around values of universality, independence, excellence, diversity, accountability, and innovation (EBU, 2014), implies a responsibility to fight information disorders by producing fact-based news content and eliciting trust.

In the European context, many different media systems exist (e.g., Hallin & Mancini, 2004, Herrero et al., 2017), and cultural variations in information structuration and audience responsiveness tend to be reflected in digitally sustained information practices. Robust PSM with ample resources and broad audience reach are typical in Northern Europe. Furthermore, factor analyses of national resilience to online disinformation indicate that particular political contexts and media use are closely connected (Humprecht et al., 2020). Populist politics challenge legacy media, diminishing trust and encouraging audiences to migrate to social media.

The same study suggests, however, that strong PSM can act as a link between society and the media, thus mitigating the fragmentation of audiences (Humprecht et al., 2020). PSM organizations are central to the information structures that promote fundamental human and communication rights (e.g., Horowitz & Nieminen, 2016). While PSM seem vulnerable to the populist and illiberal tendencies of so-called media capture (e.g., Dragomir & Horowitz, 2021), they have also proven to be the most valued source in many European countries during times of crisis (e.g., Newman et al., 2022).

All in all, the trust gap is growing between traditional and social media in Europe, and trust in quality and vetted sources seems to be the key component to combating disinformation and other online harms; in the EU, PSM are the most trusted news sources (EBU, 2022). The public's trust in public television and radio stations and the written press varies significantly between countries. For instance, in Finland, 73% of respondents trust public TV and radio stations, but this is only true for 22% of respondents in Hungary and 23% in Poland (Eurobarometer, 2022). Still, according to a 2021 European Broadcasting Union (EBU) study, people trust PSM news the most in 16 of 26 European markets (EBU, 2021). In addition, a set of correlation analyses (EBU, 2021), combining audience data and value surveys, suggests that larger national PSM audiences and increased PSM resources are linked with fewer worries about misinformation. The larger a country's PSM audience, the greater the national confidence in election reporting.

Indeed, an earlier study comparing PSM in four European countries (the Czech Republic, Finland, Spain, and the UK; Horowitz et al., 2021) reveals how, despite the global challenge of disinformation, each case country embodies different degrees of resilience to disinformation. Although the respective PSM occupy differing roles in their national media systems, there are commonalities among the case countries in both programming and services for combating disinformation: quality journalism and educational programming were highlighted in each case.

Interestingly, the study further suggests that, as much as the legacies and roles of the PSM organizations differ, the expectations that PSM actively combat information disorders are shared in each case country. Although only a few specific actions might be transferable from one PSM to another, they are invaluable tools for fighting information disorders if supported adequately. PSM must be guaranteed political, editorial, and financial independence to address information disorders responsibly and credibly.

Resilience, PSM, and Public Opinion Formation: Epistemic Considerations for Policy

The structural role of PSM in providing information resilience can be relatively simply stated in policy: PSM organizations have a key role in providing relevant information free from commercial or political imperatives. Nevertheless, suppose we understand resilience as a 'psycho-social' concept. In that case, the central aspect is how information is understood and used in people's everyday lives, for example, in discerning what is false information or what kind of information is needed for opinion formation and shared decision-making in a democratic society. In other words, epistemic resilience concerns people's capability to understand information and knowledge offered by epistemic institutions (such as the media and the like) and, based on this understanding, their ability to act for their interests and needs as well as those of society as a whole. In a democratic society, epistemic resilience means not only equality in all aspects relating to the access to and the availability of information and knowledge but symmetric relations in public communication, equality in obtaining critical literacy in information and communication, and equal protection of personal privacy from any form of public intrusion (Horowitz et al., 2024).

Indeed, the epistemic dimension of resilience becomes central when considered in the light of opinion formation for deliberative communication, advocated by all proponents of informed decision-making (Englund, 2006). Such an idea requires an accessible knowledge structure, such as open and accessible media and education, citizen engagement, and willingness to participate in dialogue, critical thinking, and decision-making. The media, striving to achieve an inclusive public sphere, where people would meet (physically or virtually) to engage in common matters, has been at the center of thinking of the current scholarship in media, political communication, and education. The idealistic side of such a public sphere rests on its social inclusion, which is far less obvious if measured against the current trends of mediated conflicts, radicalization of public discourse, and online hate speech.

Though deliberation is widely suggested as a strategy for informed opinion-making, its expectations are based on certain assumptions, such as access to information, inclusion, etc. Many of these assumptions are difficult to control and make relevant assessments. Also, deliberation is incorporated in many programs applied by policy-makers, but the practicality and political significance still cause some doubts. Policy-makers use deliberation mostly to justify political decisions. In short, deliberation is an idealized category, though the concept has a growing popularity in contemporary scholarship.

In other words, we still conceive that the journalistic profession retains the ideal of listening; however, in practice, as noted in previous sections of this essay, the (socially) mediated reality has changed dramatically, and communicative modes have shifted towards acceleration with speed-up communication. In the current predominantly digitally orchestrated and managed informational space, only a one-sided form of communication prevails, and the aspects of deliberation suffer. It is not only disinformation that is corrosive to democracy. Disinformation dramatically challenges and further disrupts the informed decision-making process. Still, the anti-systemic cynicism evident in the context of the rise of dysfunctional communication is rooted deeper in societal structures and enduring injustices and undermines the policy goals of universalism and deliberation.

All in all, proposals referring to the 'epistemic turn' towards greater wisdom and awareness (Balčytienė, 2023), or the ideas of building citizens' epistemic 'mindfulness' for resilience (Rodrigo et al., 2024) are not unique. However, PSM may be uniquely positioned to reach wider audiences than any other organization. The principle of epistemic inclusivity—as in universal access and content availability expressing various views—is not built in the commercial logic of global platforms or even national commercial press. From the perspective of the media addressing its audiences as citizens, with the civic duty of contributing to national resilience, PSM can, more securely than its commercial counterparts, foster epistemic resilience, including media and information literacy. This opportunity has already been recognized in the policy context in Resolution 2255 of the Council of Europe (2019): the resolution calls on member governments to support PSM while urging PSM organizations to prioritize countering disinformation. The Resolution sets related tasks for PSM as follows:

- Quality and innovative communication practices, especially regarding news and current affairs
- Specialized programs containing analysis and comments regarding disinformation
- Programming that stimulates critical thinking among audiences
- Targeted online communication with young people
- Projects and collaborations that address information disorders with other PSM organizations and national stakeholders

The above stipulations go beyond PSM as an information provider for opinion formation but relate to epistemic guidance for an individual's resilience. The prompt for collaborations highlights the quest for inclusivity in building epistemic resilience and trust. While not a standard policy position in individual countries, the view of the CoE is unsurprising given the central position PSM hold in many parts of Europe. PSM are still associated with high levels of trust and value in many nations (Newman et al., 2022; Sehl et al., 2020), and they can still reach a politically diverse audience (Schulz et al., 2019). Moreover, the COVID-19 pandemic and the war in Ukraine have highlighted that amidst conflicting and ever-changing information, including both accidental and purposefully false information, not only the consumption of news but also the appreciation of legacy media and journalism has a strong standing in many countries (e.g., Newman et al., 2022). A comparative analysis indicates that audiences view PSM as an organization providing special value to society (Nielsen & Newman, 2023). Indeed, it has been argued that PSM are central to 'epistemic justice' (Michalis & D'Arma, 2024): they can be a key part of the solution to the threats to epistemic rights and the foundations of democratic societies if they are given the necessary support and resources to do so.

Conclusion: Need for a Discursive Shift in PSM Policies

PSM alone cannot solve the problem of information disorder (e.g., Humprecht et al., 2020). More generally, PSM need to work together with other educational and cultural epistemic institutions to combat root causes—such as commercialization and privatization of communitive spaces and knowledge—that plague public communication in the digital era (Michalis & D'Arma, 2024). Still, the premise of PSM as a tool to counter manifestations of information disorder seems realistic and potentially highly effective, even in different national contexts. PSM can serve as a critical institution in providing structural information resilience and supporting the epistemic resilience of citizens. These two dimensions of resilience are essential in ensuring opinion formation and democratic decision-making.

The elements of disinformation and vulnerability explored in this discussion highlight the necessity for both dimensions of resilience to operate in tandem. They underscore the significance of public service media, founded on inclusion, attention, listening, and dialogic communication principles, ultimately fostering stakeholderism and sustainability.

Moreover, the level of success that PSM attains regarding inclusion, attentiveness, and dialogue should serve as a crucial determinant—a litmus test—for democracy in the examined context.

The role of PSM in building national resilience of public communication needs to be taken more seriously in the EU and national contexts. It is curious that given the enormous challenges to democratic debates in today's media landscape, and given the trend in Europe and globally, genuinely independent media are a diminishing phenomenon (Dragomir & Söderström, 2021), PSM are still challenged nationally by political and commercial adversaries, in new and robust PSM nations alike (e.g., Dragomir & Horowitz, 2021). In practice, the EU's existing policies on PSM focus on market distortion, even when research has proven that sustainable and diverse national media systems—a key focus of the European Media Freedom Act—are not disturbed by publicly funded PSM (Sehl et al., 2020). It has been indicated that strong PSM are essential to robust national media systems (Humprecht et al., 2020).

In this light, the discourse of resilience needs to enter policy conversations about PSM, to shift the claims of the role of PSM 'filling in the gap' to the central institution securing national resilience. This role, to be sure, places great demands on PSM organizations—and support to PSM from EU and national policy-making. Still, to ensure the effectiveness of PSM in combating information disorders can be benchmarked and evaluated. While the so-called public value tests, which assess the relevance and market position of PSM in national markets, have been a common practice in Europe for some time (e.g., Moe, 2010), recent rethinking has suggested the use of more nuanced, multidimensional evaluations (e.g., Mazzucato et al., 2020). If developed further, an assessment of the role and potential of PSM in tackling information disorder could include more in-depth data on what people view as disinformation, how they view other harms of information disorder, and what they want from PSM in that regard (Horowitz et al., 2021).

References

Altay, S., Nielsen, R. K., & Fletcher, R. (2023). News can help! The impact of news media and digital platforms on awareness of and belief in misinformation. *The International Journal of Press/Politics.* https://doi.org/10.1177/19401612221148981

Amazeen, M. A., & Bucy, E. P. (2019). Conferring resistance to digital disinformation: The inoculating influence of procedural news knowledge. *Journal of Broadcasting & Electronic Media, 63*(3), 415–432. https://doi.org/10.1080/08838151.2019.1653101

Balčytienė, A. (2023). Transforming epistemic communities for a healthier discourse in today's Europe. *Darbai ir dienos, 79*, 37–50. https://doi.org/10.7220/2335-8769.79.2

Balčytienė, A., & Horowitz, M. (2023). *How to assess national resilience to online disinformation? Comparing Finland and Lithuania.* DIGIRES/NORDIS/EDMO. https://nordishub.eu/wp-content/uploads/2023/03/D1.5_Policy-suggestions_DIGIRES-NORDIS-Policy-Brief.pdf

Bennett, W. L., & Livingston, S. (2018). The disinformation order: Disruptive communication and the decline of democratic institutions. *European Journal of Communication, 33*(2), 122–139. https://doi.org/10.1177/0267323118760317

Bjola, C., & Papadakis, K. (2020). Digital propaganda, counterpublics and the disruption of the public sphere: The Finnish approach to building digital resilience. *Cambridge Review of International Affairs, 33*(5), 638–666. https://doi.org/10.1080/09557571.2019.1704221

Boulianne, S., Tenove, C., & Buffie, J. (2022). Complicating the resilience model: A four-country study about misinformation. *Media and Communication, 10*(3), 169–182. https://doi.org/10.17645/mac.v10i3.5346

Buzzanell, P. M. (2010). Resilience: Talking, resisting, and imagining new normalcies into being. *Journal of Communication, 60*(1), 1–14. https://doi.org/10.1111/j.1460-2466.2009.01469.x

Carlson, M., & Lewis, S. (Eds.). (2015). *Boundaries of journalism: Professionalism, practices, and participation.* Routledge.

Chohan, S. R., & Hu, G. (2022). Strengthening digital inclusion through e-government: Cohesive ICT training programs to intensify digital competency. *Information Technology for Development, 28*(1), 16–38. https://doi.org/10.1080/02681102.2020.1841713

Christians, C., & Nordenstreng, K. (2004). Social responsibility worldwide. *Journal of Mass Media Ethics, 19*(1), 3–28. https://doi.org/10.1207/s15327728jmme1901_2

Dahlgren, P. (2006). Doing citizenship: The cultural origins of civic agency in the public sphere. *European Journal of Cultural Studies, 9*(3), 267–286. https://doi.org/10.1177/1367549406066073

Dahlgren, P. (2018). Media, knowledge, and trust: The deepening epistemic crisis of democracy. *Javnost: The Public, 25*(1–2), 20–27. https://doi.org/10.1080/13183222.2018.1418819

Dragomir, M., & Horowitz, M. (2021). Media capture and its contexts: Developing a comparative framework for public service media. In M. Túñez-López, F. Campos-Freire, & M. R. Castros (Eds.), *The values of public service media in the Internet society* (pp. 217–246). Palgrave Macmillan.

Dragomir, M., & Söderström, A. (2021). *The state of state media. A global analysis of the editorial independence of state media and an introduction of a new state media typology*. Central European University Democracy Institute. https://cmds.ceu.edu/sites/cmcs.ceu.hu/files/attachment/article/2091/thestateofstatemedia.pdf

EBU. (2014). *Public service values, editorial principles and guidelines*. European Broadcasting Union. https://www.ebu.ch/guides/public-service-values-editorial-principles

EBU. (2021). *Market insights. Trust in media 2021. Media intelligence service. Public version*. European Broadcasting Union.

EBU. (2022). *Trust in media 2022. Media intelligence service. Public version*. European Broadcasting Union. https://www.ebu.ch/files/live/sites/ebu/files/Publications/MIS/login_only/market_insights/EBU-MIS-Trust_in_Media_2022.pdf

Edelman. (2023). Edelman trust barometer. Navigating a polarized world. https://www.edelman.com/trust/2023/trust-barometer

Englund, T. (2006). Deliberative communication: A pragmatist proposal. *Curriculum Studies, 38*(5), 503–520.

Eurobarometer. (2022). *Media and news survey*. European Union. https://europa.eu/eurobarometer/surveys/detail/2832

European Commission. (2020). Documents on European Democracy Action plan (EDAP). https://commission.europa.eu/publications/documents-european-democracy-actionplan_en

European Commission. (2021). Communication from the Commission to the European Parliament, The Council, The European Economic and Social Committee and the Committee of the Regions. 2030 Digital Compass: The European way for the Digital Decade COM/2021/118 final. https://eur-lex.europa.eu/legal-content/en/ALL/?uri=CELEX:52021DC0118

Frischlich, L., & Humprecht, E. (2021). *Trust, democratic resilience, and the infodemic*. Public Policy Institute – Heinrich Böll Stiftung. https://il.boell.org/sites/default/files/2021-03/Frischlich%20%26%20Humprecht%20-%20Trust%2C%20Democratic%20Resilience%2C%20and%20the%20Infodemic.pdf

Golob, T., Makarovič, M., & Rek, M. (2021). Meta-reflexivity for resilience against disinformation. *Comunicar, 29*(66), 107–118. https://www.revistacomunicar.com/ojs/index.php/comunicar/article/view/C66-2021-09

Hallin, D. C., & Mancini, P. (2004). *Comparing media systems: Three models of media and politics.* Cambridge University Press.

Herrero, L. C., Humprecht, E., Engesser, E. S., Brüggemann, M. L., & Büchel, F. (2017). Rethinking Hallin and Mancini beyond the West: An analysis of media systems in Central and Eastern Europe. *International Journal of Communication, 11,* 4797–4823. https://ijoc.org/index.php/ijoc/article/view/6035/2196

Horowitz, M., Cushion, S., Dragomir, M., Gutiérrez Manjón, S., & Pantti, M. (2021). A framework for assessing the role of public service media organizations in countering disinformation. *Digital Journalism, 10*(5), 843–865. https://doi.org/10.1080/21670811.2021.1987948

Horowitz, M., & Nieminen, H. (2016). Public media as a human right. In G. F. Lowe & N. Yamamoto (Eds.), *Crossing borders and boundaries in public service media* (RIPE@2015) (pp. 95–106). Nordicom.

Horowitz, M., Nieminen, H., Lehtisaari, K., & D'Arma, A. (Eds.). (2024). *Epistemic rights in the era of digital disruption.* Palgrave Macmillan.

Humprecht, E., Esser, F., & Van Aelst, P. (2020). Resilience to online disinformation: A framework for cross-national comparative research. *The International Journal of Press/Politics, 25*(3), 493–516. https://doi.org/10.1177/1940161219900126

Humprecht, E., Esser, F., Van Aelst, P., Staender, A., & Morosoli, S. (2021). The sharing of disinformation in cross-national comparison: Analyzing patterns of resilience. *Information, Communication & Society, 26*(7), 1342–1362. https://doi.org/10.1080/1369118X.2021.2006744

Jakobsson, P., & Stiernstedt, F. (2023). Trust and the media: Arguments for the (irr)elevance of a concept. *Journalism Studies, 24*(4), 479–495. https://doi.org/10.1080/1461670X.2023.2169191

Jauert, P., & Lowe, G. F. (2005). Public service broadcasting for social and cultural citizenship. Renewing the Enlightenment Mission. In P. Jauert & G. F. Lowe (Eds.), *Cultural dilemmas in public service broadcasting* (RIPE@2005) (pp. 13–33).

Jerónimo, P., & Esparza, M. S. (2022). Disinformation at a local level: An emerging discussion. *Publications, 10*(2), 15. https://doi.org/10.3390/publications10020015

Juurvee, I., & Arold, U. (2021). Psychological defence and cyber security: Two integral parts of Estonia's comprehensive approach for countering hybrid threats. *ICONO 14, Revista de comunicación y tecnologías emergentes, 19*(1), 70–94. https://doi.org/10.7195/ri14.v19i1.1628

Kõuts-Klemm, R., Rožukalne, A., & Jastramskis, D. (2022). Resilience of national media systems: Baltic media in the global network environment. *Journal of Baltic Studies, 53*(4), 543–564. https://doi.org/10.1080/01629778.2022.2103162

Kreiss, D. (2021). "Social media and democracy: The state of the field, prospects for reform," edited by Nathaniel Persily and Joshua A. Tucker. *The International Journal of Press/Politics*, 26(2), 505–512. https://doi.org/10.1177/1940161220985078

Lowe, G. F., & Bardoel, J. (2008). *From public service broadcasting to public service media* (RIPE@2007). Nordicom.

Manwaring, R., & Holloway, J. (2023). Resilience to cyber-enabled foreign interference: Citizen understanding and threat perceptions. *Defence Studies*, 23(2), 334–357. https://doi.org/10.1080/14702436.2022.2138349

Mazzucato, M., Conway, R., Mazzoli, E., Knoll, E., & Albala, S. (2020). *Creating and measuring dynamic public value at the BBC.* UCL Institute for Innovation and Public Purpose, Policy Report, (IIPP WP 2020-19). https://www.ucl.ac.uk/bartlett/public-purpose/sites/public-purpose/files/final-bbc-report-6_jan.pdf

Michalis, M., & D'Arma, A. (2024). Public service media: From epistemic rights to epistemic justice. In M. Horowitz, H. Nieminen, K. Lehtisaari, & A. D'Arma (Eds.), *Epistemic rights in the era of digital disruption* (pp. 97–109). Palgrave Macmillan.

Miyamoto, I. (2021). Disinformation: Policy responses to building citizen resiliency. *Connections: The Quarterly Journal*, 20(2), 47–55.

Moe, H. (2010). Governing public service broadcasting: "Public Value Tests" in different national contexts. *Communication, Culture & Critique*, 3(2), 207–223. https://doi.org/10.1111/j.1753-9137.2010.01067.x

Newman, N., Fletcher, R., Robertson, C., Eddy, K., & Nielsen, R. K. (2022). *Digital news report 2022.* Reuters Institute for the Study of Journalism. https://reutersinstitute.politics.ox.ac.uk/digital-news-report/2022

Nielsen, R. K., & Newman, N. (2023, June 14). The importance of public service media for individuals and for society. *Reuters Institute for the Study of Journalism*. https://reutersinstitute.politics.ox.ac.uk/digital-news-report/2023/importance-public-service-media-individuals-society

Nieminen, H. (2019). Inequality, social trust and the media: Towards citizens' communication and information rights. In J. Trappel (ed.), *Digital Media Inequalities: Policies Against Divides, Distrust and Discriminations.* Gothenburg: Nordicom.

Poell, T., Nieborg, D., & van Dijck, J. (2019). Platformisation. *Internet Policy Review*, 8(4), 10.14763/2019.4.1425.

Rodrigo, P., Arakpogun, E. O., Vu, M. C., Olan, F., & Djafarova, E. (2024). Can you be mindful? The effectiveness of mindfulness-driven interventions in enhancing the digital resilience to fake news on COVID-19. *Information Systems Frontiers*, 26, 501–521. https://doi.org/10.1007/s10796-022-10258-5

Rodríguez-Pérez, C., & Canel, M. J. (2023). Exploring European citizens' resilience to misinformation: Media legitimacy and media trust as predictive variables. *Media and Communication, 11*(2), 30–41. https://doi.org/10.17645/mac.v11i2.6317

Schulz, A., Levy, D., & Nielsen, R. (2019). *Old, educated, and politically diverse: The audience of public service news*. The Reuters Institute for the Study of Journalism. https://reutersinstitute.politics.ox.ac.uk/sites/default/files/2019-09/The_audience_of_public_service_news_FINAL.pdf

Sehl, A., Fletcher, R., & Picard, R. G. (2020). Crowding out: Is there evidence that public service media harm markets? A cross-national comparative analysis of commercial television and online news providers. *European Journal of Communication, 35*(4), 389–409. https://doi.org/10.1177/0267323120903688

Shackelford, S. J., Raymond, A., Stemler, A., & Loyle, C. (2020). Defending democracy: Taking stock of the global fight against digital repression, disinformation, and election insecurity. *Washington and Lee Law Review, 77*(4), 1747–1809. https://cdn.cloud.prio.org/files/76a7e5c1-8e69-4faf-b2b8-44c0b0decbf1/Defending%20Democracy%20Taking%20Stock%20of%20the%20Global%20Fight%20Against%20Digital%20Repression%20Disinformation%20and%20Election%20Insecurity.pdf?Inline=true

UNESCO. (2001). *Public broadcasting: Why? How?* UNESCO. https://unesdoc.unesco.org/ark:/48223/pf0000124058

Van Dijck, J., Nieborg, D., & Poell, T. (2019). Reframing platform power. *Internet Policy Review, 8*(2), 10.14763/2019.2.1414.

Van Dijck, J., & Poell, T. (2014). Making public television social? Public service broadcasting and the challenges of social media. *Television and New Media, 16*(2), 148–164. https://doi.org/10.1177/1527476414527136

Wardle, C., & Derakhshan, H. (2017). *Information disorder: Toward an interdisciplinary framework for research and policymaking* (Vol. 27, pp. 1–107). Strasbourg: Council of Europe. https://edoc.coe.int/en/media/7495-information-disorder-toward-an-interdisciplinary-framework-for-research-and-policy-making.html

Welsh, M. (2014). Resilience and responsibility. *The Geographical Journal, 180*(1), 15–26. https://doi.org/10.1111/geoj.12012

Zuboff, S. (2019). *The age of surveillance capitalism: The fight for a human future at the new frontier of power*. Public Affairs.

CHAPTER 8

The Role of Public Service Media in Democratic Engagement: An Audience Perspective

Marcela Campos Rueda

INTRODUCTION

Amongst other less altruistic considerations, from a normative perspective, Public Service Broadcasting (PSB) was born to promote access to unbiased information in the hope that informed citizens would be well integrated into the community and make educated and rational decisions when exercising civil rights (Blumler, 1992). Radio and then television, with their ability to reach many, and potentially all, were also seen as too powerful and eventually too dangerous to be left unattended by the state.

The public service media policy paradigm consolidated during the post-war period and remained uncontested primarily until the 1980s (van Cuilenburg & McQuail, 2003), when a liberal shift in mainstream politics brought new private players to the field, and technological transformations disrupted the media landscape. Unfortunately, the

---

M. Campos Rueda (✉)
Universidad Carlos III de Madrid, Getafe, Spain
e-mail: marcela@marcelacampos.tv

© The Author(s), under exclusive license to Springer Nature Switzerland AG 2024
M. Goyanes, A. Cañedo (eds.), *Media Influence on Opinion Change and Democracy*, https://doi.org/10.1007/978-3-031-70231-0_8

turn-of-the-century debates were dominated by a market-driven perspective. This relegated PSB to a defensive position while failing to acknowledge its distinctiveness and foresee the tests the new media ecosystem would pose to public debate.

Since then, Europe's media, social, and political landscape has changed radically. From scarcity and transmission mode to overabundance and interactivity, from a perceived homogeneous society to the acknowledgment of diversity, from common ground to growing polarization. It has been challenging for PSB and policymakers to keep up with these transformations and adapt its services and content offer to the new environment.

The transition from PSB to Public Service Media (PSM) has been ongoing for over two decades and seems never-ending (see Bardoel & Lowe, 2007; D'Arma et al., 2024). However, at its core, the role of PSM remains unchanged: to provide tools and promote democratic engagement by fulfilling its primary information and watchdog functions, stimulating public debate and participation while nurturing social empathy and cultural identity. It is about citizenship, in all its dimensions, its enhancement, protection, and expansion through the provision of media services (Donders, 2021). This implies bringing citizens together and fostering a democratic dialogue that includes a basic agreement of who we are and what we want to pursue as a society.

Acknowledging Citizens as PSM's Main Stakeholders

As much as the goals for PSM persist, their fulfillment calls for policies and practices that are not focused on defending or trying to adapt what once worked to a radically new setting, but rather on those that allow for profound transformations, acknowledge its failings, and dare to question its practices, value parameters, and even its traditional institutional framework. The question is: how can PSM stop playing constant catch-up and take the initiative in a scenario where the state no longer controls the technological infrastructure and reach is mediated by social media, content distribution platforms, and search engines whose functioning is determined by commercial interests.

The answer is far from simple; it encompasses multiple dimensions and is inevitably linked to broader issues confronting the health of Western democracies: populist discourse, declining trust in institutions, and changes in social interactions and news consumption patterns. What has become evident is the risk of not having strong PSM to face these challenges.

At a European level, regulators have explicitly recognized the value of PSM (Council of Europe, 2018, 2024) and the Digital Service Package, which includes the Digital Markets Act (European Union, 2022a) and Digital Service Act (European Union, 2022b), finally acknowledges the need for a firmer and value-oriented regulation of platforms and search engines. Forward-thinking regulation that considers PSM's distinctive role and promotes its discoverability and reach within platformed ecosystems, together with adequate financing for innovation, vital for its survival and growth. However, it is equally crucial to recognize citizens as the primary stakeholders and ultimate source of legitimacy of PSM. For too long, citizens have been mostly left out when analyzing PSM and defining its practices; at best, they are addressed as consumers, and unfortunately, many of the PSM initiatives directed at listening to citizens' expectations account for them without considering them as a key input for policy building and designing an effective service (Van den Bulck & Raats, 2023).

A citizen-centered practice requires a new mindset within the PSM organizations, politics, regulators, and academia, one that acknowledges that PSM initiatives "be designed *with* the public, not just for them, and their relevance needs to be readily apparent to potential users" (Deane et al., 2020, p. 24). Regaining initiative and providing value to the societies they serve will not occur in the void; citizens must have contact and count on PSM's service offer to satisfy their informational and media needs and rights. The biggest existential threat for PSM is failing to (re) connect with its audiences, and their survival is dependent on citizens' attitudes and perceptions. Unless they are perceived as valuable and needed, it is only a matter of time before PSM loses relevance and become a marginalized player within the media ecosystem and the dynamics of democracy "or put another way: if public service media is to have any sort of prosperous future, the public it serves has to want and believe in that future too" (Martin, 2021, p.9).

A first step toward a citizen-centered framework is actively listening to their expectations and evaluations of PSM and their general media needs to achieve a demand-oriented response within the normative PSM framework. This requires going beyond a traditional audience research approach to explore an array of variables and potential associations that impact citizens' attitudes and perceptions toward PSM and explore further how PSM can positively impact their daily lives and empower the exercise of citizenship.

In the following sections, we discuss findings from an online panel quota-based survey representative of the adult Spanish population regarding gender, age, and education (*N* = 1717) conducted in May 2021;[1] the aim is to gain a better understanding from an audience perspective of how PSM can better fulfill its role as an active agent for society's democratic engagement.

WHAT CAN WE LEARN FROM SPANISH CITIZENS' EXPECTATIONS FOR PSM?

Similar to findings in several European countries (Fawzi & Mothes, 2020; Just, 2020), Spanish citizens show high expectations for PSM, which still align with its normative role. Respondents were presented with 21 items regarding PSM's functions and were asked whether they considered these to be primary obligations of PSM. Information (M = 7.94; SD = 2.27) and holding political power accountable (M = 7.77; SD = 2.34) topped the list, followed by "defend the free democratic order in Spain (M = 7.74; SD = 2.30)." Together with items related to programming mandates, those measuring empathy functions ("Give voice to people with different cultural backgrounds, religious views, and sexual orientation as well as to people with disabilities" M = 7.47; SD = 2.40) and analysis ("Explain complex issues" M = 7.53; SD = 2.17") also rated high. In contrast, affirmations that hinted at a prescriptive nature, mainly those related to media's mobilization role, rated the lowest ("Offer suggestions on how to solve society's problems" M = 6.92; SD = 2.43; "Guide citizens in how they can participate in political matters" M = 6.86; SD = 2.39; "Educate the audience" M = 6.81; SD = 2.58; "Serve as a mediator between politics and society" M = 6.69; SD = 2.44) (see Table 8.1).

These results, together with a still solid perception of the need for PSM at a societal level—68,5% of respondents were in complete disagreement or somewhat in disagreement with the statement "Our society can do without public media"—show that the concept and normative understanding of PSM is well entrenched in Spanish society. This seemingly

---

[1] Results of this survey were also presented as part of the author's Ph.D. dissertation, "Public Service Media from an Audience Perspective: Citizen's Attitudes and Perceptions of Spain's National Broadcaster (TVE)."

Table 8.1 Expectations-evaluations discrepancies

Item	Expectations		Evaluations		Discrepancy	
	M	SD	M	SD	M	SD
... inform citizens neutrally and precisely about events in politics and society (information).	7.94	2.27	4.94	2.71	3.00	3.47
... reveal political abuses and scandals (watchdog).	7.77	2.34	4.82	2.70	2.95	3.47
... hold political and economic elites accountable (watchdog).	7.02	2.51	4.48	2.68	2.54	3.43
... defend the free democratic order in Spain (mobilization).	7.74	2.30	5.20	2.67	2.54	3.25
... explain complex issues (analysis).	7.53	2.17	5.05	2.58	2.48	3.15
... create innovative programming (quality entertainment).	7.42	2.20	5.06	2.63	2.36	3.10
... contribute to a democratic understanding that connects the entire society (public forum).	7.33	2.29	5.01	2.57	2.32	3.16
... provide quality kids and teens programming.	7.63	2.26	5.33	2.59	2.30	3.09
... take into account interests of disadvantaged members of society (social empathy).	7.24	2.34	4.99	2.59	2.25	3.23
... share democratic norms and values (mobilization).	7.37	2.31	5.13	2.60	2.24	3.14
... highlight similarities between different political positions (analysis).	7.04	2.27	4.83	2.55	2.21	3.15
... contribute to the formation of citizens' opinions on political matters (public forum).	7.14	2.37	4.96	2.58	2.18	3.13
... give voice to people with different cultural backgrounds, religious views, and sexual orientation, as well as to people with disabilities (social empathy).	7.47	2.40	5.30	2.58	2.17	3.12
... offer suggestions on how to solve society's problems (analysis).	6.92	2.43	4.86	2.69	2.06	3.15
... arouse interest in political issues (mobilization).	7.09	2.32	5.05	2.57	2.04	3.13
... provide quality cultural programming	7.66	2.21	5.64	2.57	2.02	3.02
... guide citizens in how they can participate in political matters (mobilization).	6.86	2.39	4.85	2.59	2.01	3.15
... serve as a mediator between politics and society (public forum).	6.69	2.44	4.77	2.57	1.93	3.12

(*continued*)

Table 8.1 (continued)

Item	Expectations M	SD	Evaluations M	SD	Discrepancy M	SD
… provide quality entertainment for all audiences (quality entertainment).	7.52	2.25	5.62	2.58	1.91	3.02
… educate the audience	6.81	2.58	4.95	2.62	1.86	3.15
… produce Spanish quality fiction (quality entertainment).	7.27	2.39	5.48	2.62	1.79	2.97

Note: $N = 1717$; results are presented in decreasing order, considering the discrepancy calculated as the mean of the difference between both variables (expectations/evaluations)

positive trait must be analyzed cautiously since we do not count on previous data, and it could simply indicate that social change is slow (Just et al., 2017), particularly when we witness a constant decline in PSM consumption and low perceptions of PSM performance (see Table 8.1; Campos-Rueda, 2023a).

Nevertheless, PSM must build upon these high expectations while there is still room since they are precious amidst growing media distrust and the acceptance of populist and extreme right discourse in the mainstream debate. Our data, in consonance with previous empirical evidence, confirm consumption as the strongest predictor of positive evaluations of PSM and the perceptions of its need (see Campos-Rueda, 2023a, 2023b). At this point, we need to stress the need to analyze consumption metrics under the not-so-new digital landscape. PSM is still mainly judged by the performance of its linear services; this not only disregards the value of its much-needed expansion to other screens and points of contact with the audience but rewards catering to an older, more educated audience that is already consuming its services (see Newman et al., 2023). It also discourages testing unorthodox initiatives and does not reward the ones that are working and might need extra financing or exposure.

The audience's understanding of PSM roles as necessary for a well-functioning democracy must, therefore, be acknowledged and urgently met by reaching out to the audiences and actively pursuing their engagement with PSM. Reaching out means learning to navigate the tensions between social media and search engine algorithms with PSM ethos, exploring every new opportunity to expose the audience to the public service content, and communicating not only the services offered but also the proprietary platforms and applications where to find them and explore in a safe environment. It also involves new alliances with other public service agents and attempting new distribution strategies while fighting for discoverability and brand recognition. When social network news consumption is on the rise, over 50% of the Spanish population use social media as their primary source for news (Newman et al., 2022, 2023), the exposure of PSM content in this environment should become a priority, particularly to reach young audiences. However, being relevant and seen depends on each social network's algorithm and commercial priorities. Among our survey respondents, incidental news exposure to PSM content on social networks is low (M = 3.23; SD = 2.37). These figures and the unstoppable fall in linear consumption indicate that concepts such as "must carry" and "due prominence" must be redefined for the platform age.

Innovation strategies should also keep in mind that citizens' engagement with PSM involves participation and voice as part of the accountability and transparency process. Amongst the respondents to our survey, perceptions of participation channels being "adequate and sufficient" indicate room for improvement (M = 4.78; SD = 2.29). Participation can be a tricky concept for PSM. In 2021, following a similar 2020 campaign in France *(#Nos médias publics. Inventons ensemble les médias de demain* (#Our Public Media. Let's Invent Together the Media of Tomorrow), RTVE launched "La Gran Consulta" (The Big Consultation). It coincided with the end of a period of interim governance after a new Board and its President had been duly elected by Congress (see Ortega Gutiérrez, 2023). It was presented as "an ambitious and unprecedented transmedia campaign of citizen participation to find out the public broadcaster people want." Results were meant to be published as a White Paper and inform the drafting of a new framework remit for RTVE. Unfortunately, it was construed as more a marketing strategy than a meaningful listening or participatory exercise.

These two levels of necessary communication with the audience should never be confused. The press soon reflected flaws in the questionnaire design, which focused mainly on consumption, internal disputes regarding the budget, and the need for such an initiative (see Sánchez-Gey Valenzuela & Palomo-Domínguez, 2022). Less than a year later, the President resigned amidst cross-accusations of obstruction and wrongdoings not directly or uniquely related to "La Gran Consulta" (Gómez &

Cúe, 2022). The announced White Paper was not published; results were presented through a series of panels and scant information on the RTVE website (RTVE, 2023). The very strong communication bet on "La Gran Consulta" made its failure even more significant and, to an extent, placed a toll on future initiatives.

This experience helps reflect on the convenience of a transformational approach, particularly when trying to incorporate an audience perspective into the vision and management of PSM. Listening to the audience is a silent exercise that needs consistency and long-term goals. The focus must extend beyond merely collecting audience opinions or fostering interactions, which have always been present through call-ins and audience members being a part of show segments. PSM must define the nature and goals of listening so it can translate and flourish into actual participation and services. Co-creation is a tool that lost traction after a hype that assimilated it with simple user-generated content at the turn of the century. To date, only some broadcasters (e.g., VTR, PBS, RTVE) prioritize this form of participation (see Direito-Rebollal & Donders, 2023), which can be a way to build a more substantial representation.

Technology's opportunities for listening and establishing a constant dialogue with the audience are still underexploited. PSM should not be shy to use all the means the market puts at its disposal to connect with its audiences, but at the same time, it must make innovation a priority because "attractive content cannot reach an interested audience if it is not supported by innovative infrastructures and related technologies" (Arcidiacono, 2019, p. 2). However, the central question goes beyond technological capabilities since PSM still needs to figure out how to articulate meaningful audience participation in editorial and organizational debates.

Confronting Low Perceptions of Independence

Previous findings regarding the predictive power of perceptions of independence on PSM performance evaluations signal that trust issues and perceptions of political interventions hinder PSM's ability to fulfill its mission (Campos-Rueda & Goyanes, 2023). In Spain, despite its fully functioning democracy, PSM has never consolidated its independence and institutional stability (Bustamante, 2006). Consequently, our survey data showed high perceptions of governmental influence over PSM (M = 7.69 SD = 2.33) and instrumental use by political parties of the discourse for

PSM independence (M = 6.58 SD = 2.20). Once again, consumption is a strong predictor of a positive assessment of PSM's performance as a source of unbiased information and holding power accountable (Campos-Rueda & Goyanes, 2023), roles for which independence is a prerequisite. Citizens need to be encouraged to consume and judge for themselves what PSM has to offer. This simple premise becomes a challenge in times of fragmented audiences, an overabundance of media outlets, growing media distrust, misinformation, and constant attacks on PSM from populists, who label them as state media or the voice of the corrupt elites (Holtz Bacha, 2021).

Given Spanish PSM history and the current extremely polarized political environment, achieving more stable governance for RTVE or reaching a political agreement to prevent its instrumentalization, while desirable, is not foreseeable in the near future. Therefore, it becomes necessary to focus on strategies that build credibility and improve both factual and perceived independence, despite the overall inability to insulate PSM from political interference. This does not imply stopping to advocate and present solutions for improving PSM's functioning and institutional health. On the contrary, both academia and civil society should vigilantly act as watchdogs and be bold and proactive in proposing innovative strategies. These strategies should align with PSM's goals, considering the nuances of the local media and political landscape rather than adhering strictly to the ideal models of PSM institutions established a century ago under markedly different circumstances.

RTVE has a solid online presence and offers content and services via third-party platforms, in addition to its excellent VOD platform, RTVE Play. Contrary to its linear offer and programming strategies, online services and RTVE's innovation lab are not under constant scrutiny from the press or subject to polarized political assessments. RTVE news channel on YouTube, which includes a daily 10-minute newscast, is an excellent example of how consistent and well-formatted content can open new lines for growing viewership and connecting with younger audiences. The channel, with over 2 million subscribers, is on par with the leading commercial news media channels on the platform.[2] The fact-checking website

---

[2] As of 02/18/2024, YouTube subscribers: RTVE Noticias 2.030.000; Antena 3 Noticias 179.000; Mediaset España (They do not have a dedicated news channel) 860.000; La Sexta Noticias 429.000; Top Spanish legacy media news channel El País 2.560.000.

Verifica RTVE is another interesting space, offering an excellent but undermarketed service.

These successful services hint that a project-based approach could allow Spanish PSM to build new environments and services to grow consumption and help improve perceptions of independence. This would also allow room for new alliances and quicker iterations that integrate audience feedback.

The Trap of Populist Discourse

The mismatch between populist attitudes and the ideology underlying liberal democracies has been extensively documented and extends to PSM's values and mission (see Holtz Bacha, 2021). The threat of populism's growth to PSM can be approached from at least two perspectives. On the one hand, the entrance into the mainstream of populist discourse affects citizens' attitudes and perceptions toward PSM; on the other hand, there is the question of how PSM can effectively combat populism's divisive views.

Linear regressions using our survey results (see Campos-Rueda, 2023a) confirmed previous findings (Fawzi & Mothes, 2020) that populist attitudes, particularly those related to anti-elite sentiment, are associated with low evaluations and higher dissatisfaction with PSM services. Media in general, particularly PSM, are often the target of populist attacks, labeling them as part of or at the service of the corrupt elites. In the case of PSM, populists tend to portray them as state media questioning their independence and bias against 'the people and their true values.' In Spain, these attacks come both from extreme right parties, most often associated with populism, and the left-wing populist formations that refer to PSM as part of the 'mediatic right.' Low consumption and lower perceptions of independence make this rhetoric more pervasive, and this is particularly worrying in the case of a country where Public Service Media are in question and instrumentalized by mainstream political parties.

As much as the quality of its information, it is PSM's duty to promote a healthy public debate based on facts that, that opposed to populist discourse, can expose different views, avoiding oversimplification and labeling. The challenge is effectively integrating the emotions and needs of those who feel overlooked by traditional politics and institutions while dismantling the impact of disinformation and polarization. Combating populist discourse is not an easy task; it requires avoiding being overly tolerant of harmful visions that are difficult to tackle because they do not strictly constitute hate speech or an attack on democracy. However, the biggest task is avoiding the trap of reproducing an 'us vs. them' representation of society.

Conclusion

Our findings, supporting existing literature, underscore the significant positive correlations and predictive strength of reach, consumption, and engagement metrics in assessing PSM performance and the perceived necessity of its services. These metrics, alongside perceptions of independence, are crucial to ensure PSM's effectiveness as a key player in promoting democratic engagement. Therefore, a sustainable PSM project must include quantitative audience data and, primarily, qualitative research that provides insights into and anticipates citizens' and society's needs and challenges regarding media and information.

Universal access, informed citizenship, and the scarcity of spectrum and content were the core arguments that sustained PSM for decades. In this new context, what has become scarce? This question does not imply restricting PSM's role to a market failure perspective but acknowledges that new media needs have emerged and remain unattended in the current media ecosystem. Despite the overabundance of content, is quality information universally available? Does what has been described as a high-choice environment, truly offer free choices when guided by opaque personalization and recommendation algorithms?

While some services are overabundant, others have become difficult to reach. PSM can no longer be all about long and short-form TV and radio shows distributed across all the existing platforms. As Karen Donders suggests, it should aim to be more than a "technologically neutral version of PSB" (Donders, 2021, p. 42). If the question is how to reach citizens and how to impact their daily lives, PSM must utilize the full media tool kit at its disposal, focused not just on the provision of content in a traditional sense but on delivering much-needed services regarding disinformation and fact-checking, media literacy, and protection of privacy and attention. Considering the growing paywalls of legacy media and the partisanship of the free online and linear media offer in Spain, its core mission of providing access to unbiased information and analysis gains a renewed relevance.

Academia, regulators, and PSM managers are finally shaking off the idea of considering PSM as an institution merely tasked with covering gaps unattended by the market and the notion that new services need to be assess in reference to the market. There is a growing consensus that the public value of PSM should be measured from a mission-oriented perspective, focusing on its societal contribution to democracy and citizenship-building. To achieve its goals, PSM requires adequate funding that allows for innovation and the expansion of its services to cover new unmet needs and remain competitive in attracting hard-to-reach audiences such as younger citizens, those on the political right, or politically disengaged. It is time to stop discussing a transition and start working on theoretical, regulatory, and management frameworks that allow constant iteration and prioritize innovation.

References

Arcidiacono, A. (2019). Media innovation and Europe's digital sovereignty. *tech-i*, 42, 2. https://tech.ebu.ch/docs/tech-i/tech-i-042.pdf?_gl=1*1pwghrw*_ga*NTY0MjQwODEzLjE3MDczMTEwNDQ.*_ga_TVTB816MPW*MTcw Nzc1NjE4MS4zLjEuMTcwNzc1NjUwNy42MC4wLjA

Bardoel, J., & Lowe, G. F. (2007). From public service broadcasting to public service media: The core challenge. In G. F. Lowe & J. Bardoel (Eds.), *From public service broadcasting to public service media* (RIPE@2007) (pp. 9–26).

Blumler, J. (1992). *Televisión e interés público*. Bosch.

Bustamante, E. (2006). *Radio y televisión en España: Historia de una asignatura pendiente de la democracia*. Gedisa.

Campos-Rueda, M. (2023a). Explaining expectations-evaluation discrepancies: The role of consumption and populist attitudes in shaping citizens' perceptions of PSM performance. *Journalism Practice*. https://doi.org/10.1080/1751278 6.2023.2210531

Campos-Rueda, M. (2023b). Influence of public service media consumption on citizens' perceptions of the need for public media: The moderating role of political ideology. *International Journal of Communication*, 17, 3844–3964. https://ijoc.org/index.php/ijoc/article/view/20751/4203

Campos-Rueda, M., & Goyanes, M. (2023). Public service media for better democracies: Testing the role of perceptual and structural variables in shaping citizens' evaluations of public television. *Journalism*, 24(11), 2493–2513. https://doi.org/10.1177/14648849221114948

Council of Europe. (2018). Recommendation CM/Rec(2018)1 of the Committee of Ministers to member States on media pluralism and transparency of media ownership. https://www.coe.int/en/web/freedom-expression/committee-of-ministers-adopted-texts/-/asset_publisher/aDXmrol0vvsU/content/

recommendation-cm-rec-2018-1-1-of-the-committee-of-ministers-to-member-states-on-media-pluralism-and-transparency-of-media-ownership

Council of Europe. (2024). Proposal for a Regulation of the European Parliament and of the Council establishing a common framework for media services in the internal market (European Media Freedom Act) and amending Directive 2010/13/EU – Letter to the Chair of the European Parliament Committee on Culture and Education. https://eur-lex.europa.eu/legal-content/EN/TXT/HTML/?uri=CELEX:52022SC0286

D'Arma, A., Barclay, S., & Horowitz, M. A. (2024). Public service media and the Internet: Two decades in review. *International Journal of Communication, 18*, 248–267. https://ijoc.org/index.php/ijoc/article/download/21544/4626

Deane, J., Docquir, P. F., Mano, W., Sabry, T., & Sakr, N. (2020). *Achieving viability for public service media in challenging settings: A holistic approach.* CAMRI-University of Westminster Press. https://library.oapen.org/bitstream/handle/20.500.12657/37227/achieving-viability-for-public-service-media-in-challenging-settings.pdf?sequence=1&isAllowed=y

Direito-Rebollal, S., & Donders, K. (2023). Public service media as drivers of innovation: A case study analysis of policies and strategies in Spain, Ireland, and Belgium. *Communications, 48*(1), 43–67. https://doi.org/10.1515/commun-2021-0003

Donders, K. (2021). *Public service media in Europe: Law, theory and practice.* Routledge.

European Union. (2022a). Regulation (EU) 2022/1925 of the European Parliament and of the Council of 14 September 2022 on contestable and fair markets in the digital sector and amending Directives (EU) 2019/1937 and (EU) 2020/1828 (Digital Markets Act). https://eur-lex.europa.eu/legal-content/EN/TXT/?uri=uriserv%3AOJ.L_.2022.265.01.0001.01.ENG&toc=OJ%3AL%3A2022%3A265%3ATOC

European Union. (2022b). Regulation (EU) 2022/2065 of the European Parliament and of the Council of 19 October 2022 on a Single Market For Digital Services and amending Directive 2000/31/EC (Digital Services Act). https://eur-lex.europa.eu/legal-content/EN/TXT/?uri=celex%3A32022R2065

Fawzi, N., & Mothes, C. (2020). Perceptions of media performance: Expectation-evaluation discrepancies and their relationship with media-related and populist attitudes. *Media and Communication, 8*(3), 335–347. https://doi.org/10.17645/mac.v8i3.3142

Gómez, R., & Cúe, C. (2022, September 26). El presidente de RTVE prepara su dimisión al perder el apoyo del PSOE y Unidas Podemos. *El País.* https://elpais.com/espana/2022-09-26/el-presidente-de-rtve-prepara-su-dimision-al-perder-el-apoyo-del-psoe-y-unidas-podemos.html

Holtz Bacha, C. (2021). The kiss of death. Public service media under right-wing populist attack. *European Journal of Communication, 36*(3), 221–237. https://doi.org/10.1177/0267323121991334

Just, N. (2020). Public perceptions of public service in European Media. In J. Nussbaum (Ed.), *Oxford research encyclopedia of communication.* Oxford University Press. https://doi.org/10.1093/acrefore/9780190228613.013.894

Just, N., Büchi, M., & Latzer, M. (2017). A blind spot in public broadcasters' discovery of the public: How the public values public service. *International Journal of Communication, 11,* 992–1011. https://ijoc.org/index.php/ijoc/article/view/6591

Martin, E. N. (2021). Can public service broadcasting survive Silicon Valley? Synthesizing leadership perspectives at the BBC, PBS, NPR, CPB and local U.S. stations. *Technology in Society, 64,* 101451. https://doi.org/10.1016/j.techsoc.2020.101451

Newman, N., Fletcher, R., Eddy, K., Robertson, C. T., & Nielsen, R. K. (2022). *Digital news report 2022.* Reuters Institute for the Study of Journalism. https://reutersinstitute.politics.ox.ac.uk/digital-news-report/2022

Newman, N., Fletcher, R., Eddy, K., Robertson, C. T., & Nielsen, R. K. (2023). *Digital news report 2023.* Reuters Institute for the Study of Journalism. https://reutersinstitute.politics.ox.ac.uk/sites/default/files/2023-06/Digital_News_Report_2023.pdf

Ortega Gutiérrez, D. (2023). El tortuoso desarrollo normativo del artículo 20.3 de la constitución española. El control político sobre RTVE. *Teoría y Realidad Constitucional, 51,* 283–316. https://doi.org/10.5944/trc.51.2023.37511

RTVE. (2023). La Gran Consulta ha sumado casi 140.000 respuestas ciudadanas. *RTVE.* https://www.rtve.es/rtve/20230517/gran-consulta-sumado-casi-140000-respuestas-ciudadanas/2446469.shtml

Sánchez-Gey Valenzuela, N., & Palomo-Domínguez, I. (2022). La reforma de radiotelevisión española sometida a la opinión popular: análisis de 'La gran consulta' de RTVE. In R. Zugasti, R. Mancinas-Cháves, S. Pallarés-Navarro, & N. S.-G. Valenzuela (Eds.), *Contenidos, medios e imágenes en la comunicación política* (pp. 286–309). Fragua.

van Cuilenburg, J., & McQuail, D. (2003). Media policy paradigm shifts: Towards a new communications policy paradigm. *European Journal of Communication, 18*(2), 181–207. https://doi.org/10.1177/0267323103018002002

Van den Bulck, H., & Raats, T. (2023). Media policymaking and multistakeholder involvement: Matching audience, stakeholder and government expectations for public service media in Flanders. *European Journal of Communication, 38*(2), 132–147. https://doi.org/10.1177/02673231221112199

CHAPTER 9

Citizenship on the Public Service Internet: Citizens' Media Contribution to Reimagining Digital Democratic Communication

Luciana Musello ⓘ

INTRODUCTION

As political participation and discussion concentrate on corporate social media, public service media (PSM) have moved to digital platforms to dispute citizens' communicative space (Cañedo & Segovia, 2022). However, the platformisation of PSM threatens to undermine public service goals by subjecting public communication to the commercial logic that underpins existing digital platforms. Optimised to serve economic imperatives, the "technological encoding of sociality" (Van Dijck, 2013) on social media has eroded opportunities for meaningful communication and redefined engagement in politics as the passive circulation of content (Dean, 2005), the default form of participation afforded by existing platforms. In the process, citizens have been left with a "pseudo-digital public

L. Musello (✉)
Universidad San Francisco de Quito (USFQ), Quito, Ecuador
e-mail: lmusello@usfq.edu.ec

© The Author(s), under exclusive license to Springer Nature Switzerland AG 2024
M. Goyanes, A. Cañedo (eds.), *Media Influence on Opinion Change and Democracy*, https://doi.org/10.1007/978-3-031-70231-0_9

sphere" (Fuchs, 2021, p. 13). Corporate digital platforms act as hosts of public communication but are incompatible with public values and democratic engagement.

Amid this scenario, proposals to strengthen the public service sector on the Internet and restore public values in digital communication have flourished (Andrejevic, 2013; Murdock, 2005; Goyanes & Campos-Rueda, 2022; Rajendra-Nicolucci et al., 2023; Van Dijck et al., 2018). Among them, the initiative for a Public Service Internet (PSI) (Fuchs & Unterberger, 2021) seeks to revitalise the digital public sphere by renovating and expanding the role of PSM into the digital realm. As a vision for the future of the Internet, the PSI asserts the need to transform PSM into the central node of a new digital public communications infrastructure (Murdock, 2005). It has been conceived as an ecosystem of publicly owned and universally accessible noncommercial digital platforms, built around public values and operated by PSM institutions, in collaboration with other public and civil society organisations. Freed from economic imperatives, the PSI intends to liberate public communication from its commercial enclosure and provide a shared and open space where participation and citizenship can be realised.

An angular difference between corporate social media and the Public Service Internet is that while dominant platforms address users as consumers, public service platforms ought to interpellate users as citizens (Fuchs & Unterberger, 2021). Although this tends to be a normative distinction between corporate and public service approaches to participation and content provision, the issue of how active citizenship shall be promoted is seldom discussed. If the construction of citizens' identities is a key task of democratic politics (Mouffe, 1993), then this is also a priority for PSM and the PSI. To fulfil the interpellation "citizens", what conditions must public service platforms meet?

Drawing from Latin American thought on citizenship and communication, this chapter argues that public service platforms should align with a "citizens' media" agenda, in the sense advanced by Colombian scholar Clemencia Rodríguez (2001). Rooted in radical democracy theories that understand citizenship as engagement in daily political action (Mouffe, 1992, 1993), citizens' media designates communication practices through which citizenship is constructed and exercised (Rodríguez, 2011). The concept foregrounds grassroots groups' appropriation and use of media technologies to trigger communication interventions that can bring about change within their local communities. By examining the media as places of popular participation and emphasising a view of communication as a social process, citizens' media theory offers a way forward to reimagine digital democratic communication.

To interpellate users as citizens and further their political agency, the citizens' media framework suggests that PSM and the PSI should not only provide extended mechanisms for creative and discursive participation in the media, as aptly called for in previous PSM commentary (Cañedo & Segovia, 2022; D'Arma et al., 2021; Rodríguez-Castro et al., 2022; Vanhaeght, 2019). Citizens' media theory calls for the PSI to relinquish control over to users so that they reclaim digital public infrastructure and manage these tools as they see fit. In practice, this means decentring and broadening the PSI beyond PSM content provision to enable citizens' diverse digital endeavours. Creating or at least supporting the development of governable platforms by citizens is key. Only then can effective media-based political participation emerge.

This chapter outlines a citizens' media agenda for the Public Service Internet. It starts by systematising Latin American scholarship on citizens' media, to then elaborate on how a popular understanding of citizenship and communication can challenge the patterns of corporate digital platforms and restore democratic engagement in the digital realm.

Redefining Citizenship and Communication

In liberal approaches to citizenship, a citizen is usually conceived as a bearer of rights which in turn enable their participation in the political process (Mouffe, 1993). According to Graham Murdock (2005), this notion of citizenship historically informed the rationale for public service broadcasting. He explains that PSB's core function lies in securing access rights to the cultural resources required for substantive citizenship. These are the right to (1) comprehensive information about public issues, (2) analysis and commentary, (3) fora for collective deliberation, (4) inclusive and diverse media representations and (5) opportunities for audiences' participation in media-making and debate (Murdock, 2005, p. 217).

Yet, focused primarily on producing an educated and critical citizenry through information provision, this vision of citizenship fails to remediate the lack of effective participation opportunities on social media. Rooted in the broadcasting model, PSM's understanding of citizenship as access to media resources perpetuates an arrangement where the scope of public service is limited to content production and distribution (Andrejevic, 2013). Hence, users continue to be configured as audiences or masses to whom communication has to be brought to (Martín-Barbero, 1986). In doing so, it consolidates a passive involvement with citizenship as inscribed in the "participation" affordances provided by dominant platforms. Indeed, as Murdock (2005) and other scholars (Collins, 2010; Rincón, 2022; Vanhaeght, 2019) contend, participation continues to be the blind spot of PSM. To build a participatory alternative to the corporate Internet, the public service notion of what citizenship entails ought to be expanded.

A more active conception of citizenship and communication can be found in the work of Clemencia Rodríguez and her theory of "citizens' media" (2001). Here Rodríguez builds on Chantal Mouffe's theory of radical democracy which seeks to reframe the concept of citizenship beyond a system of rights (1992, 1993). Instead of reducing it to a mere legal status granted by formal institutions, Mouffe contends that citizenship should rather be enacted. Citizenship is a kind of political identification constructed through people's active engagement in everyday social and cultural interactions, where struggles for power can emerge. For Mouffe (1992), a democratic citizen is somebody who *acts* as a citizen and mobilises their power in a collective undertaking (p. 4).

This reconceptualisation of citizenship into active and everyday political practices led Rodríguez to produce the term "citizens' media". Citizens' media are communication spaces where people and communities can construct their citizenship (Rodríguez, 2011, p. 24). The concept highlights the processes of identity building, language appropriation, bond formation and power fragmentation that take place through communities' day-to-day media use (Rodríguez, 2020). Citizens' media enable meaning-making practices that allow grassroots groups to communicate "in their own terms", a capacity that is directly linked to people's power to undertake political action (Rodríguez, 2010, p. 18). Citizens' media are thus defined by their "performative" power (Rodríguez, 2011, p. 257) or generative role in producing lived experiences of participation in the public sphere.

In this sense, Rodríguez's theory of citizens' media breaks with the presumption that the relevance of alternative and community media is limited to their resistance to the mass media system. The concept of citizens' media extends its democratic potential by considering these media forms in terms of their empowering effects on citizens, as they gain control over media technologies and engage in communication practices directed towards their political endeavours (Rodríguez, 2010). So, while the first approach to participation is concerned with reordering media ownership and producing counter-publics, citizens' media locate participation in community governance and involvement in everyday political actions through strategic media use.

The emphasis on practice and social processes present in Rodríguez's work is a defining feature of Latin American communication thought (Stephansen & Treré, 2019). Citizens' media theory retrieves a popular theory of communication that set out to rethink communication in the region as a "praxis", beyond the transmission model (Barranquero, 2019). In his pioneering book *De los medios a las mediaciones (From the Media to Mediations)* (1987/1991), Spanish-Colombian scholar Jesús Martín-Barbero outlined a popular project that urged scholars to give up questions focused on media technologies and content, and direct their attention to what people *do* with the media.

By rejecting media-centric accounts of communication, Martín-Barbero reinserted communication studies in the domain of culture and more specifically, in the field of *lo popular* (the popular). *Lo popular* as a theory of communication seeks to foreground the creative practices in people's everyday media use (Barranquero, 2019). Grounded in Latin American theories of popular education put forward by Paulo Freire (1970/2005) and Mario Kaplún (1985), *lo popular* attempts to disentangle communication from the study of specific "instruments" or media used to impart information or knowledge from above. Instead, it argues that communication should be understood as a dialogical and participatory process aimed at cultivating people's political agency. Here, communication is a matter of "processes, practices and experiences of sharing and producing meaning" (Rincón & Marroquín, 2018, p. 64). In other words, *lo popular* invites us to evaluate the media as *places* of cultural and political identification (Rincón, 2015).

Together, Rodríguez's theory of citizens' media and Latin American theorisation of *lo popular*, offer fruitful directions to imagine what conditions should the PSI meet to revitalise citizenship in the digital realm. If we accept the citizens' media framework, then establishing pockets of public space in the corporately run Internet and securing access rights to cultural resources is crucial but not sufficient for extending citizenship. The Public Service Internet must enable people to *become* citizens and mobilise their political agency. This will demand that PSM renounce their "habitus of authority" (Collins, 2010) and that public service platforms develop into malleable and governable tools in the hands of users. If we consider *lo popular* as a way of challenging the dominant understanding of communication as information transmission, it becomes apparent that democratic communication will not sprout from creating alternative information instruments or technologies. For public service platforms to be successful, they must embrace a vision of communication as a social process, reject techno-centric approaches to democracy and attend to people's agency instead. In other words, public service platforms should enable dialogic and participatory encounters that foster cultural determination. Otherwise, they are likely to reinforce domination or remain marginal.

Overall, examining the PSI under a citizens' media lens is aimed at transforming the logic of corporate platforms which has colonised and undermined public service goals under the process of platformisation. This agenda calls for three radical shifts: moving past circulation instruments to communication practices, from mere audience engagement to popular governance and from a consumer-oriented Internet to a *citizens' Internet*. In the following sections, this chapter elaborates on the issues that existing social media poses to democratic communication and the corresponding transformations pursued by a citizens' media perspective.

From Circulation to Communication

As PSM have readily embraced digital platforms, they have yielded to a pattern of communication as circulation of content. In social media, instances of political participation merge into high-speed data streams where information is always new and abundant (Boczkowski, 2021; Poell & Van Dijck, 2015; Dean, 2005). The volume and speed of this environment have been propelled by platforms' features which encourage users to create and recirculate content in real time (Poell & Van Dijck, 2015). Massive data flows are managed by algorithms that instantly evaluate, select and serve up information to users whose preferences have already been anticipated (Gillespie, 2014).

Although this immediacy has been hailed for its democratic potential, speed attends to platforms' business models, dependent on the commodification of users' attention. The immediate nature of social media has therefore deepened the commercialisation of public discourse and rendered opportunities for engaged debate difficult. Platforms' instantaneous and algorithmic logic has turned political communication into circulating spectacles and short-lived trending topics that preclude sustained discussion about public issues (Fuchs, 2021). This real-time and event-oriented dynamic has also permeated alternative and public service media reporting, as producers start to draw from social media data streams to keep up with high-speed information flows and sustain audiences' attention (Poell & Van Dijck, 2015). In this ecosystem, users appear to be ever more exposed to circulating information but lack mechanisms or space to grasp and discuss the issues.

Indeed, news consumption on social media tends to be incidental and derivative (Boczkowski et al., 2018). In *Abundance*, Boczkowski (2021, p. 122) found that people perceive news to be "ambient", that is, they trust they will encounter news during their social media routines without actively looking for them. When news merges with other pieces of content, it becomes commodified and loses its political relevance, as users rarely engage with the stories. Hence, in accelerated environments, news consumption is expanded but remains partial in character and devoid of intentionality, leading to low political engagement (Gil de Zúñiga et al., 2017).

This is a clear instance of what political theorist Jodi Dean (2005) calls "communicative capitalism", a situation where contributions to political discourse grow but are instantly channeled into a stream of ever-circulating content, losing specificity and purpose. Dean notes that circulation devoids communication of its political potential by uncoupling messages from contexts of action, response or debate. Nonetheless, the emphasis on the expansion of opportunities to transmit and receive messages works to conceal this fact. Disseminating information on social media is perceived as political involvement when in reality our political agency has been undermined by technology acting in our stead (Dean, 2005). In Latin American thought, this disavowal of human agency is understood as "mutism". For Paulo Freire, mutism emerges when societies are denied dialogue and offered information instead (1965). He defines mutism as a response that lacks a critical character or the capacity to intervene in reality.

The high-speed circulation of information on social media is thus profoundly depoliticising and hinders the practice of citizenship. When networked technologies are only deployed to circulate content as commodity exchange among individuals, communication is deprived of its dimension of transformative action. Rodríguez and her colleagues (2014) stress that platforms' celebrated speed and efficiency tend to overshadow people's organising behind the technology. Following Martín-Barbero, they call to question such techno-centrism and opt for theoretical frameworks that fixate on human agency, shifting attention from "the media" to "mediations".

In this context, restoring an understanding of communication as a social process or "praxis" is a key issue for citizenship in the PSI. To overcome mutism, public service platforms should be more than content circulation instruments or "public" versions of dominant platforms and become places of popular communication. Drawing from Stephansen's (2016) contribution to the citizens' media framework, platforms ought to go beyond simply "making (content) public" to rather support "public-making". Citizens' media are spaces for people to come together rather than channels for individual content reception (Rodríguez, 2011).

Thus far, PSM responses to the logic of circulation have focused on reassessing content production and reception. For instance, Fuchs (2021) has called for the PSI to become "slow media", content that cultivates critical skills and requires time as well as participatory processes to be both produced and consumed. On his part, Reviglio (2022) has explored PSM's role in developing new standards for ethical information consumption in social media through algorithmic systems aligned with public values. Although these contributions are meant to decelerate the communication landscape and advance intentionality into people's information routines online, circulation as a dominant logic is left unchallenged.

To move from circulation to communication practices, PSM should be "intervened" from *lo popular* (Rincón, 2022). *Lo popular* calls for public service platforms to act as places of political identification and organisation. It foregrounds platforms that choose to establish dialogue and interaction at the centre of their technological and cultural project. In short, it prioritises popular communication spaces that contribute to the formation of networks of solidarity, learning and, ultimately, political action. The next section addresses the political participation mechanisms that a popular communication agenda promotes.

From Audience Engagement to Participation

Social media has transformed the digital public sphere by redefining the terms in which political participation is understood. Interactive features in digital platforms including publishing, liking, commenting and sharing buttons are seen as participation affordances. Consequently, metrics that quantify usage such as reach, impressions and interactions, are conceived as indicators of people's political involvement in these environments. Nonetheless, at best, these metrics only represent what José Van Dijck calls "connectivity", an algorithmic computation derived from users' social connections (2013, p. 13). By reducing people's activities into formal and manageable instances, platforms can "engineer sociality" and direct user behaviour to favour their economic interests, dependent on increased data production. This means that so-called participation features are capital accumulation mechanisms. Yet they tend to be legitimised as instances of political participation.

At first, participation affordances on social media were celebrated by media organisations as an opportunity to strengthen their connection with citizens and protect democracy at large, since audiences could finally make their voices heard (Waisbord, 2022). This is true even for PSM institutions, which welcomed new interactive online affordances as an opportunity to involve audiences in media production (Collins, 2010; Vanhaeght, 2019). However, Silvio Waisbord (2022) shows how such endeavour had only a limited impact, as the participation mechanisms favoured by the media were eventually reduced to comment sections and sharing buttons. Indeed, discursive participation enabled by social media appears to be the main participation mechanism employed by European PSM (López-Cepeda et al., 2019). In the process, expectations around participation have been reframed. For Waisbord (2022), the once-politicised "turn to the public" in journalism has mutated into a promotional take on "audience engagement". Anchored in data-driven marketing strategies, audience engagement is centred on boosting metrics and optimising content to users' preferences. Hence, in the participation rationale advanced by platforms, an understanding of citizens as political subjects is absent. Instead, they are abstracted into metrics.

Audience engagement in social media thus yields a distorted conception of political participation. Metrics promote a false equivalence between politically engaged citizens and the computation of users' reactions. Peter Dahlgren's critique of participation pinpoints the problem: "Participation is ultimately about power sharing, and if this is structurally absent or systematically undermined, then whatever is being called participation must be seen with the utmost skepticism, or indeed labeled fraudulent" (Dahlgren, 2013, p. 28). In other words, social media features may offer expressive participation opportunities for audiences but fail to promote effective interventions in the political realm. As examined before, the capture of circulating discourse as a commodity leads to the "foreclosure" of politics (Dean, 2005). In this sense, despite much optimism about digital platforms offering extended mechanisms for users to develop a voice and circulate their opinions, they neglect citizens' media goals concerned with prompting communication processes that enable the fragmentation of power. Building on Rodríguez's performance approach to citizens' media (2011), it could be argued that instead of *doing* things, platforms' participation defaults enable users to merely *say* things. Existing social media platforms are essentially removed from decision-making spheres (Dahlgren, 2013), and audience engagement metrics work to conceal such political powerlessness.

Enabling mechanisms for effective participation is thus crucial for the PSI. Following a citizens' media agenda, this endeavour is twofolded. First, by conceiving the media as places of popular communication, citizens' media promote participation strategies that cultivate interaction not between the media and their audiences, as per audience engagement, but among community members (Rodríguez et al., 2014, p. 159). Dahlgren's (2013, p. 22) distinction between participation *in* the media and participation *via* the media is a useful concept here. While the former is concerned with citizens' involvement in media production and circulation, as sought for by PSM through co-creation and engagement strategies, the latter foregrounds how media use can connect citizens to each other and to other social domains where the political resides, in true popular communication spirit. Public service platforms should then vacate PSM's intermediary function and become places where political action can be coordinated from below.

Once the subjects of communication are redefined, the PSI must strive to reconnect digital platforms with decision-making structures. One way to do this is to reframe the scale of "the political" and withdraw participation into smaller political actions. Drawing from Mouffe's conception of citizenship, the citizens' media framework understands political actions as locally situated media practices and everyday political compromises directed at reappropriating local public spheres (Rodríguez, 2011). When applied to platforms, the emphasis on situated action and community control implies devising online spaces where decision-making can be exercised by users. Here participation starts with users settling on norms, standards and purpose for their online conversations. This process of negotiation and deliberation can then build trust among members and lead to broader interventions that enable citizens to draw instances of power in their daily lives.

Some platform design directions to mobilise people's political agency in such a way can be found in the work of Rajendra-Nicolucci and Zuckerman (2022), who set out to map social media projects that work on a different logic than digital giants. Among them, "chat logic" and "civic logic" platforms figured as places where this kind of political participation could be promoted. Defined by one-to-one or small group communication, chat logic platforms enable private conversations where governance and moderation are managed by the community they cater to. Similarly, civic logic platforms are online spaces designed to foster deliberation, coordination and other civic goals. What both arrangements have in common is that they replace centralised decision-making schemes with community governance structures that address the needs of different communities. In short, they challenge dominant platforms' top-down discursive participation defaults.

These examples demonstrate that platforms can be deliberately configured to facilitate democratic participation and minimise intermediation. Nathan Schneider (2022) has posited the term "governable spaces" to describe platforms that enable users to collectively shape their communicative environments over time, and control the technical structures that affect them. He argues that getting involved in group processes of rule-setting and boundary-making is crucial to bringing democratic politics into platforms. From a citizens' media perspective, this restores the "performative" role of the media as places where people's agency is enacted or where communication is aimed at *doing*.

Now, although instances of community governance can be observed in platforms such as WhatsApp, Signal and Discord (Rajendra-Nicolucci & Zuckerman, 2022) and are certainly the merit of recent experiments with platform cooperatives and decentralised social networks (Scholz, 2016; Barabas et al., 2017), the PSI is best suited for this endeavour because public ownership or the participation of users in ownership continues to be a precondition to guarantee meaningful participation in decision-making (Fuchs, 2014). Public ownership also procures the existence of the "digital commons" (Fuchs, 2021), a library of open-access resources that communities with minimum technical knowledge will need to tailor and advance their digital spaces (Rajendra-Nicolucci & Zuckerman, 2022, p. 15). The approach to participation outlined here thus defies the consumer-oriented rationale of audience engagement and reconfigures users as decision-making citizens enabled by a scheme of public ownership. The next section delves into how the distinction between consumer and citizen plays out in the PSI, paving the way for a citizen's Internet.

From Consumers to Citizens

The dynamics examined in previous sections delineate a particular governance model at work in social media. For Tarleton Gillespie (2014), people's participation in political discourse and public life is increasingly determined by an "algorithmic logic" that steers users' connections and sorts the information flows on which citizens depend. Indeed, public communication has undergone a process of fragmentation assisted by algorithmic architectures that produce "calculated publics" (Gillespie, 2014) or consumer niches of political information. Algorithmic personalisation has perfectly coupled with media markets' long-standing commercial and advertising pressures, producing a rather fractured digital public sphere where content that appeals to specific political and commercial segments proliferates (Waisbord, 2020).

This means that an algorithmic logic has also been imputed onto content supply. Nieborg and Poell (2018) observe that public values and editorially driven processes in news production have been displaced to prioritise demand-driven content strategies informed by users' datafied indicators. They conclude that the production of knowledge and publics on social media appears to be increasingly "contingent" or dependent on platforms' economic and technological extensions, concerned with capital accumulation. In this environment, the formation of durable communities of political contestation becomes difficult. While algorithmic personalisation might generate brief instances of togetherness among users, Poell and Van Dijck (2015) note that calculated publics arise only as loosely connected networks of consumers fated to dissolve instantly, at the pace of viral content cycles.

For García-Canclini (2020), the consequence of opaque, personalised and distant algorithmic sorting is that people become alienated from the public sphere where citizenship ought to be exercised. He notes that market-oriented algorithms are unable to generate the conditions for social bonds to emerge, ushering citizens out of public communication. The algorithmic capture of people's communication practices for commercial purposes thus contributes to what García-Canclini calls "desciudadanización" (decitizenisation), understood as the championing of individualist consumer culture over citizenship as a category of collective social transformation.

By eschewing profit-making imperatives, it is argued that the PSI could nurture the "recitizenisation" of the digital public sphere. Nevertheless, citizenship will not be achieved in public service platforms as a direct result of its distinct ownership model. The theory of citizens' media is clear in pointing out that citizenship cannot be technologically instantiated. As a social process, citizenship must be constructed and thus requires producing the conditions to draw people back into the digital public sphere from which they have been displaced.

The emergence of a *citizens' Internet* is therefore characterised by processes of reappropriation of digital public infrastructure. This is a necessary step for the PSI to counter the growing alienation of users from media technologies and to reassert their collective agency in the face of algorithmic formalisation. As argued throughout this chapter, efforts to reclaim digital tools involve group processes where users engage in intentional communicative interaction to collectively decide what digital platforms are meant for and to design media interventions that transform their communities. Here citizens emerge from a process of reciprocal recognition (Martín-Barbero, 2005), a relational and horizontal dynamic of communication that challenges the predictive arrangements of algorithmic personalisation.

The marked emphasis on citizenship as a social process also implies that there is not a single ideal of citizenship to be expected from the PSI. As opposed to templatized interactions on commercial platforms, citizens' media have no prescriptive formula (Rodríguez, 2011). Citizens' media promote bottom-up "social innovation" emerging from the negotiation of people's differences and solidarities (Martín-Barbero, 2005), a process that algorithmic media neglects. For Rosa María Alfaro-Moreno (2004), whose work prefigures Rodríguez's theory of citizens' media, embracing the fact that there is not one, but various, intertwined and shifting ways of approaching citizenship is a key step to safeguarding democratic communication. Indeed, the assertion of plural expressions of citizenship against platforms' technical rationality, provides a possibility for the "recitizenisation" of the digital public sphere. Instead of striving to reconstitute a single monolithic citizenry, public service platforms have the opportunity to support the formation of diverse meaning-making communities with distinct political cultures. This approach can realistically promote people's agency while challenging algorithmic, consumer-centred economies.

Conclusion

To move from normative ideals to actual practices, the PSI project is faced with the need for a renewed framework of citizenship and communication. The citizens' media agenda outlined here provides a useful approach by placing the emphasis not on the democratic potential of media content or distinct media technologies, but on the democratic character of people's media *practices* on the Internet. It is by changing the "place of questions" (Rincón & Marroquín, 2018) and embracing a practice-based perspective of the media (Stephansen & Treré, 2019), that the vision of a Public Service Internet centred on human agency emerges. To borrow Rodríguez's original definition of citizens' media, the citizens' Internet is made up of public service platforms where people and communities can *enact* their citizenship. The citizens' Internet challenges the illusion of politics as content dissemination and instead provides spaces for users to enter into dialogic relationships directed at political action. The citizens' Internet eschews promotional or discursive approaches to participation and reconstitutes communication's performative power by enabling users to govern their platforms and engage in lived experiences alternative to engineered sociality. In other words, the citizens' Internet is a result of people retrieving control over the digital public sphere.

In the broadest sense, applying a citizen's media agenda to the PSI means integrating the political economy of public service platforms and digital community media (see Fuchs, 2021 for an extended elaboration of the differences). It is argued that while public service platforms are owned and controlled by PSM organisations, digital community media are owned and governed by their community of users. Although both types of platforms constitute the digital public sphere, insisting on their differences jeopardises the democratic potential of the PSI. Without public funding, resources and infrastructure, digital community media are set to remain marginal and precarious, and exist only as short-lived media projects. Similarly, by lacking popular appeal and insisting on a broadcasting model, public service platforms are likely to yield to the logic of content circulation and end up reinforcing people's alienation from the digital public sphere. This chapter has argued that this need not be the case. A citizen's media agenda calls for the PSI to embrace digital community media as part of its remit. Reordering Internet ownership and building a public counterforce to corporate social media is not enough for democratic communication. Public service platforms should be publicly owned to constitute a viable alternative but must be community-governed to enable popular participation. Only then can the interpellation "citizens" in the PSI be fulfilled.

REFERENCES

Alfaro-Moreno, R. M. (2004). Culturas Populares y Comunicación Participativa: En la Ruta de las Redefiniciones. *Comunicación, 126,* 13–19.

Andrejevic, M. (2013). Public service media utilities: Rethinking search engines and social networking as public goods. *Media International Australia, 146*(1), 123–132. https://doi.org/10.1177/1329878X1314600116

Barabas, C., Narula, N., & Zuckerman, E. (2017). *Defending internet freedom through decentralization: Back to the future?* MIT Media Lab. The Center for Civic Media & The Digital Currency Initiative. https://static1.squarespace.com/static/59aae5e9a803bb10bedeb03e/t/59ae908a46c3c480db42326f/1504612494894/decentralized_web.pdf

Barranquero, A. (2019). Praxis in Latin American communication thought. A critical appraisal. In H. Stephansen & E. Treré (Eds.), *Citizen media and practice. Currents, connections and challenges* (pp. 57–72). Routledge.

Boczkowski, P. J. (2021). *Abundance. On the experience of living in a world of information plenty.* Oxford University Press.

Boczkowski, P. J., Mitchelstein, E., & Matassi, M. (2018). "News comes across when I'm in a moment of leisure": Understanding the practices of incidental news consumption on social media. *New Media & Society, 20*(10), 3523–3539. https://doi.org/10.1177/1461444817750396

Cañedo, A., & Segovia, A. I. (2022). La plataformización de los medios de comunicación de servicio público. Una reflexión desde la economía política de la comunicación. In M. Goyanes & M. Campos-Rueda (Eds.), *Gestión de medios públicos en el entorno digital* (pp. 65–88) Tirant Humanidades.

Collins, R. (2010). From public service broadcasting to public service communication. In G. F. Lowe (Ed.), *The public in public service media* (RIPE@2009, pp. 53–69). Nordicom.

D'Arma, A., Fuchs, C., Horowitz, M., & Unterberger, K. (2021). The future of public service media and the internet. In C. Fuchs & K. Unterberger (Eds.), *The public service media and public service internet manifesto* (pp. 113–127). University of Westminster Press. https://doi.org/10.16997/book60.e

Dahlgren, P. (2013). *The political web. Media, participation and alternative democracy.* Palgrave Macmillan.

Dean, J. (2005). Communicative capitalism: Circulation and the foreclosure of politics. *Cultural Politics, 1*(1), 51–74. https://doi.org/10.2752/174321905778054845

Freire, P. (1965). *Educación como práctica de la libertad.* Siglo XXI Editores.
Freire, P. (2005). *Pedagogy of the oppressed* (30th Anniversary ed.). Continuum.
Fuchs, C. (2014). *Social media: A critical introduction.* Sage.
Fuchs, C. (2021). The digital commons and the digital public sphere: How to advance digital democracy today. *Westminster Papers in Communication and Culture, 16*(1), 9–26. https://doi.org/10.16997/wpcc.917
Fuchs, C., & Unterberger, K. (Eds.). (2021). *The public service media and public service internet manifesto.* University of Westminster Press. https://doi.org/10.16997/book60.e
García-Canclini, N. (2020). *Ciudadanos reemplazados por algoritmos.* Bielefeld University Press.
Gil de Zúñiga, H., Weeks, B., & Ardèvol-Abreu, A. (2017). Effects of the news-finds-me perception in communication: Social media use implications for news seeking and learning about politics. *Journal of Computer-Mediated Communication, 22*(3), 1–19. https://doi.org/10.1111/jcc4.12185
Gillespie, T. (2014). The relevance of algorithms. In T. Gillespie, P. Boczkowski, & K. Foot (Eds.), *Media technologies: Essays on communication, materiality, and society* (pp. 167–193). MIT Press.
Goyanes, M., & Campos-Rueda, M. (Eds.). (2022). *Gestión de medios públicos en el entorno digital.* Tirant Humanidades.
Kaplún, M. (1985). *El comunicador popular.* Ediciones CIESPAL.
López-Cepeda, A., López-Golán, M., & Rodríguez-Castro, M. (2019). Participatory audiences in the European public service media: Content production and copyright. *Comunicar, 60,* 93–102. https://doi.org/10.3916/C60-2019-09
Martín-Barbero, J. (1986). Prácticas de comunicación en la cultura popular: mercados, plazas, cementerios y espacios de ocio. In M. Simpson (Comp.), *Comunicación alternativa y cambio social* (pp. 284–296). Premià.
Martín-Barbero, J. (1991). *De los medios a las mediaciones* (2nd ed.). GG.
Martín-Barbero, J. (2005). Televisión pública, televisión cultural: entre la renovación y la invención. In O. Rincón (Comp.), *Televisión pública: del consumidor al ciudadano* (pp. 35–68). La Crujía.
Mouffe, C. (Ed.). (1992). *Dimensions of radical democracy: Pluralism, citizenship, community.* Verso.
Mouffe, C. (1993). *The return of the political.* Verso.
Murdock, G. (2005). Building the digital commons: Public broadcasting in the age of the internet. In P. Jauert and G. F. Lowe (Eds.), *Cultural dilemmas of public service broadcasting* (RIPE@2005, pp. 213–230). Nordicom.
Nieborg, D. B., & Poell, T. (2018). The platformization of cultural production: Theorizing the contingent cultural commodity. *New Media & Society, 20*(11), 4275–4292. https://doi.org/10.1177/1461444818769694

Poell, T., & Van Dijck, J. (2015). Social media and activist communication. In C. Atton (Ed.), *The Routledge companion to alternative and community media* (pp. 527–537). Routledge.

Rajendra-Nicolucci, C., & Zuckerman, E. (2022). *An illustrated field guide to social media*. The Knight First Amendment Institute at Columbia University. https://knightcolumbia.org/blog/an-illustrated-field-guide-to-social-media

Rajendra-Nicolucci, C., Sugarman, M., & Zuckerman, E. (2023). *The three legged stool: A manifesto for a smaller, denser internet*. Initiative for Digital Public Infrastructure, UMass Amherst. https://tinyurl.com/idpi3leg

Reviglio, U. (2022). Sistemas de personalización ética e integridad atencional. ¿Nuevas prioridades de los medios de servicio público? In M. Goyanes & M. Campos-Rueda (Eds.), *Gestión de medios públicos en el entorno digital* (pp. 129–160) Tirant Humanidades.

Rincón, O. (2015). Lo popular en la comunicación: culturas bastardas + ciudadanías celebrities. In A. Amado & O. Rincón (Eds.), *La comunicación en mutación* (pp. 23–42). Centro de Competencia en Comunicación para América Latina - FES Comunicación.

Rincón, O. (2022). Las públicas cool, pop y popular. In O. Rincón (Ed.), *TV Pública Cool* (pp. 39–74). FES Comunicación - FLACSO Argentina.

Rincón, O., & Marroquín, A. (2018). Los aportes del popular latinoamericano al pop mainstream de la comunicación. *Perspectivas de la Comunicación, 11*(2), 61–81. https://www.perspectivasdelacomunicacion.cl/ojs/index.php/perspectivas/article/view/1166

Rodríguez, C. (2001). *Fissures in the mediascape: An international study of citizens' media*. Hampton Press.

Rodríguez, C. (2010). De medios alternativos a medios ciudadanos: trayectoria teórica de un término. *Folios, Revista de la Facultad de Comunicaciones y Filología, 21–22*, 13–25. https://revistas.udea.edu.co/index.php/folios/article/view/6416

Rodríguez, C. (2011). *Citizens' media against armed conflict: Disrupting violence in Colombia*. The University of Minnesota Press.

Rodríguez, C. (2020). Deambulando por el sendero de la comunicación popular. In C. Rodríguez, C. Magallanes Blanco, A. Marroquín Parducci, & O. Rincón (Eds.), *Mujeres de la comunicación* (pp. 157–172) Centro de Competencia en Comunicación para América Latina - FES Comunicación.

Rodríguez, C., Ferron, B., & Shamas, K. (2014). Four challenges in the field of alternative, radical and citizens' media research. *Media, Culture & Society, 36*(2), 150–166. https://doi.org/10.1177/0163443714523877

Rodríguez-Castro, M., Maroto-González, I., & Campos-Freire, F. (2022). Participación ciudadana y valor público: en búsqueda de la legitimidad del servicio audiovisual público. In M. Goyanes & M. Campos-Rueda (Eds.), *Gestión de medios públicos en el entorno digital* (pp. 13–34). Tirant Humanidades.

Schneider, N. (2022). Governable spaces: A feminist agenda for platform policy. *Internet Policy Review*, *11*(1), 1–19. https://doi.org/10.14763/2022.1.1628

Scholz, T. (2016). *Platform cooperativism – Challenging the Corporate Sharing Economy*. Rosa Luxemburg Stiftung. https://rosalux.nyc/wp-content/uploads/2020/11/RLS-NYC_platformcoop.pdf

Stephansen, H. C. (2016). Understanding citizen media as practice. Agents, processes, publics. In M. Baker & B. Blaagaard (Eds.), *Citizen media and public spaces: Diverse expressions of citizenship and dissent*. Routledge.

Stephansen, H. C., & Treré, E. (2019). Practice what you preach? Currents, connections, and challenges in theorizing citizen media and practice. In H. C. Stephansen & E. Treré (Eds.), *Citizen media and practice: Currents, connections, challenges* (pp. 1–34). Routledge.

Van Dijck, J. (2013). *The culture of connectivity: A critical history of social media*. Oxford University Press.

Van Dijck, J., Poell, T., & De Waal, M. (2018). *The platform society: Public values in a connective world*. Oxford University Press.

Vanhaeght, A. S. (2019). The need for not more, but more socially relevant audience participation in public service media. *Media, Culture & Society*, *41*(1), 120–137. https://doi.org/10.1177/0163443718798898

Waisbord, S. (2020). ¿Es válido atribuir la polarización política a la comunicación digital? Sobre burbujas, plataformas y polarización afectiva. *Revista SAAP*, *14*(2), 249–279. https://doi.org/10.46468/rsaap.14.2.A1

Waisbord, S. (2022). Trolling journalists and the risks of digital publicity. *Journalism Practice*, *16*(5), 984–1000. https://doi.org/10.1080/17512786.2020.1827450

PART III

Opinion Change and Democracy in Social Media Platforms

CHAPTER 10

Origin and Evolution of the News Finds Me Perception: Review of Theory and Effects

Homero Gil de Zúñiga ● *and Zicheng Cheng* ●

WHAT IS THE NEWS FINDS ME PERCEPTION? ORIGINS

Social Media Is Everywhere

For almost two decades, society has witnessed the thriving of social media as a global phenomenon (McFarland & Ployhart, 2015). The popularity of social media has steadily grown since the early 2000s in both developing and more established democracies (e.g., Mitchell et al., 2018; Newman

---

This chapter was previously published as a journal article in Gil de Zúñiga, H. & Cheng, Z. (2022). Origin and evolution of the News Finds Me perception: Review of theory and effects. *Profesional De La información, 30*(3). https://doi.org/10.3145/epi.2021.may.21

H. Gil de Zúñiga (✉)
Universidad de Salamanca, Salamanca, Spain

Pennsylvania State University, University Park, PA, USA

Universidad Diego Portales, Santiago, Chile
e-mail: hgzn@psu.edu

© The Author(s), under exclusive license to Springer Nature Switzerland AG 2024
M. Goyanes, A. Cañedo (eds.), *Media Influence on Opinion Change and Democracy*, https://doi.org/10.1007/978-3-031-70231-0_10

151

et al., 2017). News organizations have embraced social media as a new way to produce news and to engage with their audience (Alejandro, 2010), where professional journalists report original news content and interact with their followers on social media platforms (Gil de Zúñiga et al., 2018; Hermida, 2012). Likewise, news users increasingly integrate social media news use within their daily media routine. According to existing data from *Smart Insights* (2021), the number of social media users worldwide has surpassed two billion, and a recent *Pew Research Center* survey of U.S. adults (Auxier & Anderson, 2021) showed that 69% of U.S. adults use Facebook. With this unprecedented widespread usage, social media has profoundly changed the way people get entertained, socialize, and more importantly for this study, gain and disseminate information in their daily lives (Sterrett et al., 2019).

Social media was initially designed as a space where people can get life updates from their friends and social contacts (Lewis, 2010), but now it has also organically become one important source for getting public affairs information. About 86% of U.S. adults indicate they often use a digital device to get news while traditional news sources like television (68%), radio (50%), and print news (32%) are much less used for this purpose.

One of social media distinct news features revolves around the prosumer theoretical accolade, converging consumer and producing aspects of the news (Ritzer et al., 2012). On the one hand, users have access to various kinds of either professionally curated or individually generated news from journalists, strategic communicators, individual media users, social contacts, and algorithmic filters (Thorson & Wells, 2016). As the media environment increasingly move toward digital and mobile realms, people progressively enjoy more access to news information in a much more rapid and convenient way (Boczkowski et al., 2018). On the other hand, users can create and share news contents to social contacts in one's social network, which deals with the producing aspects of the news cycle (Holton et al., 2013; Newman et al., 2017). As many social media news users create political content, or just share news with others, inevitably, other users within the same social network will effortlessly see the news content shared or created by their friends and contacts (Fletcher & Nielsen, 2018; Kim et al., 2013).

Z. Cheng
The University of Arizona, Tucson, AZ, USA
e-mail: zichengcheng@arizona.edu

News Are Always On

This widespread use of mobile devices and social networking platforms enable people to constantly stay connected, which leads to individuals' ambient awareness of the social others (Levordashka & Utz, 2016). The asynchronous, lightweight, and always-on online communication system gives birth to an ambient journalism (Hermida, 2010), in which citizens can easily access digitally fragmented news from both official and unofficial sources. Micro-blogging spaces such as Twitter (now known as X), for instance, provide means for citizens to gain immediate awareness of political information. Social networking sites serve as news awareness systems where users receive public affairs' information revolving around people's consciousness (Hermida, 2010; Markopoulos et al., 2009). Given this context, the "News Finds Me" (NFM) has been defined as "the extent to which individuals believe they can indirectly stay informed about public-affairs – despite not actively following news – through Internet use, information received from peers and online social networks" (Gil de Zúñiga et al., 2017, p. 107).

Prior research argued that the need for surveillance is on decline as the media choices become more diverse (Hopmann et al., 2016). An excessive reliance on the ambient informational environment might detach oneself from the traditional surveillance use of news media, which is characterized by the purposeful gathering of the information. An alternative view suggests that the surveillance practice has shifted from news media sources to peer groups (e.g., Gil de Zúñiga & Diehl, 2019). In the past, people remain informed about the news by actively seeking news outlets which informed them about the latest events; now they believe they just need to stay connected with their social feeds and online social networks to maintain the same informational objective.

One explanation for the shift from news outlets to social network feeds is that the ambient information environment is overwhelming, thus creating an information overload for digital news users. To manage the influx of information, citizens depend on other social ties and their networks to filter the news for them (Pentina & Tarafdar, 2014). These news users rely on those who, in general, more actively discuss political news in social media as they tend to be perceived as opinion leaders in one's network, and they are more likely to be trusted (Owen, 2017; Turcotte et al., 2015).

Perceptions Matter

Perception is the process of information selection, organization, and interpretation (Fiske & Taylor, 1984). It affects how individuals communicate as every individual respond to environmental stimuli in a different way. At times, particularly within the political arena, people's perception toward other objects or phenomena can be biased, misleading, or not reflective of the reality (Gil de Zúñiga et al., 2022). This is important because perception has historically played an important role in the development of communication theories. One example is the third-person effect hypothesis, which suggests that individuals tend to *perceive* the mass media message will exert a greater influence on others than on themselves (Davison, 1983; Gunther & Thorson, 1992). The spiral of silence theory also specifies that a *perceived* opinion dominance affects one's opinion expression (Glynn & Park, 1997; Noelle-Neumann, 1974), as those who *perceive* themselves in the minority are less likely to speak up in front of others (Noelle-Neumann, 1974; Gearhart & Zhang, 2014). Similarly, drawing on cultivation theory, people's *perceived* realism judgments over a message narrative affect their level of trust in the personalities that emit those messages, and its persuasiveness capabilities (Lippman et al., 2014; Quick, 2009). These are just few examples to illustrate the role of perception in information interpretation processes, particularly showing how individuals assign meaning to their daily experiences based on perceptions.

Similarly, social media algorithms, which contain user-driven (user-tracking) algorithms and socially driven (peer-filtering) algorithms (Feezell et al., 2021; Thurman et al., 2019), can elicit individual's perception of *being well-informed* about current news events and political affairs. Prior studies on algorithmic journalism have provided three theoretical pathways to explain the being well informed perception. First of all, machine algorithms as an information source can activate what has been coined as "machine heuristic" (Sundar, 2008), or the propensity to perceive machines as more objective, credible, and bias free (Clerwall, 2014; Gillespie, 2014). Second, as social influence theory suggests, individuals tend to be influenced by those who are in their social circles (Hong & Rojas, 2016; Katz et al., 1955). People are more likely to select and trust the news that are endorsed by close friends and family members than strangers or media institutions (e.g. Anspach, 2017; Messing & Westwood, 2012; Turcotte et al., 2015). Third, people are exposed to enormous amount of information on social media, including constant news updates.

This avalanche of information might lead to the belief that they are informed about the political world and their surveillance needs may have already been thoroughly satisfied (Van Erkel & Van Aelst, 2020).

But there is a problem. This perception of being well-informed is not necessarily true. According to utility maximization theory literature from the field of economics, the expected value of some utility function is defined by its prospective payoff (Meyer, 1987). That is, people will choose to do what they think will provide them with the maximum benefit, but with the least effort (Tversky & Kahneman, 1973). In this regard, individuals may perceive that social media provide them with maximum informational benefit at minimum news surveillance effort.

But what is perhaps most useful about the utility maximization theory is that at many instances, subjects are simply wrong (Kahneman, 2003; Loewenstein et al., 2003). For instance, depending on how hungry an individual may perceive she is, one may overestimate the amount of "pizza" she is able to consume over a week period, purchasing more than what they could possibly consume with the minimal effort of a single trip to the grocery store. This person "has made a forecasting error that has led to a bad choice" (Kahneman & Thaler, 2006, p. 222).

Similarly, individuals may overestimate how well they can be informed by only relying on their social networks to inform them about important news and public affair issues. Like the naive and unsuspecting shopper from the prior example, this person may be simply wrong. NFM may deceive subjects into thinking they do not need to seek information about public affairs as they will remain well informed without any active effort (Gil de Zúñiga & Diehl, 2019; Gil de Zúñiga et al., 2017; Lee, 2020).

With social media news displayed in "preview mode," bombing headlines, snack news features, and a waterfall of text snippets, users only know the broad idea of a story rather than a full-detailed narrative, which can hardly be considered as a knowledge internalization process (Fletcher & Nielsen, 2018). This may be one of the explanations as for why prior research has shown a null or negative relationship between social media news use and surveillance political knowledge (Bode, 2016; Oeldorf-Hirsch, 2018; Shehata & Strömbäck, 2018). In addition, social media users tend to follow the "similar others" and actively or passively tune algorithms to access news contents aligned with their ideology and past behavior (Bisgin et al., 2010; Fletcher & Nielsen, 2018), which might create echo chambers online (Pariser, 2011).

Previous NFM literature concluded the phenomenon encompasses three conceptual dimensions: being informed, not seeking, reliance on peers (Gil de Zúñiga et al., 2017; Lee, 2020; Song et al., 2020; Strauß et al., 2021). The following section captures these three dimensions and proposes a new one named *reliance on algorithmic news*.

DIMENSIONS OF THE NEWS FINDS ME PERCEPTION: THEORY

Being Informed

NFM people hold the epistemic belief that they are well informed about current political affairs and public events (Gil de Zúñiga et al., 2017; Song et al., 2020; Strauß et al., 2021). To point out, different from news avoiders (Newman et al., 2017), NFM people do have the intention to stay informed about the news as they take place, just engaging less actively and more strategically. It is the ambient news environment that leads to the belief that they will be informed without actively seeking the news (Lee & Xenos, 2019), generating the passive news consumption habit. The passive browsing behavior will elicit an ambient awareness of the activities by one's friends, colleagues, and family members (Levordashka & Utz, 2016). Furthermore, fragmented digital news disseminated on new media platforms, also referred as para-journalism, helps citizens reach immediate awareness and instant knowledge of the surrounding information (Sunstein, 2006; Hermida, 2010). This fast, lightweight, always-on mode of information acquisition on social media supports the mental *news around me* model, which is featured with low requirement of time and thought investment (Java et al., 2007).

Peer Reliance

Building on the original incidental news exposure hypothesis (Tewksbury et al., 2001), it is natural to think that when people use social media, they will inadvertently encounter news posted by their friends (Kim et al., 2013; Park & Kaye, 2020). NFM theory argues that one intends to stay informed through peers and online social networks. This hypothesis can be traced back to the two-step-flow theory (Lazarsfeld et al., 1948), which suggests that peers can reduce the cognitive efforts of seeking political information by facilitating the diffusion and acquisition of opinion elite information. News users can easily receive political news updates from their opinion leaders in the online social network, which will satisfy one's information surveillance need (Weeks et al., 2017a). DeVito (2017) identified that friend relationships is one of the key predictors of the news feed presented on one's Facebook feed. For instance, social influence of familiar individuals, with friends and family at the forefront, will become a better predictor of one's news selection than ideological cues on Facebook (Anspach, 2017), relying on mental shortcuts or heuristic cues to evaluate the information (Sundar, 2008) and fostering a dependance on peer and social network to get information, over other sources. Ultimately, receiving information from socially proximate sources can legitimate the validity of information shared in one's network, even though the accuracy of the news contents is uncertain (Gil de Zúñiga et al., 2022; Tandoc et al., 2017).

Not Seeking

NFM people believe that the important public news will find them eventually anyway. Looking way back to the mass media era, traditional news gathering behavior is a purposeful and directed activity, which requires people to deliberately seek news to stay informed (Ostertag, 2010; Tewksbury et al., 2001). However, the dynamics of social media have increased the likelihood for people to encounter news as a byproduct of their online activities and majority of people have become passive news consumers (Nielsen & Schrøder, 2014), perceiving news consumption to be an unintentional activity. For NFM people, social media provides them news from different sources simultaneously, including professional media outlets, citizen journalists and the proximate social networks (Park & Kaye, 2020). Thanks to social media, people can consume brief news pieces and obtain an overview of news events with little effort, as a part of their checking cycle each day (Costera-Meijer & Groot-Kormelink, 2015). To some degree, the technical affordances of social media enable users to choose whom to interact with, which information source to follow and further curate the information flow on one's news feed (Lee & Ma, 2012).

Algorithmic Reliance

The most current empirical instrument of the NFM includes six items, two per dimension, tapping on the three dimensions of the construct (see Table 10.1; for similar results with Austrian data, see Song et al., (2020)). Drawing on survey data collected in 2019 in the USA, and in 2020 in Italy

Table 10.1 Question wording for NFM and its subdimensions in the USA, Italy, and Portugal

Items	Dimension	Item wordings	M (SD)
1	Peers reliance	I rely on my friends to tell me what's important when news happen	4.57 (2.61)
2		I rely on information from my friends based on what they like or follow through social media	3.98 (2.49)
3	Well-informed	I do not worry about keeping up with news because I know news will find me	4.63 (2.68)
4		I can be well-informed even when I don't actively follow the news	5.38 (2.59)
5	Not seeking	I do not have to actively seek news because when important public affairs break, they will get to me in social media	4.78 (2.75)
6		I'm up-to-date and informed about public affairs news, even when I do not actively seek news myself	5.79 (2.46)
7	Algorithmic reliance	I rely on social media algorithms to tell me what's important when news happen	
8		I rely on social media algorithms to provide me with important news and public affairs	

Note: N = 3363; the newly theorized two-item subdimension of *Algorithmic reliance* is included

and Portugal, results indicate the three-factor construct of NFM has a much better fit for the data than a single-factor construct (Table 10.2). These results support the notion of a three-interrelated-dimensional NFM phenomenon. Building on this instrument, this chapter offers the inclusion of *algorithmic reliance* in the theoretical and empirical concept explication as a fourth NFM dimension, since people are increasingly more likely to also rely on algorithmic news gatekeeping and editorial selection in social media to introduce useful political information in their lives (Bodó et al., 2019). That is, we argue that as much as there is an expectation that one's social network is working toward providing important information as it happens, social media users will be equally expecting that automated algorithmic mechanisms will present them with important current events and public affairs information as news break.

In fact, there is initial empirical evidence suggesting this may be indeed the case. Algorithmic news provides the benefit of presenting a coherent and legitimated array of news information to social media users (Carlson, 2018; Gillespie, 2014; Thurman et al., 2019). Additionally, news users perceive machine-generated news to be more informative, accurate, and

Table 10.2 NFM confirmatory factor analysis comparison of a single factor vs. three-factor models

Models	Chisq (df)	CFI	TLI	RMSEA [90% CIs]	SRMR
Single factor	987.86 (9)***	0.840	0.733	0.18*** [0.170, 0.189]	0.07
Three-factor	230.96 (6)***	0.963	0.908	0.10*** [0.094, 0.117]	0.03

Note: Model fit comparison yields χ^2-diff = 756.9, df = 3, p < 0.001, showing fully theorized three-factor model fits significantly better to the data than the single-factor model, N = 3363

objective than those selected by human journalists (Clerwall, 2014), and automated news can elicit people's machine heuristic where the algorithmic news carries higher credibility and bias-free (Sundar, 2008; Waddell, 2019). Besides, social media covers a wide mix of professionally generated news content and user-generated content (Bode, 2016), satisfying news users' surveillance needs. News users tend to believe that social recommendation makes them become aware of a broad range of news information (Hermida et al., 2012), have access to more diverse views (Sveningsson, 2015) ,and also will be presented with more important news than what legacy news can offer (Hogan & Quan-Haase, 2010). Algorithm news driven by social recommendation and user behaviors also decreases information overload (Pentina & Tarafdar, 2014) laying out grounds to positively evaluating the role of social media in offering news, and perfectly catering political information with the least possible effort. In short, NFM would also encompass the belief that machines, via algorithmic curated information, will help people to be well informed without actively surveilling or seeking for news.

Why the News Finds Me Perception Matters: Effects

Extant literature on NFM suggest the theory is valuable at explaining a diverse array of effects, encompassing different levels. A first level of effects may be directly related to news and media consumption habits, explaining how people further interact with news ecosystems. A second level of effects highlights a diverse set of effects over democracy determinants. Last, a final level of effects in the literature deal with the antecedent, moderating, and mediating mechanisms that the NFM facilitate in assessing other phenomena.

First Level of Effects: News Ecosystem

Previous research shows that NFM is directly and negatively associated with traditional news use (Gil de Zúñiga et al., 2017; Park & Kaye, 2020). It also partially explains the ways in which incidental exposure to news decreases further active traditional news use (Park & Kaye, 2020). As citizens develop the NFM, they will be less likely to tune into traditional news such as TV news, newspaper, and radio news, because they do not further find an active news engagement to be required to be fully informed. They only become more actively involved in social media news use. Algorithmic recommendations online and on social media, and the 24/7 availability of social media news provides the perfect means for NFM people to consume information, either directly (Gil de Zúñiga et al., 2017, 2020) or by means of incidental exposure to news (Park & Kaye, 2020). What's more, qualitative evidence shows that young people with higher NFM are heavily reliant on social media news, where information is discovered via social connections, algorithms, and social curation (Swart, 2021). Building on this argument, Toff and Nielsen (2018) suggest that as people change their news reading habits and increasingly rely on distributed discovery on social media and online platforms, NFM can be seen as a folk theory (i.e., people's confidence in remaining informed about the public affairs information through the social networks and social media algorithms) which helps users navigate information about public affairs in the distributed media environment.

But NFM not only explains news use patterns. It also contributes to clarifying other news ecosystem features. For instance, NFM is also found to influence the perceived accuracy and factuality of news. Those who report higher NFM levels are more likely to rate news articles as accurate and factual, implying that NFM people tend to lower the expectation about the news and are less critical about news information (Segado-Boj et al., 2020), or they simply expect that news curated and presented by friends and social connections are previously filtered, eliminating inaccurate and nonfactual information. Also, recent research has started to investigate the link between NFM and fake news and misinformation cognitive processing. For example, Chadwick et al. (2021) have bridged the gap between media diet and vaccine hesitancy. Deploying a comprehensive study in the UK, findings reveal a stronger tendency toward discouragement of vaccine inoculation as peoples' NFM increases. In addition, Giglietto et al. (2019) suggest that NFM exposes people to conflicting news information, although confirmation bias remains the most important principle guiding people's information processing.

Second Level of Effects: Democracy Determinants

Valuable NFM effects are increasingly rooted within democratic features and determinants. The effects revolve around NFM and people's political knowledge, political interest, political cynicism, and voting behaviors. NFM elicits a type of self-delusion of being informed about the political affairs when people consume online and social media news. In this context, NFM proliferates, and political learning is less likely to occur (Gil de Zúñiga et al., 2017, 2018; Gil de Zúñiga & Diehl, 2019) as the reliance on social media platforms and social networks to feed important news actually lowers citizens' political knowledge (Lee & Xenos, 2019; Yamamoto et al., 2018). This effect has also been corroborated either directly or indirectly, by linking the relationship between social media usage and decreased political knowledge (Lee, 2020). Likewise, qualitative evidence also supports this empirical stance, as NFM does not motivate people to deeply learn about the news subject matter (Oeldorf-Hirsch & Srinivasan, 2021). This is troubling because NFM people will consume less information, will engage more superficially with it, and ultimately, considering how NFM people get news from their personal networks, will foster filter bubbles and homogeneous opinions (Gil de Zúñiga et al., 2022), partially explained by some of the deleterious effects of incidental information consumption on political learning from three perspectives (Boczkowski et al., 2018):

1. The users of social network services (SNS) have less time to devote to detailed news stories.
2. The loss of hierarchy and recontextualization of news report.
3. The reliance on acquaintances rather than professional media outlets or journalists for news information.

Overall, the NFM literature continues to accumulate robust evidence on the effect of NFM on political learning.

An important nuance that deserves attention within the NFM and political knowledge context is the difference between perceived knowledge and actual knowledge acquisition. That is, the perceived knowledge, understood as a subdimension of NFM negatively relates to tangible political learning. According to Feezell and Ortiz (2019), social media news use, particularly the information presented incidentally on Facebook, does not necessarily lead to real knowledge acquisition. Instead, incidental exposure to political news can change one's perception about what we think we know about the political world. Similarly, Schäfer (2020) found that SNS news increases people's perceived knowledge rather than actual knowledge. As the author argues, the algorithmic nature of SNS news—frequent repetition of topics and the favoring of similar posting—is related to a failure of actual knowledge acquisition. These findings on NFM and political knowledge showcase a rising concern about how new media technology can have negative consequences for a system of shared public knowledge (Carlson, 2020). Prior scholarship suggests the connection of political knowledge and social media may be contingent upon features of specific social media platforms. For example, Boukes (2019) found that the effect of social media news use on political knowledge is moderated by the content on social media platforms and user characteristics. Whereas some of these characteristics may provide people with successful paths toward political learning within social media, NFM is clearly not one of these effective pathways.

NFM not only affects people's political knowledge. It is also inversely related to political interests over time (Gil de Zúñiga & Diehl, 2019; Gil de Zúñiga et al., 2020). When individuals rely heavily on their own social network and curated news flow on social media as a backbone to acquire information, they are more likely to consume news more sporadically (Molyneux, 2018). Gradually, the absence of regular active exposure to news makes it less likely for users to cultivate political interests, and importantly, this steady decrease in political interest is further negatively associated to a decrease in voting (Gil de Zúñiga & Diehl, 2019; Gil de Zúñiga et al., 2020). Additionally, NFM has been linked with political cynicism, especially the reliance on peer dimension of NFM, indicating that an overreliance on peers from one's social network to provide political information may result in the detachment from the political process, thus increasing people's political cynicism (Song et al., 2020).

Third Level of Effects: Antecedents, Mediators, and Moderators

Although comparatively less developed, another strand of NFM literature specifically examined the antecedents of NFM, and the mediating and moderating variables that can affect the influence of NFM. Concluding from the diverse existing research on NFM, those who are younger (Gil de Zúñiga & Diehl, 2019; Gil de Zúñiga et al., 2020; Strauß et al., 2021), less educated (Gil de Zúñiga et al., 2020; Strauß et al., 2021), belonging to ethnic minorities (Gil de Zúñiga & Diehl, 2019; Strauß et al., 2021), with less income (Gil de Zúñiga & Diehl, 2019), higher social media use frequency (Park & Kaye, 2020), and with stark social media news use patterns (Gil de Zúñiga et al., 2017, 2020; Lee, 2020; Park & Kaye, 2020) and citizen journalism use (Gil de Zúñiga et al., 2017) tend to develop the perception that the news finds them. Similarly, individuals who report more group memberships, higher discussion frequency, and lower information elaboration and live in countries with lower GDP (Gil de Zúñiga et al., 2020; Strauß et al., 2021), lower political interests (Gil de Zúñiga & Diehl, 2019; Park & Kaye, 2020), lower internal political efficacy (Park & Kaye, 2020), and lower political knowledge (Gil de Zúñiga et al., 2017; Gil de Zúñiga & Diehl, 2019) are also more likely to show higher NFM levels.

In terms of relevant mediating mechanisms, empirical data suggests that NFM negatively mediates the relationship between social media usage and political knowledge (Lee, 2020), while Gil de Zúñiga et al. (2017) failed to find a significant indirect association for this connection. NFM mediates the relationship between incidental exposure to social media news and active news consumption on both online and social media news over time (Park & Kaye, 2020), which suggests that those who encounter news incidentally on social media tend to develop the NFM, which in turn, facilitates further news exposure but only in virtual spaces. As indicated above, there is a negative influence of NFM on voting behavior, wholly mediated by political knowledge and political interests (Gil de Zúñiga & Diehl, 2019). NFM also negatively mediates the relationship between social media news use and political cynicism, with nuanced disparate effects between NFM subdimensions (Song et al., 2020). As for the moderating effects, Lee (2020) shows that when NFM mediates the relationship between social media and political knowledge, the mediating mechanism is moderated by the degree of traditional news use. In other words, those who use social media as well as traditional media for news will be less vulnerable to the negative effect of social media use on political knowledge. Clearly, the available research on the potential moderating variables that contribute to clarifying NFM effects is rather limited, introducing a fruitful avenue for future studies.

NFM Future Directions

This chapter contends that NFM construct should continue to be refined by including a reliance on algorithmic news subdimension, particularly knowing that recent research has already linked some NFM features such as network reliance, with positive attitudes toward algorithmic news selection and gatekeeping process (Bodó et al., 2019; Scheffauer et al., 2021). We argue that NFM people will show positive attitudes and evaluations of algorithmic selecting news for them, as they will (wrongfully) expect algorithms to help them (1) be aware of a broader range of news information (affecting the "being informed" dimension), (2) obtain brief news pieces with little effort as their daily news checking cycle (affecting the "not seeking" dimension), and (3) stay informed through peers and online social network (affecting the "peer reliance" dimension). Therefore, future research should integrate the reliance on algorithmic news dimension when measuring NFM and should provide empirical evidence to support this theoretical proposition (see Table 10.1 for specific items).

Future studies may also have a closer look into NFM differential effects across various social media platforms. Current theory on social networking platforms already advocates for a more nuanced empirical observation of social media effects, considering distinct social media architectures and their audiences (Bossetta, 2018; Boukes, 2019). Different social networking sites potentially serve varying informational or social purposes. As pointed out by Gil de Zúñiga and Diehl (2019), the need for entertainment and social bonding might be more salient on some social networking sites. For example, Facebook has an architecture oriented toward bidirectional relationships, and the algorithms favor social network matters over public affairs content (Lee & Oh, 2013). Conversely, Twitter is an information-sharing, sending-oriented community, with an emphasis on one-directional relationships (Davenport et al., 2014). The social structure of connections, and the perceptions that these different social and informational interactions generate, may also be distinct. Accordingly, for example, some social media platforms may better enable perceptions about how one can rely on others to provide information, fostering the being well-informed perception, and so on, while other social media platforms may potentially attenuate this effect.

Likewise, the way people consume news in social media, and how they interact with information in these contexts may also matter. NFM people may exhibit varying degrees of engagement and interaction with news and its contents. Having the perception that the news will find me should have an effect not only on whether a person decides to consume and pursue information but also on how this news engagement takes place. From reading to sharing, liking, and commenting, NFM people would interact with the news content differently. Previous research suggests that news users tend to relate differently to digital news (Sang et al., 2020), carrying unique effects with regard to knowledge acquisition (Beam et al., 2016; Lee & Yang, 2014), political efficacy (Moeller et al., 2014), and political participation (Hyun & Kim, 2015). We expect NFM people to devote less reading and cognitive efforts when engaging with news information.

Future research should investigate the preference of different news contents, information overload, and news avoidance as possible antecedents or correlates of NFM. People who prefer soft news rather than hard news may be more likely to select algorithmic news that are based on what their friends have read (Fletcher & Nielsen, 2019), implying that a preference for soft news can predict higher level of NFM. Additionally, news content might serve as a moderating variable in the relationship between NFM and political learning. Gil de Zúñiga and Diehl (2019) pointed out that a deeper understanding is required about what kinds of news contents (e.g., entertainment, news reporting, soft news) would lead to the formation of the "being well-informed and up to date" perception. Some scholars argue that news information on social media fails to provide people with pragmatic increased in political learning (Bright, 2016). Thus, it will be interesting to investigate people NFM levels, the specific news contents people consume on social media, and how the varying contents might moderate the political learning process. Second, information overload and news avoidance are two additional concepts that are closely related to NFM perception. Prior research has found that information overload leads to avoidance of news consumption on social media (Lee et al., 2017; Park, 2019; Song et al., 2016), and recent empirical research shows that news overload positively predicts news avoidance behavior and social filtering of news (Goyanes et al., 2021), signaling that news avoidance serves as a coping strategy when news users face oversupply of news information (Lee et al., 2017). The reliance on news stories that are filtered and curated by their friends on social media are a less effort-requiring tactic for news consumption (Lerman, 2007). Unpacking the relationship between news content type, information overload, news avoidance, and NFM warrants a fruitful theoretical contribution to the literature.

NFM research may also delve into other communicative community structure effects. For instance, over time, people's discussion and information networks may be shaped by individuals' levels of NFM. Reporting higher levels of NFM could potentially explain why citizens create homogenous political discussion groups and information sources, fueling homophilic virtual and face-to-face social groups. This will strengthen the tendency for people to associate with like-minded individuals or congenial news viewpoints on social media (Gil de Zúñiga et al., 2022). Although whether the information tailoring practices create echo chambers is still under debate (e.g., Bruns, 2017; Dutton et al., 2017; Flaxman et al., 2016; Garrett, 2009), NFM and social media algorithms enable users to tailor their news feed based on user inputs and peer filters (Thurman, 2011), which might be particularly related to homophilic social media news use, creation of filter bubbles, and ideological segregation (Auxier & Vitak, 2019; Barberá, 2020).

Political polarization and populist attitudes might also serve as NFM antecedents. Populists tend to hold an anti-elitist attitude toward the political and media systems. Social media gives them a platform to consume, articulate, and circulate their own messages (Engesser et al., 2017; Schumann et al., 2021). Therefore, it stands to reason that the populists may be more likely to rely on their peers to stay informed about public affair news rather than simply relying on governmental, mainstream news sources or other "elitists" out-groups beyond "the people" (Gerbaudo, 2018). With respect to political polarization, Feezell et al. (2021) have found that algorithmic news do not generally predict people's political schism. However, it remains to be investigated whether political polarization will be related to NFM. Partisans choose media contents that are aligned with their existing attitudes and interests (Iyengar & Hahn, 2009; Peterson et al., 2019; Stroud, 2010), and a partisan selective exposure to news is further driven by social media algorithms that enable news users to personalize their news feeds (Pariser, 2011). According to this line of research, we expect political polarization to positively relate to higher levels of NFM.

Prior work established that NFM is negatively associated with political knowledge (Gil de Zúñiga et al., 2017; Gil de Zúñiga & Diehl, 2019; Lee, 2020). Future research can explore the mediating variables in the relationship between NFM and political knowledge, for example news sharing behavior (Weeks et al., 2017b) and media efficacy (Kim et al., 2018). Another promising direction is to test the influence of media efficacy or news epistemic efficacy on NFM and knowledge acquisition. The former refers to perceived helpfulness of the news media in understanding political issues and is found to fully mediate the relationship between social media news use and news elaboration (Kim et al., 2018). The latter deals with whether citizens are able to find the truth in politics which also elicit essential cognitive processes to better understand complex issues within the political realm (Pingree, 2011). The cognitive mediation model (Eveland Jr., 2001) has suggested that attention and elaboration mediate the news and discussion process explaining knowledge gain. It will be reasonable to further test whether media efficacy, epistemic efficacy, and cognitive elaboration sequentially or altogether mediate the relationship between NFM and political knowledge.

An alternative exciting direction of NFM research is to examine how NFM news consumption habits will relate to people's conspiracy mentality and fake news exposure processing. Prior work suggested that those who are reliant on social media for news are more vulnerable to unverified news and misinformation (Chadwick et al., 2018). A recent research has shown that those with higher NFM and news avoidance levels posed serious challenges for public health communication campaigns during Covid-19 pandemic. These people became the hardest ones to reach on social media and had lesser opportunities to learn about the Covid-19 vaccines information online (Chadwick et al., 2021). Importantly, we argue that the reliance on friends-recommended contents might play a role in misinformation dissemination processes. Today's social media dynamics have enabled fake news stories to rapidly disseminate through "short-attention-span social sharers" (Rainie et al., 2017, p. 11). When it comes to news sharing, source characteristics will influence the likelihood of individuals sharing misinformation on social media (Buchanan & Benson, 2019), and individuals are more likely to trust news stories that are shared by sources they trust, such as close friends and family members (Sterrett et al., 2019). Based on these findings, NFM people who are reliant on peers to feed them with important news as they break, might be more likely to trust peer-generated contents, which does not necessarily correspond to verified factual professional news sources.

Last, research revolving NFM should broaden current available methodological choices by going beyond qualitative studies, survey research, and experimental designs, by, for instance, applying computational techniques collecting social trace data or modeling agents to simulate community behavior. Existing research on NFM mostly applied either qualitative interviews or survey research methods (e.g., Gil de Zúñiga et al., 2017; Song et al., 2020; Lee, 2020; Park & Kaye, 2020; Toff & Nielsen, 2018; Oeldorf-Hirsch & Srinivasan, 2021), which is prone to measurement error, including social desirability bias and inaccurate recalls, failing to fully capture detailed context underneath the concept. For example, when measuring social media use, we can't capture the specific news content and sources that users have consumed. Another example is the measurement of political knowledge. Existing studies measure factual knowledge, disregarding other types of knowledge such as connotative information (Eveland Jr. et al., 2004). Future research can measure knowledge by incorporating the knowledge structure density (KSD) to measure user's ability to connect various political issues and concepts (Eveland Jr. et al., 2004). Second, the advantage of the experiment method is increasing the power in making claims of causal relationships, which is particularly useful in investigating the antecedents and consequences of NFM. Third, a combination of physiological measures and self-reported measurement is another viable option. Promising studies have developed both eye-tracking method and NFM questionnaire to evaluate the perceived believability of the news stories (Sümer et al., 2021). Finally, traditional qualitative methods including in-depth interview and focus group data (Kümpel, 2019; Oeldorf-Hirsch & Srinivasan, 2021; Swart, 2021; Toff & Nielsen, 2018) offered more NFM detailed insights, which creatively helped discover unexplored subdimensions and possible consequences of NFM, so as to develop comprehensive sets of measurement items about NFM and advance the theorization of NFM (Song et al., 2020). All in all, NFM research will become more prominent as social media news use continues to gradually permeate across societies.

References

Alejandro, J. (2010). *Journalism in the age of social media*. Reuters Institute Fellowship Paper. https://reutersinstitute.politics.ox.ac.uk/our-research/journalism-age-social-media

Anspach, N. M. (2017). The new personal influence: How our Facebook friends influence the news we read. *Political Communication, 34*(4), 590–606. https://doi.org/10.1080/10584609.2017.1316329

Auxier, B. E., & Anderson, M. (2021). *Social media use in 2021*. Pew Research Center. https://www.pewresearch.org/internet/2021/04/07/social-media-use-in-2021

Auxier, B. E., & Vitak, J. (2019). Factors motivating customization and echo chamber creation within digital news environments. *Social Media + Society*, *5*(2). https://doi.org/10.1177/2056305119847506

Barberá, P. (2020). Social media, echo chambers, and political polarization. In N. Persily & J. Tucker (Eds.), *Social media and democracy: The state of the field* (pp. 34–55). Cambridge University Press. ISBN: 9781108835558.

Beam, M. A., Hutchens, M. J., & Hmielowski, J. D. (2016). Clicking vs. sharing: The relationship between online news behaviors and political knowledge. *Computers in Human Behavior*, *59*, 215–220. https://doi.org/10.1016/j.chb.2016.02.013

Bisgin, H., Agarwal, N., & Xu, X. (2010). Investigating homophily in online social networks. In *IEEE/WIC/ACM international conference on web intelligence and intelligent agent technology* (Vol. 1, pp. 533–536). IEEE. ISBN: 9780769541914. https://dl.acm.org/doi/proceedings/10.5555/1913791

Boczkowski, P. J., Mitchelstein, E., & Matassi, M. (2018). 'News comes across when I'm in a moment of leisure': Understanding the practices of incidental news consumption on social media. *New Media & Society*, *20*(10), 3523–3539. https://doi.org/10.1177/1461444817750396

Bode, L. (2016). Political news in the news feed: Learning politics from social media. *Mass Communication and Society*, *19*(1), 24–48. https://doi.org/10.1080/15205436.2015.1045149

Bodó, B., Helberger, N., Eskens, S., & Möller, J. (2019). Interested in diversity: The role of user attitudes, algorithmic feedback loops, and policy in news personalization. *Digital Journalism*, *7*(2), 206–229. https://doi.org/10.1080/21670811.2018.1521292

Bossetta, M. (2018). The digital architectures of social media: Comparing political campaigning on Facebook, Twitter, Instagram, and Snapchat in the 2016 US election. *Journalism & Mass Communication Quarterly*, *95*(2), 471–496. https://doi.org/10.1177/1077699018763307

Boukes, M. (2019). Social network sites and acquiring current affairs knowledge: The impact of Twitter and Facebook usage on learning about the news. *Journal of Information Technology & Politics*, *16*(1), 36–51. https://doi.org/10.1080/19331681.2019.1572568

Bright, J. (2016). The social news gap: How news reading and news sharing diverge. *Journal of Communication*, *66*(3), 343–365. https://doi.org/10.1111/jcom.12232

Bruns, A. (2017). Echo chamber? What echo chamber? Reviewing the evidence. In *6th Biennial Future of Journalism Conference (FOJ17)*. https://eprints.qut.edu.au/113937

Buchanan, T., & Benson, V. (2019). Spreading disinformation on Facebook: Do trust in message source, risk propensity, or personality affect the organic reach of fake news? *Social Media + Society,* 5(4). https://doi.org/10.1177/2056305119888654

Carlson, M. (2018). Automating judgment? Algorithmic judgment, news knowledge, and journalistic professionalism. *New Media & Society,* 20(5), 1755–1772. https://doi.org/10.1177/1461444817706684

Carlson, M. (2020). Journalistic epistemology and digital news circulation: Infrastructure, circulation practices, and epistemic contests. *New Media & Society,* 22(2), 230–246. https://doi.org/10.1177/1461444819856921

Chadwick, A., Vaccari, C., & O'Loughlin, B. (2018). Do tabloids poison the well of social media? Explaining democratically dysfunctional news sharing. *New Media & Society,* 20(11), 4255–4274. https://doi.org/10.1177/1461444818769689

Chadwick, A., Kaiser, J., Vaccari, C., Freeman, D., Lambe, S., Loe, B. S., Vanderslott, S., Lewandowsky, S., Conroy, M., Ross, A. R. N., Innocenti, S., Pollard, A. J., Waite, F., Larkin, M., Rosebrock, L., Jenner, L., McShane, H., Giubilini, A., Petit, A., & Yu, L. (2021). Online social endorsement and Covid-19 vaccine hesitancy in the United Kingdom. *Social Media + Society,* 7(2). https://doi.org/10.1177/20563051211008817

Clerwall, C. (2014). Enter the robot journalist: Users' perceptions of automated content. *Journalism Practice,* 8(5), 519–531. https://doi.org/10.1080/17512786.2014.883116

Costera-Meijer, I., & Groot-Kormelink, T. (2015). Checking, sharing, clicking and linking: Changing patterns of news use between 2004 and 2014. *Digital Journalism,* 3(5), 664–679. https://doi.org/10.1080/21670811.2014.937149

Davenport, S. W., Bergman, S. M., Bergman, J. Z., & Fearrington, M. E. (2014). Twitter versus Facebook: Exploring the role of narcissism in the motives and usage of different social media platforms. *Computers in Human Behavior,* 32, 212–220. https://doi.org/10.1016/j.chb.2013.12.011

Davison, W. P. (1983). The third-person effect in communication. *Public Opinion Quarterly,* 47(1), 1–15. https://doi.org/10.1086/268763

DeVito, M. A. (2017). From editors to algorithms: A values-based approach to understanding story selection in the Facebook news feed. *Digital Journalism,* 5(6), 753–773. https://doi.org/10.1080/21670811.2016.1178592

Dutton, W. H., Reisdorf, B., Dubois, E., & Blank, G. (2017). Social shaping of the politics of internet search and networking: Moving beyond filter bubbles, echo chambers, and fake news. *Quello Center Working Paper, 2944191.* https://papers.ssrn.com/sol3/papers.cfm?abstract_id=2944191

Engesser, S., Ernst, N., Esser, F., & Büchel, F. (2017). Populism and social media: How politicians spread a fragmented ideology. *Information, Communication & Society,* 20(8), 1109–1126. https://doi.org/10.1080/1369118X.2016.1207697

Eveland, W. P., Jr. (2001). The cognitive mediation model of learning from the news: Evidence from non-election, off-year election, and presidential election contexts. *Communication Research, 28*(5), 571–601. https://doi.org/10.1177/009365001028005001

Eveland, W. P., Jr., Marton, K., & Seo, M. (2004). Moving beyond 'just the facts': The influence of online news on the content and structure of public affairs knowledge. *Communication Research, 31*(1), 82–108. https://doi.org/10.1177/0093650203260203

Feezell, J. T., & Ortiz, B. (2019). "I saw it on Facebook": An experimental analysis of political learning through social media. *Information, Communication & Society.* https://doi.org/10.1080/1369118X.2019.1697340

Feezell, J. T., Wagner, J. K., & Conroy, M. (2021). Exploring the effects of algorithm-driven news sources on political behavior and polarization. *Computers in Human Behavior, 116,* 106626. https://doi.org/10.1016/j.chb.2020.106626

Fiske, S. T., & Taylor, S. E. (1984). *Social cognition.* Addison-Wesley.

Flaxman, S., Goel, S., & Rao, J. M. (2016). Filter bubbles, echo chambers, and online news consumption. *Public Opinion Quarterly, 80*(S1), 298–320. https://doi.org/10.1093/poq/nfw006

Fletcher, R., & Nielsen, R.-K. (2018). Are people incidentally exposed to news on social media? A comparative analysis. *New Media & Society, 20*(7), 2450–2468. https://doi.org/10.1177/1461444817724170

Fletcher, R., & Nielsen, R.-K. (2019). Generalised scepticism: How people navigate news on social media. *Information, Communication & Society, 22*(12), 1751–1769. https://doi.org/10.1080/1369118X.2018.1450887

Garrett, R. K. (2009). Echo chambers online?: Politically motivated selective exposure among Internet news users. *Journal of Computer-Mediated Communication, 14*(2), 265–285. https://doi.org/10.1111/j.1083-6101.2009.01440.x

Gearhart, S., & Zhang, W. (2014). Gay bullying and online opinion expression: Testing spiral of silence in the social media environment. *Social Science Computer Review, 32*(1), 18–36. https://doi.org/10.1177/0894439313504261

Gerbaudo, P. (2018). Social media and populism: An elective affinity? *Media, Culture & Society, 40*(5), 745–753. https://doi.org/10.1177/0163443718772192

Giglietto, F., Iannelli, L., Valeriani, A., & Rossi, L. (2019). "'Fake news' is the invention of a liar": How false information circulates within the hybrid news system. *Current Sociology, 67*(4), 625–642. https://doi.org/10.1177/0011392119837536

Gil de Zúñiga, H., & Diehl, T. (2019). News finds me perception and democracy: Effects on political knowledge, political interest, and voting. *New media & society, 21*(6), 1253–1271.

Gil de Zúñiga, H., Weeks, B., & Ardèvol-Abreu, A. (2017). Effects of the news-finds-me perception in communication: Social media use implications for news seeking and learning about politics. *Journal of Computer-Mediated Communication, 22*(3), 105–123. https://doi.org/10.1111/jcc4.12185

Gil de Zúñiga, H., Diehl, T., & Ardèvol-Abreu, A. (2018). When citizens and journalists interact on Twitter: Expectations of journalists' performance on social media and perceptions of media bias. *Journalism Studies, 19*(2), 227–246. https://doi.org/10.1080/1461670X.2016.1178593

Gil de Zúñiga, H., Strauß, N., & Huber, B. (2020). The proliferation of the News Finds Me perception across societies. *International Journal of Communication, 14*, 1605–1633. https://ijoc.org/index.php/ijoc/article/view/11974/3011

Gil de Zúñiga, H., Cheng, Z., & González-González, P. (2022). Effects of the News Finds Me perception on algorithmic news attitudes and social media political homophily. *Journal of Communication, 72*(5), 578–591.

Gillespie, T. (2014). The relevance of algorithms. In *Media technologies: Essays on communication, materiality, and society* (p. 167). MIT Press. https://doi.org/10.7551/mitpress/9780262525374.003.0009

Glynn, C. J., & Park, E. (1997). Reference groups, opinion intensity, and public opinion expression. *International Journal of Public Opinion Research, 9*(3), 213–232. https://doi.org/10.1093/ijpor/9.3.213

Goyanes, M., Ardèvol-Abreu, A., & Gil de Zúñiga, H. (2021). Antecedents of news avoidance: Competing effects of political interest, news overload, trust in news media, and 'News Finds Me' perception. *The Association for Education in Journalism and Mass Communication.* https://www.aejmc.org

Gunther, A. C., & Thorson, E. (1992). Perceived persuasive effects of product commercials and public service announcements: Third-person effects in new domains. *Communication Research, 19*(5), 574–596. https://doi.org/10.1177/009365092019005002

Hermida, A. (2010). Twittering the news: The emergence of ambient journalism. *Journalism Practice, 4*(3), 297–308. https://doi.org/10.1080/17512781003640703

Hermida, A. (2012). Social journalism: Exploring how social media is shaping journalism. In E. Siapera & A. Veglis (Eds.), *The handbook of global online journalism* (Chapter 17, pp. 309–328). https://doi.org/10.1002/9781118313978.ch17

Hermida, A., Fletcher, F., Korell, D., & Logan, D. (2012). Share, like, recommend: Decoding the social media news consumer. *Journalism Studies, 13*(5–6), 815–824. https://doi.org/10.1080/1461670X.2012.664430

Hogan, B., & Quan-Haase, A. (2010). Persistence and change in social media. *Bulletin of Science, Technology & Society, 30*(5), 309–315. https://doi.org/10.1177/0270467610380012

Holton, A. E., Coddington, M., & Gil de Zúñiga, H. (2013). Whose news? Whose values? Citizen journalism and journalistic values through the lens of content creators and consumers. *Journalism Practice, 7*(6), 720–737. https://doi.org/10.1080/17512786.2013.766062

Hong, Y., & Rojas, H. (2016). Agreeing not to disagree: Iterative versus episodic forms of political participatory behaviors. *International Journal of Communication, 10,* 1743–1763. https://ijoc.org/index.php/ijoc/article/view/5030

Hopmann, D. N., Wonneberger, A., Shehata, A., & Höijer, J. (2016). Selective media exposure and increasing knowledge gaps in Swiss referendum campaigns. *International Journal of Public Opinion Research, 28*(1), 73–95. https://doi.org/10.1093/ijpor/edv002

Hyun, K. D., & Kim, J. (2015). Differential and interactive influences on political participation by different types of news activities and political conversation through social media. *Computers in Human Behavior, 45,* 328–334. https://doi.org/10.1016/j.chb.2014.12.031

Iyengar, S., & Hahn, K. S. (2009). Red media, blue media: Evidence of ideological selectivity in media use. *Journal of Communication, 59*(1), 19–39. https://doi.org/10.1111/j.1460-2466.2008.01402.x

Java, A., Song, X., Finin, T., & Tseng, B. (2007). Why we Twitter: Understanding microblogging usage and communities. In *Proceedings of the 9th WebKDD and 1st SNA-KDD 2007 workshop on Web mining and social network analysis* (pp. 56–65). https://ebiquity.umbc.edu/paper/html/id/367/Why-We-Twitter-Understanding-Microblogging-Usage-and-Communities

Kahneman, D. (2003). A perspective on judgment and choice: Mapping bounded rationality. *American Psychologist, 58*(9), 697–720. https://doi.org/10.1037/0003-066X.58.9.697

Kahneman, D., & Thaler, R. H. (2006). Anomalies: Utility maximization and experienced utility. *The Journal of Economic Perspectives, 20*(1), 221–234. https://doi.org/10.1257/089533006776526076

Katz, E., Lazarsfeld, P. F., & Roper, E. (1955). *Personal influence: The part played by people in the flow of mass communication.* Free Press.

Kim, Y., Chen, H. T., & Gil de Zúñiga, H. (2013). Stumbling upon news on the Internet: Effects of incidental news exposure and relative entertainment use on political engagement. *Computers in Human Behavior, 29,* 2607–2614. https://doi.org/10.1016/j.chb.2013.06.005

Kim, J. W., Chadha, M., & Gil de Zúñiga, H. (2018). News media use and cognitive elaboration. The Mediating role of media efficacy. *Revista Latina de Comunicación Social, 73,* 168–183. http://www.revistalatinacs.org/073paper/1251/10en.html

Kümpel, A. S. (2019). The issue takes it all? Incidental news exposure and news engagement on Facebook. *Digital Journalism, 7*(2), 165–186. https://doi.org/10.1080/21670811.2018.1465831

Lazarsfeld, P. F., Berelson, B., & Gaudet, H. (1948). *The people's choice.* Columbia University Press.

Lee, S. (2020). Probing the mechanisms through which social media erodes political knowledge: The role of the news-finds-me perception. *Mass Communication and Society, 23*(6), 810–832. https://doi.org/10.1080/15205436.2020.1821381

Lee, C. S., & Ma, L. (2012). News sharing in social media: The effect of gratifications and prior experience. *Computers in Human Behavior, 28*(2), 331–339. https://doi.org/10.1016/j.chb.2011.10.002

Lee, E. J., & Oh, S. Y. (2013). Seek and you shall find? How need for orientation moderates knowledge gain from Twitter use. *Journal of Communication, 63*(4), 745–765. https://doi.org/10.1111/jcom.12041

Lee, S., & Xenos, M. (2019). Social distraction? Social media use and political knowledge in two US Presidential elections. *Computers in Human Behavior, 90*, 18–25. https://doi.org/10.1016/j.chb.2018.08.006

Lee, H., & Yang, J. (2014). Political knowledge gaps among news consumers with different news media repertoires across multiple platforms. *International Journal of Communication, 8*, 597–617. https://ijoc.org/index.php/ijoc/article/view/2455

Lee, S. K., Lindsey, N. J., & Kim, K. S. (2017). The effects of news consumption via social media and news information overload on perceptions of journalistic norms and practices. *Computers in Human Behavior, 75*, 254–263.

Lerman, K. (2007). Social information processing in news aggregation. *IEEE Internet Computing, 11*(6), 16–28. https://doi.org/10.1109/MIC.2007.136

Levordashka, A., & Utz, S. (2016). Ambient awareness: From random noise to digital closeness in online social networks. *Computers in Human Behavior, 60*, 147–154. https://doi.org/10.1016/j.chb.2016.02.037

Lewis, B. K. (2010). Social media and strategic communication: Attitudes and perceptions among college students. *Public Relations Journal, 4*(3) https://prjournal.instituteforpr.org/wp-content/uploads/2010Lewis.pdf

Lippman, J. R., Ward, L. M., & Seabrook, R. C. (2014). Isn't it romantic? Differential associations between romantic screen media genres and romantic beliefs. *Psychology of Popular Media Culture, 3*(3), 128–140. https://doi.org/10.1037/ppm0000034

Loewenstein, G., O'Donoghue, T., & Rabin, M. (2003). Projection bias in predicting future utility. *Quarterly Journal of Economics, 118*(4), 1209–1248. https://doi.org/10.1162/003355303322552784

Markopoulos, P., Ruyter, B. D., & Mackay, W. (2009). *Awareness systems: Advances in theory, methodology, and design.* Springer.

McFarland, L. A., & Ployhart, R. E. (2015). Social media: A contextual framework to guide research and practice. *Journal of Applied Psychology, 100*(6), 1653–1677. https://psycnet.apa.org/doi/10.1037/a0039244

Messing, S., & Westwood, S. J. (2012). How social media introduces biases in selecting and processing news content. *ResearchGate.* https://www.researchgate.net/publication/265673993_How_Social_Media_Introduces_Biases_in_Selecting_and_Processing_News_Content

Meyer, J. (1987). Two-moment decision models and expected utility maximization. *The American Economic Review, 77*(3), 421–430. https://www.jstor.org/stable/1804104

Mitchell, A., Simmons, K., Matsa, K. E., & Silver, L. (2018). *Publics globally want unbiased news coverage, but are divided on whether their news media deliver.* Pew Research Center. https://www.pewresearch.org/global/2018/01/11/publics-globally-want-unbiased-news-coverage-but-are-divided-on-whether-their-news-media-deliver.

Moeller, J., De-Vreese, C., Esser, F., & Kunz, R. (2014). Pathway to political participation: The influence of online and offline news media on internal efficacy and turnout of first-time voters. *American Behavioral Scientist, 58*(5), 689–700. https://doi.org/10.1177/0002764213515220

Molyneux, L. (2018). Mobile news consumption: A habit of snacking. *Digital Journalism, 6*(5), 634–650. https://doi.org/10.1080/21670811.2017.1334567

Newman, N., Fletcher, R., Kalogeropoulos, A., Levy, D. A. L., & Nielsen, R. K. (2017). *Reuters Institute Digital News Report 2017.* Reuters Institute for the Study of Journalism. https://reutersinstitute.politics.ox.ac.uk/sites/default/files/Digital%20News%20Report%202017%20web_0.pdf

Nielsen, R. K., & Schrøder, K. C. (2014). The relative importance of social media for accessing, finding, and engaging with news: An eight-country cross-media comparison. *Digital Journalism, 2*(4), 472–489. https://doi.org/10.1080/21670811.2013.872420

Noelle-Neumann, E. (1974). The spiral of silence, a theory of public opinion. *Journal of Communication, 24*(2), 43–51. https://doi.org/10.1111/j.1460-2466.1974.tb00367.x

Oeldorf-Hirsch, A. (2018). The role of engagement in learning from active and incidental news exposure on social media. *Mass Communication and Society, 21*(2), 225–247. https://doi.org/10.1080/15205436.2017.1384022

Oeldorf-Hirsch, A., & Srinivasan, P. (2021). An unavoidable convenience: How post-millennials engage with the news that finds them on social and mobile media. *Journalism.* https://doi.org/10.1177/1464884921990251

Ostertag, S. (2010). Establishing news confidence: A qualitative study of how people use the news media to know the news-world. *Media, Culture & Society, 32*(4), 597–614. https://doi.org/10.1177/0163443710367694

Owen, L. H. (2017). Avoiding articles from "the creep": People trust news based on who shared it, not on who published it. *Nieman Lab.* http://www.niemanlab.org/2017/03/avoiding-articles-from-thecreep-people-trust-news-based-on-who-shared-it-not-on-who-published-it

Pariser, E. (2011). *The filter bubble: How the new personalized web is changing what we read and how we think.* Penguin.

Park, C. S. (2019). Learning politics from social media: Interconnection of social media use for political news and political issue and process knowledge. *Communication Studies, 70*(3), 253–276. https://doi.org/10.1080/1051097 4.2019.1581627

Park, C. S., & Kaye, B. K. (2020). What's this? Incidental exposure to news on social media, news-finds-me perception, news efficacy, and news consumption. *Mass Communication and Society, 23*(2), 157–180. https://doi.org/10.108 0/15205436.2019.1702216

Pentina, I., & Tarafdar, M. (2014). From 'information' to 'knowing': Exploring the role of social media in contemporary news consumption. *Computers in Human Behavior, 35,* 211–223. https://doi.org/10.1016/j.chb.2014.02.045

Peterson, E., Goel, S., & Iyengar, S. (2019). Partisan selective exposure in online news consumption: Evidence from the 2016 presidential campaign. *Political Science Research and Methods, 9*(2), 242–258. https://doi.org/10.1017/psrm.2019.55

Pingree, R. J. (2011). Effects of unresolved factual disputes in the news on epistemic political efficacy. *Journal of Communication, 61*(1), 22–47. https://doi.org/10.1111/j.1460-2466.2010.01525.x

Quick, B. L. (2009). The effects of viewing Grey's Anatomy on perceptions of doctors and patient satisfaction. *Journal of Broadcasting & Electronic Media, 53*(1), 38–55. https://doi.org/10.1080/08838150802643563

Rainie, L., Anderson, J., & Albright, J. (2017). *The future of free speech, trolls, anonymity and fake news online.* Pew Research Center. https://www.pewresearch.org/internet/2017/03/29/the-future-of-free-speech-trolls-anonymity-and-fake-news-online

Ritzer, G., Dean, P., & Jurgenson, N. (2012). The coming of age of the prosumer. *American Behavioral Scientist, 56*(4), 379–398. https://doi.org/10.1177/0002764211429368

Sang, Y., Lee, J. Y., Park, S., Fisher, C., & Fuller, G. (2020). Signalling and expressive interaction: Online news users' different modes of interaction on digital platforms. *Digital Journalism, 8*(4), 467–485. https://doi.org/10.1080/21670811.2020.1743194

Schäfer, S. (2020). Illusion of knowledge through Facebook news? Effects of snack news in a news feed on perceived knowledge, attitude strength, and willingness for discussions. *Computers in Human Behavior, 103,* 1–12. https://doi.org/10.1016/j.chb.2019.08.031

Scheffauer, R., Goyanes, M., & Gil de Zúñiga, H. (2021). *Professional journalists versus social media algorithmic editorial news selection: Effects of gatekeeping on traditional and social media news trust*. Presented at The International Communication Association, Denver, CO, USA (virtual conference).

Schumann, S., Boer, D., Hanke, K., & Liu, J. (2021). Social media use and support for populist radical right parties: Assessing exposure and selection effects in a two-wave panel study. *Information, Communication & Society, 24*(7), 921–940. https://doi.org/10.1080/1369118X.2019.1668455

Segado-Boj, F., Díaz-Campo, J., Navarro-Asencio, E., & Remacha-González, L. (2020). Influence of News-Finds-Me perception on accuracy, factuality and relevance assessment. Case study of news item on climate change. *Revista Mediterránea de Comunicación, 11*(2), 85–103. https://doi.org/10.14198/MEDCOM2020.11.2.12

Shehata, A., & Strömbäck, J. (2018). Learning political news from social media: Network media logic and current affairs news learning in a high-choice media environment. *Communication Research, 48*(1), 125–147. https://doi.org/10.1177/0093650217749354

Smart Insights. (2021). Global social media research summary 2021, March 11. https://www.smartinsights.com/social-media-marketing/social-media-strategy/new-global-social-media-research

Song, H., Jung, J., & Kim, Y. (2016). Perceived news overload and its cognitive and attitudinal consequences for news usage in South Korea. *Journalism & Mass Communication Quarterly, 94*(4), 1172–1190. https://doi.org/10.1177/1077699016679975

Song, H., Gil de Zúñiga, H., & Boomgaarden, H. G. (2020). Social media news use and political cynicism: Differential pathways through "news finds me" perception. *Mass Communication and Society, 23*(1), 47–70. https://doi.org/10.1080/15205436.2019.1651867

Sterrett, D., Malato, D., Benz, J., Kantor, L., Tompson, T., Rosenstiel, T., Sonderman, J., & Loker, K. (2019). Who shared it?: Deciding what news to trust on social media. *Digital Journalism, 7*(6), 783–801. https://doi.org/10.1080/21670811.2019.1623702

Strauß, N., Huber, B., & Gil de Zúñiga, H. (2021). Structural influences on the News Finds Me perception: Why people believe they don't have to actively seek news anymore. *Social Media + Society, 7*(2). https://doi.org/10.1177/20563051211024966

Stroud, N. J. (2010). Polarization and partisan selective exposure. *Journal of Communication, 60*(3), 556–576. https://doi.org/10.1111/j.1460-2466.2010.01497.x

Sümer, Ö., Bozkir, E., Kübler, T., Grüner, S., Utz, S., & Kasneci, E. (2021). FakeNewsPerception: An eye movement dataset on the perceived believability of news stories. *Data in Brief,* 35, 106909. https://doi.org/10.1016/j. dib.2021.106909

Sundar, S. S. (2008). *The MAIN model: A heuristic approach to understanding technology effects on credibility* (pp. 73–100). MacArthur Foundation Digital Media and Learning Initiative. https://www.issuelab.org/resources/875/875.pdf

Sunstein, C. R. (2006). *Infotopia: How many minds produce knowledge.* Oxford University Press.

Sveningsson, M. (2015). 'It's only a pastime, really': Young people's experiences of social media as a source of news about public affairs. *Social Media + Society,* 1(2). doi:https://doi.org/10.1177/2056305115604855

Swart, J. (2021). Experiencing algorithms: How young people understand, feel about, and engage with algorithmic news selection on social media. *Social Media + Society,* 7(2). doi:https://doi.org/10.1177/20563051211008828

Tandoc, E. C., Ling, R., Westlund, O., Duffy, A., Goh, D., & Wei, L. Z. (2017). Audiences' acts of authentication in the age of fake news: A conceptual framework. *New Media & Society,* 20(8), 2745–2763. https://doi.org/10.1177/1461444817731756

Tewksbury, D., Weaver, A. J., & Maddex, B. D. (2001). Accidentally informed: Incidental news exposure on the World Wide Web. *Journalism & Mass Communication Quarterly,* 78(3), 533–554. https://doi.org/10.1177/107769900107800309

Thorson, K., & Wells, C. (2016). Curated flows: A framework for mapping media exposure in the digital age. *Communication Theory,* 26(3), 309–328. https://doi.org/10.1111/comt.12087

Thurman, N. (2011). Making 'The Daily Me': Technology, economics and habit in the mainstream assimilation of personalized news. *Journalism,* 12(4), 395–415. https://doi.org/10.1177/1464884910388228

Thurman, N., Moeller, J., Helberger, N., & Trilling, D. (2019). My friends, editors, algorithms, and I: Examining audience attitudes to news selection. *Digital Journalism,* 7(4), 447–469. https://doi.org/10.1080/21670811.2018.1493936

Toff, B., & Nielsen, R. K. (2018). I just Google it: Folk theories of distributed discovery. *Journal of Communication,* 68(3), 636–657. https://doi.org/10.1093/joc/jqy009

Turcotte, J., York, C., Irving, J., Scholl, R. M., & Pingree, R. J. (2015). News recommendations from social media opinion leaders: Effects on media trust and information seeking. *Journal of Computer-Mediated Communication,* 20(5), 520–535. https://doi.org/10.1111/jcc4.12127

Tversky, A., & Kahneman, D. (1973). Availability: A heuristic for judging frequency and probability. *Cognitive Psychology,* 5(2), 207–232. https://doi.org/10.1016/0010-0285(73)90033-9

Van Erkel, P. F. A., & Van Aelst, P. (2020). Why don't we learn from social media? Studying effects of and mechanisms behind social media news use on general surveillance political knowledge. *Political Communication.* https://doi.org/10.1080/10584609.2020.1784328

Waddell, T. F. (2019). Can an algorithm reduce the perceived bias of news? Testing the effect of machine attribution on news readers' evaluations of bias, anthropomorphism, and credibility. *Journalism & Mass Communication Quarterly, 96*(1), 82–100. https://doi.org/10.1177/1077699018815891

Weeks, B. E., Ardèvol-Abreu, A., & Gil de Zúñiga, H. (2017a). Online influence? Social media use, opinion leadership, and political persuasion. *International Journal of Public Opinion Research, 29*(2), 214–239.

Weeks, B. E., Lane, D. S., Kim, D. H., Lee, S. S., & Kwak, N. (2017b). Incidental exposure, selective exposure, and political information sharing: Integrating online exposure patterns and expression on social media. *Journal of Computer-Mediated Communication, 22*(6), 363–379. https://doi.org/10.1111/jcc4.12199

Yamamoto, M., Kushin, M. J., & Dalisay, F. (2018). How informed are messaging app users about politics? A linkage of messaging app use and political knowledge and participation. *Telematics and Informatics, 35*(8), 2376–2386. https://doi.org/10.1016/j.tele.2018.10.008

CHAPTER 11

From Mass Media to Social Media: Political Persuasion in the Field of Communication

Beatriz Jordá and *R. Lance Holbert*

INTRODUCTION

Persuasion is pervasive in politics. It permeates the statements and speeches of politicians, the opinions that interest groups and elites express in public, and is also present in much of the content that everyday citizens post on social media. Persuasion is built into the fabric of everyday life because we are social creatures, and by default then political creatures as well. The essential nature of persuasion has made it a storied research topic in various fields such as communication, social psychology and political science (O'Keefe, 2015; Perloff, 2020). However, despite academic efforts, persuasion research remains fragmented, disconnected and sometimes contradictory. It has become clear that social influence operates at different

B. Jordá (✉)
Universidad Carlos III de Madrid, Getafe, Spain

Saint Louis University, Madrid, Spain

R. L. Holbert
Annenberg Public Policy Center, University of Pennsylvania, Philadelphia, PA, USA

© The Author(s), under exclusive license to Springer Nature Switzerland AG 2024
M. Goyanes, A. Cañedo (eds.), *Media Influence on Opinion Change and Democracy*, https://doi.org/10.1007/978-3-031-70231-0_11

levels of analysis and involves multiple components that intertwine, which makes the immediate, direct effects (i.e., a magic bullet) of persuasion unfeasible (Druckman, 2022). At the same time, the emergence of new technologies, especially social media, has posed new challenges for persuasion research. People now have access to a wider range of information sources which can be persuasive, even if they are not always reliable or accurate.

In this chapter, we provide an overview of political persuasion research in the field of communication, from the early studies on the influence of mass media to the current state of the literature, which mainly focuses on social media effects (Robinson et al., 2018). We also offer various suggestions for future studies to illuminate and improve our understanding of persuasion in social media. The chapter begins with a brief introduction to persuasion and media effects scholarship and a summary of the phases traditionally considered to reflect the evolution of media effects research. Next, we present an overview of the two strands of research that argue for and against the polarizing effects of social media platforms. We also describe recent scholarship on political attitude change on social media. The chapter concludes with three suggestions for future work and some final remarks.

POLITICAL PERSUASION IN THE FIELD OF COMMUNICATION

The study of persuasion is long-standing with the broader undertaking of communication research. Since the birth of the field in the 1920s, scholars have been interested in understanding how, why, when and where media produce effects (Borah, 2016; McQuail, 2010; Vorderer et al., 2019). These questions—profoundly linked to persuasion-based processes—still occupy a central position in the field today. However, despite the numerous studies and mounting evidence, we are still unable to provide definitive answers to these core queries. It is "difficult, if not impossible" to grasp how empirical and theoretical studies of media effects work together to understand the impact of media on society (Holbert & Tchernev, 2013, p. 48). This lack of clarity mirrors a broader pattern in persuasion research. After providing a brief overview of findings, Druckman (2022) concludes that "persuasion is unconstrained or extremely limited by prior opinions, campaigns are persuasive or they are not, and persuasion effects taper or endure" (p. 67). The study of persuasion is indeed complex and multifaceted, with no consensus even for its definition and facets (Miller, 2013;

Perloff, 2020), and if there is one thing that characterizes persuasion research, it is its fragmented, disconnected and sometimes contradictory nature. In fact, the elaboration likelihood model (Petty & Cacioppo, 1986), one of the most well-known models to the study of persuasion, was created as a means to organize all the seemingly disparate findings.

Communication scientists, social psychologists, sociologists and political scientists study persuasion, but tend to focus on different aspects of the phenomenon (O'Keefe, 2015; Perloff, 2020). In the field of communication, media effects research has traditionally focused on attitude change (or lack thereof). The history of media effects research "is very nearly the history of attitude change research" (McLeod & Reeves, 2013, p. 25), although persuasion scholars have often considered other dimensions of the phenomenon. According to Miller (2013), there are three different persuasion effects: attitude *formation*, attitude *reinforcement* and attitude *change*. Attitude formation regards the process by which individuals shape their opinions about something as they discover and inform themselves about it. Attitude reinforcement refers to persuasive transactions that strengthen a person's existing opinions. Finally, attitude change as persuasion corresponds to the common use of the word and refers to modifications in preexisting attitudes about how favorable or unfavorable something is.

The common approach in communication research of viewing persuasion as attitude change or even using the two phenomena synonymously has been criticized over the years. Various scholars have pointed out that this focus places an artificial boundary around persuasion and its possible outcomes and fails to capture its full breadth (Holbert et al., 2010; Miller, 2013; Perloff, 2020). Yet, this criticism has not prevented the media effects tradition from being structured around this equation. This line of inquiry, like other persuasion research, is characterized by conflicting and contradictory paradigms shaped by the circumstances of time and place (McQuail, 2010; Vorderer et al., 2019), and these paradigmatic shifts that have taken shape over time have led to alternative notions of the persuasive power of media that range from the all-powerful to minimal effects.

In the early days of the field, generally considered to be the 1920s and 1930s, the media were seen as an all-powerful, corrupting influence that could *change* the behavior and opinions of citizens. During this era, the audience was considered a homogeneous passive mass that responded identically to media messages and could not resist their influence (Borah, 2016; McQuail, 2010; Vorderer et al., 2019). This idea was soon abandoned. As the transition to empirical research took shape, Paul Lazarsfeld and his colleagues conducted a series of voting studies, culminating in the publication of *The People's Choice* (1948) and *Personal Influence* (1955). In these studies, they found to their surprise that media messages tended to *reinforce* rather than *change* citizens' attitudes and behaviors. It was also highlighted that the reported direct flow of influence from the mass media to the audience was actually mediated by preexisting social connections called opinion leaders (i.e., two-step flow). The idea of *reinforcement* of political opinions as the main media effect characterized this second phase of research, which became known as the "minimal effects era" and which continues to influence an important part of the field today (Holbert et al., 2013; Vorderer et al., 2019).

In the 1950s and 1960s, a new generation of scholars challenged the minimal effects paradigm by finding significant media effects through refined methodological approaches. These researchers criticized earlier studies for treating the media solely as an agent of persuasion and thus failing to acknowledge its role as a source of information or to examine other media effects (Borah, 2016; Holbert et al., 2013). Accordingly, instead of investigating short-term effects, these studies rediscovered strong media influence by focusing on *cumulative change* and cognitive aspects rather than behavioral ones. This third stage of "moderate" effects calls for a "return to the concept of powerful mass media" and shatters the myth of "no-effect" or rather "only-reinforcement effect" (McQuail, 2010; Noelle-Neumann, 1973). Three theories stand out: agenda-setting theory, the spiral of silence theory and cultivation theory.

Toward the end of the 1970s, a new approach to media effects emerged as scholars' attention began to move beyond *attitude change*. In this phase, termed "social constructivist," researchers emphasized the creation of meaning, a process in which audiences play an active role along personal experiences and immediate social context, and which may make citizens more or less resistant to persuasion (Borah, 2016; McQuail, 2010). Shortly thereafter, however, the advent of the Internet (Web 1.0) and social media (Web 2.0) changed citizens' everyday information needs and behavior. These new technologies expanded media choice and an ability for citizens to seek out and engage in partisan news sources, facilitating users' self-selection of like-minded, reaffirming information (Cinelli et al., 2021; Stroud, 2011). As a result, scholars began to argue that the digital environment was ushering in "a new era of minimal effects" (Bennett & Iyengar, 2008).

This view encouraged a return to the idea of *reinforcement* as the main outcome of media exposure and is now the prevailing one in both academic and popular circles (Barberá, 2020; Bruns, 2021). However, there are also ardent critics who have cogently argued that the Internet and social media facilitate conversation across lines of political difference. This group of studies looks at a more positive side of social media and the Internet and opens up new avenues for research into attitude change.

Persuasion on Social Media: Echoing and Diversifying Political Views

Within the framework of studies on social media effects, two major strands of research have crystallized. On the one hand, some studies suggest that social media users tend to nest themselves within like-minded networks of information that can only reinforce their preexisting beliefs (e.g., Cinelli et al., 2021; Flaxman et al., 2016; Sunstein, 2017). Given that social media has become a major gateway to news in recent decades (Newman et al., 2023), advocates of this approach also believe that these platforms pose a threat to democracy and may be partly responsible for the growing success of extremist ideas around the world. On the other hand, other studies have countered this view showing that users report encountering more disagreeable viewpoints on social media than in other settings (Barnidge, 2017) and that, although prevalent, like-minded sources are not polarizing (Nyhan et al., 2023). These two bodies of research provide evidence for and against the alleged contribution of social media to political polarization and have each put forward a number of arguments in support of their positions.

The first line of inquiry generally emphasizes that the psychological biases in human behavior can only facilitate the emergence of echo chambers in which continued exposure to agreeable views is ensured and opinions become more extreme (Cinelli et al., 2021; Flaxman et al., 2016; Sunstein, 2017). The psychological processes underlying this argument are homophily, people's natural preference to interact with similar others (McPherson et al., 2001), and selective exposure, people's tendency to seek out sources of information that match their preexisting attitudes and interests. Research on selective exposure has its theoretical foundations in the seminal studies of the "minimal effects era" (Katz & Lazarsfeld, 1955; Klapper, 1960; Lazarsfeld et al., 1948) and has seen a resurgence in the digital era, with evidence of this consumption pattern found in different settings, topics, countries and research designs (e.g., Cardenal et al., 2019; Cinelli et al., 2021; Stroud, 2011). According to these studies, people prefer ideologically congruent information sources to avoid cognitive dissonance, a state of psychological discomfort caused by the consumption of divergent information (Festinger, 1957), and to minimize the cognitive effort required to process information (Stroud, 2011).

Furthermore, it is argued that there are other aspects of social media that further homogenize the information that users consume. First, the platforms' algorithms. By creating a personalized universe of content based on users' preferences, algorithms may potentially create filter bubbles that limit the ideological diversity of information (Cardenal et al., 2019; Flaxman et al., 2016; Pariser, 2011). Second, users' filtering tactics. On social media, users may customize their feeds to their liking by unfriending/unfollowing, hiding or even blocking. Being confronted with uncongenial information online may evoke negative emotions in recipients, and deploying these tactics is one of the possible reactions they may have, which may in turn lead them to greater affective polarization (Lin et al., 2023).

The second strand of research, conversely, provides a much more complex and nuanced story of social media effects, criticizing the former studies for their alarmist narratives and their lack of rigorous empirical evidence (Barberá, 2020; Bruns, 2021). It generally argues that exposure to disagreement on social media is more prevalent than commonly believed and that it occurs regardless of people's preferences, algorithms and filtering strategies. It draws on two main arguments: the lack of selective avoidance and the affordances and social logics that govern these platforms.

First, the extent to which people eliminate dissonant viewpoints in their feeds has been found to be overstated. Although the litany of studies on selective exposure show that users do have a preference for attitude-consistent information, it has also been noted that users do not necessarily avoid attitude-discrepant content when they inadvertently stumble upon it (Messing & Westwood, 2014; Holbert et al., 2010, 2013). Overall, studies on selective exposure only show that users prioritize reinforcing information, but do not systematically filter out disagreeable content when it reaches them. In addition, even if citizens do attempt to selectively avoid information that runs counter to their preexisting worldview, they are not highly effective at doing so on social media platforms. Ineffective avoidance is high, with people still reporting contact with content they try to stay away from (Annenberg IOD Collaborative, 2023).

Second, the first line of research overlooks the primary reasons why citizens use social media and the users with whom they interact there. Several studies have pointed this out: most citizens do not access these platforms to inform themselves about politics, or that is at least not their main goal (Kümpel, 2019; Matthes et al., 2023). They access them to connect with friends, pass time or consume entertainment content and get informed as a by-product of this use (Matthes et al., 2020). This is a good thing because studies show that the likelihood of being confronted with disagreement is greater in online spaces not dedicated to politics than in overly political environments (Wojcieszak et al., 2024), and because it improves on the previous situation. Before the advent of social media, a person who was not very knowledgeable or politically interested could easily opt out of news in favor of entertainment options (Prior, 2007). These platforms have made this more difficult because they allow users only partial control over what they consume and because users tend not to make connections based on ideology (Bode, 2016). As a result, citizens are often surprised by the political opinions of their contacts and end up being exposed to political disagreement (Bakshy et al., 2015; Barnidge, 2017; Silver et al., 2019).

In their everyday lives, research suggests that citizens tend to talk about politics with like-minded people with whom they already agree such as their friends or family (Barnidge, 2017; McPherson et al., 2001; Granovetter, 1973). When discrepancies arise, common ground is quickly sought to avoid arguments (Conover et al., 2002). However, this is not the case in social media, as users typically have a much more diverse network of contacts. Over time, users' online feeds become an amalgam of collapsed contexts that bring together family members and close friends with weak ties such as acquaintances, coworkers, or former classmates (Marwick & boyd, 2014). Even if not everything these people post is liked by recipients, users are compelled to maintain these connections for social reasons. These contacts will thus be the ones that may foster the transmission of novel information that cuts across lines of political difference (Granovetter, 1973) and the ones that surpass partisan cues and prompt users to select counter-attitudinal news articles (Messing & Westwood, 2014).

On these grounds, these studies have suggested, for instance, that social media users report encountering more disagreement there than in other settings (Barnidge, 2017), that people on social media interact with people from both sides of the political spectrum (Bakshy et al., 2015; Silver et al., 2019) and that the increase in political polarization was lower among younger people, who also form the age cohort that uses social media more frequently (Boxell et al., 2017). Like-minded sources may be prevalent in these digital spaces, but they do not necessarily lead to a more polarized electorate (Nyhan et al., 2023).

Political Attitude Change on Social Media

Implicit in the second line of research is the idea that social media may facilitate political attitude change. That is, if citizens increasingly use social media as a source of information and tend to encounter political disagreement, it is reasonable to think that this will sometimes lead them to change their political opinions. In this context, an emerging line of inquiry has focused on investigating the antecedents that lead users to be politically persuaded in these ecologies. These studies speak of persuasion and have mostly examined self-reported attitude change, noting that users who use social media to get informed, discuss politics or consume political content may ultimately change opinions about political issues, but also those who use it for social interaction or who encounter fake news (Chang et al., 2018; Diehl et al., 2016; Gil de Zúñiga et al., 2022; Jordá & Goyanes, 2022; Jordá et al., 2024).

This growing body of research reveals the potential of social media to challenge and change users' opinions. It has also brought back to the table the importance of studying this persuasive effect and the relevance of doing so in the context of social media. Classic media effects research emphasized the importance of interpersonal communication (Katz & Lazarsfeld, 1955). Such communication and its possibilities have expanded in social media, as the posts and opinions of ordinary people may reach and persuade a larger audience across borders (Chang et al., 2018; Greenwood et al., 2016). This may be beneficial for society because when citizens increase their openness to political opinion change, the exchange of viewpoints becomes more fruitful and tolerant, and political polarization is discouraged (Gil de Zúñiga et al., 2023). This accounts for the positive side of persuasion in social media, a side that must be acknowledged to do justice to the phenomenon. Academic discussions often speak of the undemocratic influence that social media may have on society, but social media persuasion may also be a natural extension of counter-attitudinal exposure which makes users realize other perspectives or information that they were unaware of.

Advancing the Study of Political Attitude Change in Communication Research

With many studies noting that the attitude change dimension of political persuasion in social media merits scholarly attention, it is time for the literature to explore new avenues for how this persuasive effect is manifested. In this section, three recommendations for future research are put forward to address this phenomenon in a systematic fashion: (1) narrative persuasion on social media, (2) entertainment-oriented and political entertainment content on social media and (3) a holistic approach to political persuasion. The first two regard content and uses of social media that although widespread, have received little attention: narrative persuasion and entertainment-oriented use and content. The third recommendation addresses the lack of studies that look at persuasion holistically.

Narrative Persuasion on Social Media

Narratives refer to symbolic representations of events through a story or a person's experience, with an identifiable structure, characters and a message about the topic, be it explicit or implicit (Bilandzic & Busselle, 2013). Narrative persuasion thus refers to influence processes that involve this type of evidence. Accordingly, studies have shown that this type of persuasion can be effective in changing people's attitudes on issues as diverse as same-sex marriage, citizenship for immigrants, wealth inequality, the refugee crisis, climate change or health-conscious behavior (Polletta & Redman, 2020; Wojcieszak & Kim, 2016).

Narrative persuasion has a unique way of capturing the audience that is fundamentally different from that of non-narrative messages. According to transportation theory (Green, 2008), personal narratives cause recipients to develop a strong cognitive and affective connections with characters as they become involved in stories. This experience links mental images with the beliefs implied in the narrative, transporting individuals and enhancing their empathy, which in turn facilitates persuasion. This occurs because, in the midst of transportation, narratives are perceived as less threatening and as not even having persuasive intent, which causes persuasion to go unnoticed and overcome resistance (Bilandzic & Busselle, 2013; Polletta & Redman, 2020). Some studies have also emphasized that the identification that recipients experience in transportation may be further enhanced by perceived similarity (e.g., Igartua et al., 2024), as people tend to feel more connected to characters that are similar to them in terms of demographic, social and psychological characteristics.

The persuasive potential of narratives is clear. However, the literature has tended to examine such type of influence more in written and audiovisual stories in short and long format, overlooking other narratives that citizens now consume very frequently: those of social media users. People often post personal content about experiences they have had in a relatable way. Authenticity or "realness" is increasingly valued on social media, and what is more real than a layperson telling a personal story? Additionally, these narrative posts come from people with whom the recipients share many socio-demographic characteristics. If these posts are about sociopolitical issues, they could certainly evoke empathy and transport recipients, potentially nudging changes in political viewpoints. The possibilities of narrative persuasion in social media are plentiful and yet we do not know much about it empirically.

Entertainment-Oriented and Political Entertainment Content on Social Media

As noted earlier, citizens tend to use social media for nonpolitical and non-news purposes (Kümpel, 2019; Matthes et al., 2020). On the contrary, many people access these digital spaces seeking entertainment, although such use tends to be ignored by scholars in political communication (Matthes et al., 2023). These studies have tended to focus on the political muscle of social media as if it were widespread or as if it could be separated from the consumption of entertainment-related content. In users' feeds, news and political discussions may get mixed with memes and jokes, which sometimes also deal with public affairs and politics (Greenwood et al., 2016; Holbert et al., 2010).

Both citizens' entertainment-oriented use of social media and the political entertainment content they encounter may have persuasive effects on users. For this reason, more scholarly efforts are needed to study them. Research has found that people tend to choose entertainment over politics when they are given the choice (Anspach, 2017), and a nonpolitical use of social media (i.e., social interaction) has already been noted to directly influence political persuasion (Diehl et al., 2016). However, whether this applies to other nonpolitical uses of social media is unknown. Likewise, although much research on political entertainment has investigated the effects of infotainment talk shows and other satire content, there are few studies conducted in the context of social media. One notable exception is the experimental study by Greenwood et al. (2016), in which it was found that political comedy on Facebook can influence attitudes.

In sum, entertainment content certainly matters to users, although it may seem trivial to some scholars. It is the users who determine which content is politically relevant (Coles, 2024), and this may include entertainment. Future work should thus further examine such content and use to understand the effects that reflect the actual usage that citizens make of these platforms.

A Holistic Approach to Political Persuasion

In this chapter, we have described how media effects research has traditionally tended to focus on the attitude change dimension of persuasion, and how it still tends to equate persuasion and attitude change as if they were interchangeable concepts. Research in reinforcement has also been a common one. However, studies of this effect have been accompanied by misleading notions such as "minimal effects," which led scholars to perceive that political media have "no-effect" (Holbert et al., 2010). Thus, if we take a critical look at media effects research, it becomes apparent that these studies generally examine one persuasive effect at a time, mostly going back and forth from change to reinforcement.

In the course of its history, communication research has tended toward a reductionist view of this multidimensional phenomenon. For this reason, we argue for a holistic view of persuasion that does not reduce it to an isolated variable or a single dimension, but considers it as a whole. When Miller (2013) wrote his distinction of the three dimensions of persuasion, namely, change, formation and reinforcement, he also specified that these dimensions are not mutually exclusive. What factors foster someone to change, form or reinforce an opinion? What are the overlaps between the three effects? We lack a holistic approach to the phenomenon that preserves its complexity and helps us to understand how the different dimensions interrelate and complement each other.

Conclusion

In this chapter, we have summarized political persuasion research in the field of communication, including classic media effects scholarship and more recent studies on social media. We point out that media effects research has always been closely linked to certain dimensions of persuasion and that the influence of social media on political polarization remains an open question that requires further work. We also argue for the relevance of studying political attitude change on these platforms. Finally, we have put forward three suggestions for future research in the hope that they will prove to be useful starting points for media effects and persuasion studies in relation to a wider range of online content and a broader view of persuasion. Political persuasion will undoubtedly remain one of the core areas of communication research for many years to come. However, further work is needed to achieve a proper understanding of this important topic.

References

Annenberg IOD Collaborative. (2023). *Democracy amid crises: Polarization, pandemic, protests, and persuasion*. Oxford University Press.

Anspach, N. M. (2017). The new personal influence: How our Facebook friends influence the news we read. *Political Communication, 34*(4), 590–606. https://doi.org/10.1080/10584609.2017.1316329

Bakshy, E., Messing, S., & Adamic, L. A. (2015). Exposure to ideologically diverse news and opinion on Facebook. *Science, 348*(6239), 1130–1132. https://doi.org/10.1126/science.aaa1160

Barberá, P. (2020). Social media echo chambers, and political polarization. In N. Persily & J. A. Tucker (Eds.), *Social media and democracy: The state of the field and prospects for reform* (pp. 34–55). Cambridge University Press.

Barnidge, M. (2017). Exposure to political disagreement in social media versus face-to-face and anonymous online settings. *Political Communication, 34*(2), 302–321. https://doi.org/10.1080/10584609.2016.1235639

Bennett, W. L., & Iyengar, S. (2008). A new era of minimal effects? The changing foundations of political communication. *Journal of Communication, 58*(4), 707–731. https://doi.org/10.1111/j.1460-2466.2008.00410.x

Bilandzic, H., & Busselle, R. (2013). Narrative persuasion. In J. P. Dillard & L. Shen (Eds.), *The SAGE handbook of persuasion: Developments in theory and practice* (pp. 200–219). Sage.

Bode, L. (2016). Political news in the news feed: Learning politics from social media. *Mass Communication and Society, 19*(1), 24–48. https://doi.org/10.1080/15205436.2015.1045149

Borah, P. (2016). Media effects theory. In G. Mazzoleni (Ed.), *The international Encyclopedia of political communication* (pp. 1–12). Hoboken: John Wiley & Sons.
Boxell, L., Gentzkow, M., & Shapiro, J. M. (2017). Greater Internet use is not associated with faster growth in political polarization among US demographic groups. *Proceedings of the National Academy of Sciences, 114*(40), 10612–10617. https://doi.org/10.1073/pnas.1706588114
Bruns, A. (2021). Echo chambers? Filter bubbles? The misleading metaphors that obscure the real problem. In M. Pérez-Escolar & J. M. Noguera-Vivo (Eds.), *Hate speech and polarization in participatory society* (pp. 33–48). Routledge.
Cardenal, A. S., Aguilar-Paredes, C., Galais, C., & Pérez-Montoro, M. (2019). Digital technologies and selective exposure: How choice and filter bubbles shape news media exposure. *The International Journal of Press/Politics, 24*(4), 465–486. https://doi.org/10.1177/1940161219862988
Chang, J. H., Zhu, Y. Q., Wang, S. H., & Li, Y. J. (2018). Would you change your mind? An empirical study of social impact theory on Facebook. *Telematics and Informatics, 35*(1), 282–292. https://doi.org/10.1016/j.tele.2017.11.009
Cinelli, M., De Francisci Morales, G., Galeazzi, A., Quattrociocchi, W., & Starnini, M. (2021). The echo chamber effect on social media. *Proceedings of the National Academy of Sciences, 118*(9), e2023301118. https://doi.org/10.1073/pnas.2023301118
Coles, S. M. (2024). Conceptualizing evaluations of the political relevance of media texts: The politically relevant media model. *Communication Theory, 34*(2), 71–81. https://doi.org/10.1093/ct/qtae004
Conover, P. J., Searing, D. D., & Crewe, I. M. (2002). The deliberative potential of political discussion. *British Journal of Political Science, 32*(1), 21–62.
Diehl, T., Weeks, B. E., & Gil de Zúñiga, H. (2016). Political persuasion on social media: Tracing direct and indirect effects of news use and social interaction. *New Media & Society, 18*(9), 1875–1895. https://doi.org/10.1177/1461444815616224
Druckman, J. N. (2022). A framework for the study of persuasion. *Annual Review of Political Science, 25*, 65–88. https://doi.org/10.1146/annurev-polisci-051120-110428
Festinger, L. (1957). *A theory of cognitive dissonance*. Row.
Flaxman, S., Goel, S., & Rao, J. M. (2016). Filter bubbles, echo chambers, and online news consumption. *Public Opinion Quarterly, 80*(S1), 298–320. https://doi.org/10.1093/poq/nfw006
Gil de Zúñiga, H., González-González, P., & Goyanes, M. (2022). Pathways to political persuasion: Linking online, social media, and fake news with political attitude change through political discussion. *American Behavioral Scientist.* https://doi.org/10.1177/00027642221118272

Gil de Zúñiga, H. G., Marné, H. M., & Carty, E. (2023). Abating dissonant public spheres: Exploring the effects of affective, ideological and perceived societal political polarization on social media political persuasion. *Political Communication*, *40*(3), 327–345. https://doi.org/10.1080/1058460 9.2022.2139310

Granovetter, M. S. (1973). The strength of weak ties. *American Journal of Sociology*, *78*(6), 1360–1380. https://www.jstor.org/stable/2776392

Green, M. C. (2008). Transportation theory. In W. Donsbach (Ed.), *The international Encyclopedia of communication* (1st ed., pp. 1–7). John Wiley & Sons.

Greenwood, M. M., Sorenson, M. E., & Warner, B. R. (2016). Ferguson on Facebook: Political persuasion in a new era of media effects. *Computers in Human Behavior*, *57*, 1–10. https://doi.org/10.1016/j.chb.2015.12.003

Holbert, R. L., & Tchernev, J. M. (2013). Media influence as persuasion. In J. P. Dillard & L. Shen (Eds.), *The SAGE handbook of persuasion: Developments in theory and practice* (pp. 36–52). Sage.

Holbert, R. L., Garrett, R. K., & Gleason, L. S. (2010). A new era of minimal effects? A response to Bennett and Iyengar. *Journal of Communication*, *60*(1), 15–34. https://doi.org/10.1111/j.1460-2466.2009.01470.x

Holbert, R. L., Weeks, B. E., & Esralew, S. (2013). Approaching the 2012 US presidential election from a diversity of explanatory principles: Understanding, consistency, and hedonism. *American Behavioral Scientist*, *57*(12), 1663–1687. https://doi.org/10.1177/0002764213490693

Igartua, J. J., González-Vázquez, A., & Arcila-Calderón, C. (2024). The effect of similarity to a transitional role model of an entertainment–education narrative designed to improve attitudes toward immigrants: Evidence from three European countries. *Media Psychology*, *27*(2), 211–242. https://doi.org/1 0.1080/15213269.2023.2235574

Jordá, B., & Goyanes, M. (2022). The rear window effect: How users respond to political discussions and persuasive discourses in social media. *International Journal of Communication*, *16*, 19.

Jordá, B., Goyanes, M., Borah, P., & Gil de Zúñiga, H. (2024). Social media symbiosis: Understanding the dynamics of online political persuasion in social media ecologies. *Journalism*, *0*(0). https://doi.org/10.1177/14648849241272164

Katz, E., & Lazarsfeld, P. F. (1955). *Personal influence: The part played by people in the flow of mass communication*. Free Press.

Klapper, J. T. (1960). *The effects of mass communication*. Free Press.

Kümpel, A. S. (2019). The issue takes it all? Incidental news exposure and news engagement on Facebook. *Digital Journalism*, *7*(2), 165–186. https://doi.org/10.1080/21670811.2018.1465831

Lazarsfeld, P. F., Berelson, B., & Gaudet, H. (1948). *The people's choice*. Columbia University Press.

Lin, H., Wang, Y., Lee, J., & Kim, Y. (2023). The effects of disagreement and unfriending on political polarization: A moderated-mediation model of cross-cutting discussion on affective polarization via unfriending contingent upon exposure to incivility. *Journal of Computer-Mediated Communication, 28*(4). https://doi.org/10.1093/jcmc/zmad022

Marwick, A. E., & boyd, d. (2014). Networked privacy: How teenagers negotiate context in social media. *New Media & Society, 16*, 1051–1067. https://doi.org/10.1177/1461444814543995

Matthes, J., Nanz, A., Stubenvoll, M., & Heiss, R. (2020). Processing news on social media. The political incidental news exposure model (PINE). *Journalism, 21*(8), 1031–1048. https://doi.org/10.1177/1464884920915371

Matthes, J., Heiss, R., & van Scharrel, H. (2023). The distraction effect. Political and entertainment-oriented content on social media, political participation, interest, and knowledge. *Computers in Human Behavior, 142*, 107644. https://doi.org/10.1016/j.chb.2022.107644

McLeod, J. M., & Reeves, B. (2013). On the nature of mass media effects. In S. Withey & R. Abeles (Eds.), *Television and social behavior: Beyond violence and children* (pp. 17–54). Lawrence Erlbaum.

McPherson, M., Smith-Lovin, L., & Cook, J. M. (2001). Birds of a feather: Homophily in social networks. *Annual Review of Sociology, 27*(1), 415–444. https://doi.org/10.1146/annurev.soc.27.1.415

McQuail, D. (2010). *McQuail's mass communication theory*. Sage.

Messing, S., & Westwood, S. J. (2014). Selective exposure in the age of social media: Endorsements trump partisan source affiliation when selecting news online. *Communication Research, 41*(8), 1042–1063. https://doi.org/10.1177/0093650212466406

Miller, G. R. (2013). On being persuaded: Some basic distinctions. In J. P. Dillard & L. Shen (Eds.), *The SAGE handbook of persuasion: Developments in theory and practice* (pp. 70–82). Sage.

Newman, N., Fletcher, R., Eddy, K., Robertson, C. T., & Nielsen, R. K. (2023). *Digital news report 2023*. Reuters Institute for the Study of Journalism. https://reutersinstitute.politics.ox.ac.uk/sites/default/files/2023-06/Digital_News_Report_2023.pdf

Noelle-Neumann, E. (1973). Return to the concept of the powerful mass media. *Studies in Broadcasting, 9*, 67–112.

Nyhan, B., Settle, J., Thorson, E., Wojcieszak, M., Barberá, P., Chen, A. Y., ... & Tucker, J. A. (2023). Like-minded sources on Facebook are prevalent but not polarizing. *Nature, 620*(7972), 137–144. https://doi.org/10.1038/s41586-023-06297-w

O'Keefe, D. J. (2015). *Persuasion: Theory and research*. Sage.

Pariser, E. (2011). *The filter bubble: What the internet is hiding from you*. Viking.

Perloff, R. M. (2020). *The dynamics of persuasion: Communication and attitudes in the 21st century*. Routledge.

Petty, R. E., & Cacioppo, J. T. (1986). *Communication and persuasion: Central and peripheral routes to attitude change*. Springer.

Polletta, F., & Redman, N. (2020). When do stories change our minds? Narrative persuasion about social problems. *Sociology Compass, 14*(4). https://doi.org/10.1111/soc4.12778

Prior, M. (2007). *Post-broadcast democracy: How media choice increases inequality in political involvement and polarizes elections*. Cambridge University Press.

Robinson, N. W., Zeng, C., & Holbert, R. L. (2018). The stubborn pervasiveness of television news in the digital age and the field's attention to the medium, 2010–2014. *Journal of Broadcasting & Electronic Media, 62*(2), 287–301. https://doi.org/10.1080/08838151.2018.1451857

Silver, L., Huang, C., & Taylor, K. (2019). *In emerging economies, smartphone and social media users have broader social networks*. Pew Research Center. https://www.pewresearch.org/internet/wp-content/uploads/sites/9/2019/08/PI-PG_2019-08-22_social-networks-emerging-economies_FINAL.pdf

Stroud, N. J. (2011). *Niche news: The politics of news choice*. Oxford University Press.

Sunstein, C. R. (2017). *#republic. Divided democracy in the age of social media*. Princeton University Press.

Vorderer, P., Park, D. W., & Lutz, S. (2019). A history of media effects research traditions. In M. B. Oliver, A. Raney, & J. Bryant (Eds.), *Media effects: Advances in theory and research* (pp. 1–15). Routledge.

Wojcieszak, M., & Kim, N. (2016). How to improve attitudes toward disliked groups: The effects of narrative versus numerical evidence on political persuasion. *Communication Research, 43*(6), 785–809. https://doi.org/10.1177/0093650215618480

Wojcieszak, M., Menchen-Trevino, E., Clemm von Hohenberg, B., de Leeuw, S., Gonçalves, J., Davidson, S., & Gonçalves, A. (2024). Non-news websites expose people to more political content than news websites: Evidence from browsing data in three countries. *Political Communication, 41*(1), 129–151. https://doi.org/10.1080/10584609.2023.2238641

CHAPTER 12

Fake News Exposure and Political Persuasion

Samuel Toledano ⓘ, *Sheila Guerrero Rojas* ⓘ,
and Alberto Ardèvol-Abreu ⓘ

INTRODUCTION

In a dystopian 1984, the Ministry of Truth held the responsibility of ensuring that there was no other reality beyond the one established by the party. The regime's communication strategy, encapsulated in a series of authoritarian slogans, systematically eliminated the past, leading to its eventual erasure from public memory. This deliberate process culminated in a state where lies metamorphosed into accepted truths. Orwell's (1949) fictional universe was deeply informed by his understanding of the political and media environments of his time. In this milieu, words were (and

---

S. Toledano
Universidad de La Laguna (ULL), San Cristóbal de La Laguna, Spain

Laboratorio de Investigación sobre Medios y sus Efectos (LIME, ULL), San Cristóbal de La Laguna, Spain
e-mail: stoledano@ull.edu.es

S. Guerrero Rojas
Universidad de La Laguna (ULL), San Cristóbal de La Laguna, Spain
e-mail: sguerrer@ull.edu.es

© The Author(s), under exclusive license to Springer Nature Switzerland AG 2024
M. Goyanes, A. Cañedo (eds.), *Media Influence on Opinion Change and Democracy*, https://doi.org/10.1007/978-3-031-70231-0_12

continue to be) not mere tools of expression but builders of reality, with the dual concepts of truth and falsehood at the heart of both authoritarian and democratic systems. This perspective finds its roots in the modern state and connects with Rousseau's social contract theory. The individual's commitment to the general will—effectively, a commitment to themselves—is hardly conceivable without an entry point into social reality, an access to truth. It is this truth, "or what is perceived as such, what fundamentally constitutes the bond of the social body" (Hude, 1982, p. 216).

In real-life political contexts, akin to those depicted in *1984*, the quest for truth is more often motivated by the desire to manipulate it for the acquisition or maintenance of power rather than by noble aspirations. Arendt contends that, in such scenarios, the truth most politically significant truth is factual rather than rational. She maintains that while rational truths are grounded in axioms and debatable theories, factual truths, noted for their irrefutability, are fundamentally distinct. Arendt further notes that factual truths are intrinsically more vulnerable than theoretical constructs: "once they are lost, no rational effort will ever bring them back" (Arendt, 2006, pp. 223–259). Expanding on this argument, she posits that for political opinions to be considered legitimate they need to align with the underlying facts they are based upon. Transitioning to the present climate of mass manipulation, Arendt advanced a relevant question:

> if the modern political lies are so big that they require a complete rearrangement of the whole factual texture—the making of another reality, as it were, into which they will fit without seam, crack, or fissure, exactly as the facts fitted into their own original context—what prevents these new stories, images, and non-facts from becoming an adequate substitute for reality and factuality? (Arendt, 2006, p. 249)

A. Ardèvol-Abreu (✉)
Universidad de La Laguna (ULL), San Cristóbal de La Laguna, Spain

Laboratorio de Investigación sobre Medios y sus Efectos (LIME, ULL), San Cristóbal de La Laguna, Spain

Instituto Universitario de Neurociencia (IUNE, ULL), San Cristóbal de La Laguna, Spain
e-mail: aardevol@ull.edu.es

Arendt identified the realm of factual statements as the battleground where deliberate falsehoods, or plain lies, come into play. In this regard, "unwelcome opinion can be argued with, rejected, or compromised upon, but unwelcome facts possess an infuriating stubbornness that nothing can move except plain lies" (Arendt, 2006, p. 236). Echoing Machiavelli, who noted that "we've had examples of leaders who've done great things without worrying too much about keeping their word" (2014, p. 69), Arendt highlights the modern phenomenon where dictators and statesmen alike resort to falsehoods as necessary and justifiable instruments. "If we understand political action in terms of the means-end category, we may very well come to the seemingly paradoxical conclusion that lying can very well serve to establish or safeguard the conditions for the search after truth" (Arendt, 2006, p. 224).

Decades after Arendt's analysis, Kellyanne Conway, Counselor to President Donald Trump, exemplified this struggle for control over the narrative through her use of the term "alternative facts." She employed this term as a means to navigate current affairs, coinciding with the emergence of the fake news phenomenon. As Klein (2017) observes, "in Trump's world, and according to the internal logic of his brand, lying with impunity is all part of being the big boss. Being tethered to the fixed, boring facts is for losers" (p. 56). This approach has proven effective, as seen with Donald Trump's electoral base (Klein, 2017) and as previously reflected in Machiavelli's portrayal of the *Prince*: "People are so gullible and so caught up with immediate concerns that a con man will always find someone ready to be conned" (2014, p. 70). This is also reminiscent of the 'non-lies' of former President Richard Nixon and his famous assertion: "I was not lying. I said things that later on seemed to be untrue" ("Nixon: I wasn't," 1978).

Huxley noted that in democracies, as opposed to dictatorships where facts are often censored or distorted, voters are supplied "with adequate information and persuaded to make realistic choices in the light of that information." He drew a nuanced distinction—not in his dystopian *Brave New World* but in his later revisited essay—, an anti-democratic variation of this provision of information to citizens within the "machinery of mass communication." This variant exploits people's vulnerabilities for commercial profit, which, while economically advantageous, is detrimental to individuals both in their capacity as voters and as human beings (Huxley, 1994, pp. 69–70).

Despite these considerations, it would not be fair to attribute the emergence of fake news in the media to Conway's "alternative facts" and Trump's adoption of them as a central aspect of his political communication strategies. The phenomenon of disinformation and the prevailing low trust in politics and journalism are not recent developments. The portrayal of Vietnam and Iraq in the media, along with the undemocratic nature of political and media deception as highlighted in Herman and Chomsky's (1988) propaganda model, serve as prime examples of this long-standing trend. Lies in these instances were not opinions but published facts, which compelled apologies from the *New York Times*, notably for their reporting of the (nonexistent) weapons of mass destruction in Iraq: "Looking back, we wish we had been more aggressive in re-examining the claims as new evidence emerged—or failed to emerge" ("From the editors," 2004). Similarly, in the years leading upon to the Great Financial Crisis, a trend of insufficiently accountable journalism was evident in numerous countries. Journalists subsequently acknowledged a deficiency in rigor in their business reporting (Strauß, 2019). News media and journalists often justify their actions by claiming they are fulfilling their professional duty to seek journalistic truth, which necessitates adhering to the facts. However, they frequently hide behind the myth of objectivity and propagate certain 'facts' without questioning their existence.

Consequently, the contemporary term 'fake news' has garnered renewed attention, although it essentially reflects an enduring dichotomy of falsehood versus truth (see Farkas & Schou, 2018). The concept is further complicated by the introduction of notions like 'post-truth', reflecting a more philosophical approach to the current era of informational confusion. More commonly, 'post-truth' is also associated with disinformation, which, unlike misinformation, is characterized by a deliberate intent to deceive the public, thus aligning closely with the definition of fake news: "made-up news, manipulated to look like credible journalistic reports that are designed to deceive us" (Brennen, 2017, p. 180). The deception does not necessarily involve a false statement but aims to make someone believe something known to be untrue (Robinson et al., 2018).

Alongside the disinformative aspects of fake news as a genre, it is also important to consider its role as a label. This refers to "the weaponization of the term fake news," or, in simpler words, its use by politicians to delegitimize journalists and the news media (Egelhofer & Lecheler, 2019, p. 105). Both dimensions of the fake news issue highlight a "power struggle between the journalistic field and the political field," which implies, in the last instance, a struggle to define what is "truthful, who can portray social reality accurately" (Farkas & Schou, 2018, p. 308). The true novelty of fake news lies in unprecedented volume and the speed and ease of its spread, enabled by digital advancements (Bennett & Livingston, 2018). This shift allows disinformation to enter mainstream discourse, challenging traditional elite communication and contributing to decreased public trust in media and journalism's accuracy and credibility (Egelhofer & Lecheler, 2019, p. 112; Farhall et al., 2019).

It is clear that the rise of fake news, coinciding with the emergence of the Internet and social media, represents a communicative democratization of deception and its role in political discourse. However, it is not coincidental that concepts such as 'populism' and 'fake news' have surfaced almost simultaneously, especially at a time when mainstream media and established political entities are ceding influence on those emerging from 'the fringes.' This appears to be a terminological battle reminiscent of Orwellian newspeak and its prominence in current affairs (Toledano, 2006). The digital landscape is now a battleground for redefining power in media and politics, with media organizations and political parties vying to present the factual truths they want citizens to believe.

POLITICAL MISPERCEPTIONS AND MOTIVATED REASONING

For decades, scholars across various disciplines have expressed concerns about the implications of *un*informed public opinion for democracy and civic life. However, what may be even more concerning than *un*informed citizenry is the prevalence of *mis-* or *dis*informed citizenry (Flynn et al., 2017; Kuklinski & Quirk, 2000). Intentionally disseminated false information can have adverse consequences for political life, both in democracies and authoritarian regimes. Despite being a long-standing issue, the unique aspect of disinformation in the age of the Internet, social media, and Artificial Intelligence (AI) is the ease and affordability with which malicious agents can inject and viralize falsehoods within the media system. These players are commonly individual or institutional actors driven by economic gain, as seen with the Macedonian fake news creators during the 2016 Trump campaign (Subramanian, 2017), or states engaging in disinformation campaigns as a form of warfare (see Xia et al., 2019).

The principles of participatory democracy presuppose that citizens hold accurate beliefs about political events and proposals, allowing them to freely participate in the decision-making process. However, these assumptions are compromised when audiences are misled by disinformation. Amid scenarios marked by divergent public opinion and decisions made with narrow margins, the potential for influence by evil-intentioned entities becomes evident. This may include actions such as manipulating election outcomes, inciting social upheaval, or hindering the effectiveness of governments and their measures. Currently, the diffusion of disinformation can also be a driving factor behind the affective polarization that appears to arise among certain groups as a consequence of their use of social media (see Allcott et al., 2020). Indeed, there is evidence suggesting that some political partisans actively spread news, whether real or fake, as a means to target and undermine the opposing party (Osmundsen et al., 2021).

Perhaps the moment when the world became aware of these systemic vulnerabilities was in 2018, with the revelation of the Cambridge Analytica scandal. Following a series of publications in the British newspaper *The Observer*, the global public learned that the private consultancy Cambridge Analytica irregularly used Facebook data to craft psychological profiles of millions of individuals (up to 15% of the US population; see Confessore, 2018; Heawood, 2018). The consultancy traded this data and employed it in strategic communication tactics in the United States (US) and the United Kingdom (UK), aiming to micro-target individual voters through highly personalized political messages, which included disinformation (Scott, 2018). In other words, they attempted to manipulate voters to influence electoral outcomes.

When viewed through a rational-cognitive lens, the prerequisite for disinformation to shape attitudes and affect behaviors is the acceptance or belief in disinformation—be it a specific piece of fake news or a collection of deceptive disinformation. From this perspective, disinformation represents a "threat to the rational processes of sensemaking and decision-making" (Bastick, 2021, p. 106633). Put differently, the democratic implications of disinformation stem from its potential to generate political misperceptions, defined as "factual beliefs that are false or contradict the best available evidence in the public domain" (Flynn et al., 2017, p. 128).

Sometimes the mere repetition of a message enhances its perceived truthfulness, irrespective of its factual accuracy. Indeed, Adolf Hitler and his renowned Propaganda Minister Joseph Goebbels relied on the repetition to instill the misperception that there was a Jewish conspiracy to attack Germany and dominate the world. This phenomenon, recognized academically since the 1970s, is termed the "truth effect" (Hasher et al.,

1977; Unkelbach & Speckmann, 2021). In today's media landscape, repeated falsehoods disseminated across various channels and platforms can engender a sense of familiarity and be accepted as truth. This effect of repetition may provide insight into why, for example, in 2015, 42% of Americans still believed that US troops uncovered weapons of mass destruction during their 2003 invasion of Iraq, despite the lack of evidence supporting their existence or the presence of facilities for their production (Breitman, 2015).

Beyond the simple repetition, understanding the mechanisms by which disinformation translates into political misperceptions hinges significantly on motivated reasoning. This connects with the manner in which individuals apply varying standards to assess the credibility of facts and the robustness of opinions based on the way they make them feel. While individuals may be motivated to be accurate and hold correct beliefs, this seems to be less common when it comes to evaluating political information or opinions. Indeed, people *want* to believe in things that make them feel good and *do not want* to believe in things that make them feel bad. Three fundamental processes guide motivated reasoning: the prior attitude effect, confirmation bias, and disconfirmation bias (Taber & Lodge, 2006; Zaller, 1992; see also Ardèvol-Abreu & Gil de Zúñiga, 2020). First, congenial arguments are commonly perceived as more robust and persuasive compared to challenging viewpoints, illustrating the prior attitude effect. Second, people frequently subject information and arguments they dislike to more intense scrutiny, often resulting in the rejection of opposing viewpoints while readily accepting agreeable information—a phenomenon recognized as disconfirmation bias. Third, individuals exhibit a tendency to gravitate towards information that reinforces their existing beliefs while avoiding contradictory perspectives, a phenomenon termed selective exposure.

In the domain of political disinformation, partisan affiliation and ideological leanings significantly influence the mechanisms of motivated reasoning. These factors frequently determine whether a message evokes positive or negative sentiments in individuals, subsequently impacting their inclination to accept or challenge it. This dynamic explains why disinformation tends to circulate within politically homogeneous networks, where the message resonates positively and is thus more readily embraced. For instance, "strategic lies" regarding the purported benefits of Brexit for the budget of the UK's National Health Service or the imminent accession of Turkey to the EU were more likely to circulate among *Brexiteers* than among detractors of Brexit (see Gaber & Fisher, 2021; Parnell, 2023). Similarly, misinformation regarding the involvement of 5G technologies in transmitting the COVID-19 virus is more readily accepted and spread within preexisting conspiracist communities (Bruns et al., 2021).

Another facet of research complements this perspective by emphasizing the influence of *partisan motivations* on the dissemination of fake news. Osmundsen and colleagues (2021) posit that, within the realm of political expression and discussion on social media, certain fervent partisans consistently tailor their online behaviors to align with partisan goals, notably including the denigration and vilification of the opposing party. Within this framework, some partisans may leverage disinformation as a means to attack out-parties, irrespective of its authenticity. As the authors assert: "Partisans' decisions to share both fake and real news sources depend on how politically useful they are in derogating the out-party," and in some cases they will not "pay attention to the veracity dimension of the information at all" (Osmundsen et al., 2021, pp. 1001–1012). In other words, the circulation of fake news is not always a result of ignorance or an individual's inability to distinguish facts from falsehoods.

Influence of Fake News on Political Behavior: Conscious and Unconscious Paths

How do manipulation-induced shifts in behavior, such as altering voting preferences or stimulating protest mobilization, take place within the target audience? The answer to this question is nuanced, drawing insights from cognitive and social psychology, political science, and communication studies. Arguably, the most traditional and explored academic explanations rely on models of indirect effects that operate through the modification of perceptions, beliefs, and attitudes—the precursors to behavior. Simply put, if the initial stimulus, namely, disinformation, successfully changes certain relevant beliefs and attitudes, the probability of modifying the objective behavior increases. Indirect effects models are not novel in the study of political communication and campaign effects (Valkenburg et al., 2016). For instance, within the well-established Elaboration Likelihood Model, scholars have theorized and provided evidence that persuasive communication has the capability to modify attitudes by engaging a central or a peripheral route of information processing. Subsequently, altered attitudes, especially those resulting from central processing, are predictive of associated behaviors (see Petty et al., 2009).

It is easy to intuitively think of examples of how certain beliefs (e.g., political misperceptions) can impact the quality of the democratic process or influence political participation in one direction or another. For instance, one might have the misperception that Barack Obama was born in Kenya, and therefore, his candidacy violates the US Constitution, leading them to vote for John McCain. Certainly, empirical evidence indicates that exposure to disinformation triggers attitudinal and behavioral processes influencing political dynamics. Although the magnitude of these effects is typically modest, they can pose a notable challenge to the legitimacy of the democratic process, particularly in closely contested elections or within multiparty systems. This is precisely what Zimmermann and Kohring (2020) discovered in a longitudinal study on disinformation during the 2017 federal elections in Germany. In this national context, exposure to xenophobic "disinforming news" concerning refugees and Muslim immigrants led voters away from the ruling party (the Christian Democrats of the CDU/CSU) and towards the embrace of the far-right populist AfD. Similarly, in a randomized online experiment, Barrera and colleagues (2020) found that exposure to misleading statements by French far-right candidate Marine Le Pen significantly heightened the intention to vote for her. What's particularly striking in this latter study is that the increase in voting intentions persisted even when participants were subjected to fact-checking from official sources. In the realm of public health, some research suggests that exposure to COVID-19-related disinformation may have been linked to a decreased adherence to protective measures, as evidenced by a lowered intention to download contact-tracing apps (Greene & Murphy, 2021). Moreover, there is anecdotal evidence indicating occurrences in countries such as the US, Spain, or Germany, where the far-right strategically employed COVID-19-related disinformation to further antidemocratic agendas and actively oppose lockdown measures (Fominaya, 2024).

A limitation of the rational-cognitive perspectives on disinformation is their inability to comprehensively explain all effects on behavior and attitudes, as not all can be attributed to conscious mechanisms. In the broader context of media influence, it has long been acknowledged that the persuasive impact of messages is also shaped by emotions, whether consciously or unconsciously experienced (Hasell & Weeks, 2016; Petty et al., 2009). Additionally, psychological research has long highlighted the existence of implicit attitudes—those of which individuals are unaware—which can impact the way people think or behave. Given that fake news is structured around "emotionally satisfying beliefs" (Bennett & Livingston, 2018, p. 32), it has the potential to unconsciously alter the emotions, attitudes, and subsequently, behaviors of individuals exposed to it.

This line of research into the potential unconscious influence of disinformation is still in its early stages, with a focus on fundamental actions that could "cascade into more complex behaviors" (Bastick, 2021, p. 106633). For example, Bastick (2021) found that a singular exposure to a piece of fake news in an experimental setting could unconsciously influence the tapping speed of participants. To examine this, he used a traditional neuropsychological test known as the Finger Tapping Test (FTT). Participants in the experimental groups were instructed to tap a finger as rapidly as possible both before and after exposure to two different disinformative (fake) texts. These texts discussed the virtues or vices associated with individuals tapping at a high speed: intelligence in one group and criminality in the other.

Bastick's interpretation for the unconscious change in tapping speed (a moderate effect of more than 5% increase in one of the experimental conditions) is not straightforward, as the literature on the impact of cognitions and emotions on the test performance has not fully elucidated this aspect. The author suggests that emotions and implicit attitudes induced by exposure to the fake text may explain the effect, and proposes that "real-world effects that assume psychometrically optimized content, micro-targeted audiences, and repeated exposure can be expected to be larger" (Bastick, 2021, p. 106633).

Assessing Protective Measures Against Fake News Manipulation

Expanding on the earlier mentioned rational-cognitive perspective, a significant portion of the literature in the context of fake news and disinformation has concentrated on protective measures that enable individuals exposed to disinformation to identify it. The foundational concept driving this research posits that if individuals can successfully identify misinformation, the impact on their beliefs and attitudes will be null or, at the very least, diminished in magnitude, thereby preventing subsequent effects on their behaviors. For instance, a specific line of research has delved into the potentially safeguarding role of different facets of media-related literacy, which equips citizens "with the skillset needed to discern facts from falsehoods" (Jones-Jang et al., 2019, p. 372). The results are promising, although overall, the effects are of small magnitude, and not all types of media-related literacy prove effective. For example, information literacy—defined as the proficiency to locate, comprehend, assess, and apply information—appears to be associated with improved recognition of fake news (Jones-Jang et al., 2019; see also Podgornik et al., 2016). However, other literacies, such as media, news, and digital literacies, do not seem to contribute to recognizing such disinforming news. In the same vein of research, training in fake news detection appears to improve, to a certain extent, the ability to spot it and decrease the likelihood of sharing disinformation (Adjin-Tettey, 2022).

Another potentially protective strategy could stem from the collaboration between content distributors and fact-checkers, who might label contested, deceptive, or outright false content, especially on social media. Yet, once again, research in this area suggests that fact-checking labels have, at best, a modest protective effect on the audience. On the one hand, this may be because many social media users do not pay sufficient attention to these labels (Ardèvol-Abreu et al., 2020; Brandtzaeg & Følstad, 2017; Oeldorf-Hirsch et al., 2020). Another reason may have to do with the reconstructive nature of human memory and the so-called continued influence effect (CIE) of misinformation. The term refers to the significant challenge of eradicating false information from memory once it was initially accepted as true: "Misinformation continues to affect behavior, even if people explicitly acknowledge that this information has been retracted, invalidated, or corrected" (Ecker et al., 2010, p. 1087). Among the few interventions that have demonstrated effectiveness in minimizing the CIE is adding causal alternatives to corrections, aiming to avoid a "gap" in the audience's mental model. For instance, the retraction of information claiming that a Mexican journalist presented extraterrestrial mummies in the Mexican Congress will be more effective if the correction additionally explains precisely what the journalist presented: a forgery, a mixture of animal and human bones with synthetic glue serving as a base for their assembly (Ecker et al., 2011; see also Guerrero, 2023).

A third reason why corrections are only relatively effective is that some individuals—especially those most vulnerable to disinformation—lack confidence in fact-checkers. Disinformation, as previously noted, does not spread uniformly across all social spheres; rather, it tends to proliferate more within social circles characterized by low levels of trust in institutional actors such as mainstream media, fact-checkers, and sometimes the political system as a whole (Ardèvol-Abreu et al., 2020; Brandtzaeg & Følstad, 2017; Zimmermann & Kohring, 2020). As a result, individuals within these circles of 'generalized distrust' often approach labels and corrections from representatives of the establishment with skepticism, regarding them as unreliable. Furthermore, the coalescence of ideological uniformity and political radicalism, common characteristics of online 'echo chambers,' reinforces the predominance of directional goals as outlined in motivated reasoning theory (see Frischlich et al., 2021; van Kessel et al., 2021). Consequently, within these ideologically segregated environments, individuals tend to perceive information that aligns with their beliefs and political stances as more truthful, even at the expense of accuracy. Worse still, in the era of post-truth, some suggest that "a portion of society no longer adheres to the conventional principles of factual reasoning" (Zimmermann & Kohring, 2020, p. 216), supported by evidence of individuals knowingly sharing information they suspect to be false (Ardèvol-Abreu et al., 2020; see also Chadwick et al., 2018).

Epilogue

The overview provided in this section encapsulates the challenges brought forthby disinformation. The advent of social media has streamlined the production and dissemination of disinformation, jeopardizing crucial elements for the functioning of democratic societies, such as the informed participation of citizens. Political actors are sometimes exploiting this new landscape, where lies can transform into truths through alternative facts that craft a new reality. Fake news, a contemporary term for traditional falsehoods, has evolved from a mere genre into a discursive tool used to delegitimize opponents and secure a dominant position in the current power struggle between journalism and politics. However, the impact of disinformation on attitudes and behaviors seems relatively limited across the general population, though it cannot be dismissed, especially during times of political polarization and fragmentation when decisions are made within narrow margins. Furthermore, disinformation thrives in polarized environments, creating a vicious cycle of disinformation fueling polarization, and vice versa.

Turning to potential solutions and opportunities, certain interventions, such as enhancing media-related literacy or bolstering fact-checking processes, may alleviate the issue. However, they encounter scalability challenges and often lag behind the strategies employed by disinformation disseminators. Nowadays, AI holds promise in developing tools to detect and curb disinformation, yet these tools may inadvertently give rise to new threats: AI has the capacity to amplify the quantity and specificity of disinformation, contributing to micro-targeting individuals based on their specific vulnerabilities. Relying exclusively on the cognitive-rational pathway may not be prudent, as both emerging and established research on media persuasion suggests the existence of non-conscious routes to influence.

References

Adjin-Tettey, T. D. (2022). Combating fake news, disinformation, and misinformation: Experimental evidence for media literacy education. *Cogent Arts & Humanities*, *9*(1), 2037229. https://doi.org/10.1080/23311983 .2022.2037229

Allcott, H., Braghieri, L., Eichmeyer, S., & Gentzkow, M. (2020). The welfare effects of social media. *American Economic Review*, *110*(3), 629–676. https://doi.org/10.1257/aer.20190658

Ardèvol-Abreu, A., & Gil de Zúñiga, H. (2020). "Obstinate partisanship": Political discussion attributes effects on the development of unconditional party loyalty. *International Journal of Communication*, *14*, 22. https://ijoc.org/index.php/ijoc/article/viewFile/12464/2910

Ardèvol-Abreu, A., Delponti, P., & Rodríguez-Wangüemert, C. (2020). Intentional or inadvertent fake news sharing? Fact-checking warnings and users' interaction with social media content. *Profesional de la información*, *29*(5). https://doi.org/10.3145/epi.2020.sep.07

Arendt, H. (2006). *Between past and future. Eight exercises in political thought*. Penguin.

Barrera, O., Guriev, S., Henry, E., & Zhuravskaya, E. (2020). Facts, alternative facts, and fact checking in times of post-truth politics. *Journal of Public Economics*, *182*. https://doi.org/10.1016/j.jpubeco.2019.104123

Bastick, Z. (2021). Would you notice if fake news changed your behavior? An experiment on the unconscious effects of disinformation. *Computers in Human Behavior*, *116*, 106633. https://doi.org/10.1016/j.chb.2020.106633

Bennett, W. L., & Livingston, S. (2018). The disinformation order: Disruptive communication and the decline of democratic institutions. *European Journal of Communication*, *33*(2), 122–139. https://doi.org/10.1177/0267323118760317

Brandtzaeg, P. B., & Følstad, A. (2017). Trust and distrust in online fact-checking services. *Communications of the ACM*, *60*(9), 65–71. https://doi.org/10.1145/3122803

Breitman, K. (2015, January 7). Poll: Half of Republicans still believe WMDs found in Iraq. *Politico.* https://www.politico.com/story/2015/01/poll-republicans-wmds-iraq-114016

Brennen, B. (2017). Making sense of lies, deceptive propaganda, and fake news. *Journal of Media Ethics, 32*(3), 179–181. https://doi.org/10.1080/23736992.2017.1331023

Bruns, A., Harrington, S., & Hurcombe, E. (2021). Coronavirus conspiracy theories: Tracing misinformation trajectories from the fringes to the mainstream. In M. Lewis, E. Govender, & K. Holland (Eds.), *Communicating COVID-19* (pp. 229–249). Palgrave Macmillan.

Chadwick, A., Vaccari, C., & O'Loughlin, B. (2018). Do tabloids poison the well of social media? Explaining democratically dysfunctional news sharing. *New Media & Society, 20*(11), 4255–4274. https://doi.org/10.1177/1461444818769689

Confessore, N. (2018, April 4). Cambridge Analytica and Facebook: The scandal and the fallout so far. *The New York Times.* https://www.nytimes.com/2018/04/04/us/politics/cambridge-analytica-scandal-fallout.html

Ecker, U. K., Lewandowsky, S., & Tang, D. T. (2010). Explicit warnings reduce but do not eliminate the continued influence of misinformation. *Memory & Cognition, 38,* 1087–1100. https://doi.org/10.3758/MC.38.8.1087

Ecker, U. K., Lewandowsky, S., & Apai, J. (2011). Terrorists brought down the plane!—No, actually it was a technical fault: Processing corrections of emotive information. *Quarterly Journal of Experimental Psychology, 64*(2), 283–310. https://doi.org/10.1080/17470218.2010.497927

Egelhofer, J. L., & Lecheler, S. (2019). Fake news as a two-dimensional phenomenon: A framework and research agenda. *Annals of the International Communication Association, 43*(2), 97–116. https://doi.org/10.1080/23808985.2019.1602782

Farhall, K., Carson, A., Wright, S., Gibbons, A., & Lukamto, W. (2019). Political elites' use of fake news discourse across communications platforms. *International Journal of Communication, 13,* 4353–4375.

Farkas, J., & Schou, J. (2018). Fake news as a floating signifier: Hegemony, antagonism and the politics of falsehood. *Javnost - The Public, Journal of the European Institute for Communication and Culture, 25*(3), 298–314. https://doi.org/10.1080/13183222.2018.1463047

Flynn, D. J., Nyhan, B., & Reifler, J. (2017). The nature and origins of misperceptions: Understanding false and unsupported beliefs about politics. *Political Psychology, 38,* 127–150. https://doi.org/10.1111/pops.12394

Fominaya, C. F. (2024). Mobilizing during the Covid-19 pandemic: From democratic innovation to the political weaponization of disinformation. *American Behavioral Scientist, 68*(6), 829–852. https://doi.org/10.1177/00027642221132178

Frischlich, L., Hellmann, J. H., Brinkschulte, F., Becker, M., & Back, M. D. (2021). Right-wing authoritarianism, conspiracy mentality, and susceptibility to distorted alternative news. *Social Influence, 16*, 24–64. https://doi.org/10.1080/15534510.2021.1966499

From the Editors; The Times and Iraq. (2004, May 26). *The New York Times*. https://www.nytimes.com/2004/05/26/world/from-the-editors-the-times-and-iraq.html

Gaber, I., & Fisher, C. (2021). "Strategic lying": The case of Brexit and the 2019 U.K. election. *The International Journal of Press/Politics, 27*(2), 460–477. https://doi.org/10.1177/1940161221994100

Greene, C. M., & Murphy, G. (2021). Quantifying the effects of fake news on behavior: Evidence from a study of COVID-19 misinformation. *Journal of Experimental Psychology: Applied, 27*(4), 773–784. https://doi.org/10.1037/xap0000371

Guerrero, T. (2023, September 14). Un ufólogo muestra en la Cámara de Diputados de México dos supuestos extraterrestres: "Es una farsa, un burdo montaje". *El Mundo*. https://www.elmundo.es/ciencia-y-salud/ciencia/2023/09/13/6501b5e0e85ece7b518b45cd.html

Hasell, A., & Weeks, B. E. (2016). Partisan provocation: The role of partisan news use and emotional responses in political information sharing in social media. *Human Communication Research, 42*(4), 641–661. https://doi.org/10.1111/hcre.12092

Hasher, L., Goldstein, D., & Toppino, T. (1977). Frequency and the conference of referential validity. *Journal of Verbal Learning and Verbal Behavior, 16*(1), 107–112. https://doi.org/10.1016/S0022-5371(77)80012-1

Heawood, J. (2018). Pseudo-public political speech: Democratic implications of the Cambridge Analytica scandal. *Information Polity, 23*(4), 429–434. https://doi.org/10.3233/IP-180009

Herman, E. S., & Chomsky, N. (1988). *Manufacturing consent: The political economy of the mass media*. Pantheon Books.

Hude, H. (1982). Política y verdad en Rousseau. *Anuario Filosófico, 15*(2), 215–219.

Huxley, A. (1994). *Brave new world revisited*. Flamingo.

Jones-Jang, S. M., Mortensen, T., & Liu, J. (2019). Does media literacy help identification of fake news? Information literacy helps, but other literacies don't. *American Behavioral Scientist, 65*(2), 371–388. https://doi.org/10.1177/0002764219869406

Klein, N. (2017). *No is not enough. Defeating the new shock politics*. Penguin.

Kuklinski, J. H., & Quirk, P. J. (2000). Reconsidering the rational public: Cognition, heuristics, and mass opinion. In A. Lupia, M. D. McCubbins, & S. L. Popkin (Eds.), *Elements of reason: Understanding and expanding the limits of political rationality* (pp. 153–182). Cambridge University Press.

Machiavelli, N. (2014). *The prince*. Penguin.

Nixon: 'I wasn't lying. I said things that later on seemed to be untrue'. (1978, November 28). *The Washington Post.* https://www.washingtonpost.com/archive/politics/1978/11/29/nixon-i-wasnt-lying-i-said-things-that-later-on-seemed-to-be-untrue/3756f600-6d07-4335-b504-fed52f3fef77/

Oeldorf-Hirsch, A., Schmierbach, M., Appelman, A., & Boyle, M. P. (2020). The ineffectiveness of fact-checking labels on news memes and articles. *Mass Communication and Society, 23*(5), 682–704. https://doi.org/10.1080/15205436.2020.1733613

Orwell, G. (1949). *1984.* Secker & Warburg.

Osmundsen, M., Bor, A., Vahlstrup, P. B., Bechmann, A., & Petersen, M. B. (2021). Partisan polarization is the primary psychological motivation behind political fake news sharing on Twitter. *American Political Science Review, 115*(3), 999–1015. https://doi.org/10.1017/S0003055421000290

Parnell, T. (2023). Brexit and disinformation. In S. M. Maci, M. Demata, M. McGlashan, & P. Seargeant (Eds.), *The Routledge handbook of discourse and disinformation* (pp. 187–200). Routledge.

Petty, R. E., Briñol, P., & Priester, J. R. (2009). Mass media attitude change: Implications of the elaboration likelihood model of persuasion. In J. Bryant & M. B. Oliver (Eds.), *Media effects: Advances in theory and research* (pp. 125–164). Routledge.

Podgornik, B. B., Dolničar, D., Šorgo, A., & Bartol, T. (2016). Development, testing, and validation of an information literacy test (ILT) for higher education. *Journal of the Association for Information Science and Technology, 67*, 2420–2436. https://doi.org/10.1002/asi.23586

Robinson, P., Miller, D., Herring, E., & Bakir, V. (2018). Lying and deception in politics. In J. Meibauer (Ed.), *The Oxford handbook of lying* (pp. 529–540). Oxford University Press. https://doi.org/10.1093/oxfordhb/9780198736578.013.42

Scott, M. (2018, March 27). Cambridge Analytica helped 'cheat' Brexit vote and US election, claims whistleblower. *Politico.* https://www.politico.eu/article/cambridge-analytica-chris-wylie-brexit-trump-britain-data-protection-privacy-facebook/

Strauß, N. (2019). Financial journalism in today's high-frequency news and information era. *Journalism, 20*(2), 274–291. https://doi.org/10.1177/1464884917753555

Subramanian, S. (2017, February 15). Inside the Macedonian fake-news complex. *Wired.* https://www.wired.com/2017/02/veles-macedonia-fake-news/

Taber, C. S., & Lodge, M. (2006). Motivated skepticism in the evaluation of political beliefs. *American Journal of Political Science, 50*(3), 755–769. https://doi.org/10.1111/j.1540-5907.2006.00214.x

Toledano, S. (2006). La neolengua de Orwell en la prensa actual. La literatura profetiza la manipulación mediática del lenguaje. *Revista Latina de Comunicación Social, 61*, 1–8. https://doi.org/10.4185/RLCS-200601

Unkelbach, C., & Speckmann, F. (2021). Mere repetition increases belief in factually true COVID-19-related information. *Journal of Applied Research in Memory and Cognition, 10*(2), 241–247. https://doi.org/10.1016/j.jarmac.2021.02.001

Valkenburg, P. M., Peter, J., & Walther, J. B. (2016). Media effects: Theory and research. *Annual Review of Psychology, 67*, 315–338. https://doi.org/10.1146/annurev-psych-122414-033608

van Kessel, S., Sajuria, J., & Van Hauwaert, S. (2021). Informed, uninformed or misinformed? A cross-national analysis of populist party supporters across European democracies. *West European Politics, 44*(3), 585–610. https://doi.org/10.1080/01402382.2019.1700448

Xia, Y., Lukito, J., Zhang, Y., Wells, C., Kim, S. J., & Tong, C. (2019). Disinformation, performed: Self-presentation of a Russian IRA account on Twitter. *Information, Communication & Society, 22*(11), 1646–1664. https://doi.org/10.1080/1369118X.2019.1621921

Zaller, J. R. (1992). *The nature and origins of mass opinion*. Cambridge University Press.

Zimmermann, F., & Kohring, M. (2020). Mistrust, disinforming news, and vote choice: A panel survey on the origins and consequences of believing disinformation in the 2017 German parliamentary election. *Political Communication, 37*(2), 215–237. https://doi.org/10.1080/10584609.2019.1686095

CHAPTER 13

Content Sharing Dynamics and Political Polarization in Social Media

Natalia Aruguete ⓘ

INTRODUCTION

The social media have been a central vector of the public crisis unleashed by political violence, digital attack, and deliberate dissemination of falsehoods in contexts of high polarization, with negative effects on the already eroded support for democratic consensus, whose pillars have been citizen participation, political tolerance, and public deliberation. Distrust in social and political institutions includes the media, which are undergoing processes of news avoidance and selective disconnection by their audiences. In response, media celebrities cling to editorial exaltation as a necessary tool to retain their loyal audiences. But neither algorithms nor media perceived as ideologically biased alone explains polarization and identity divisions. In a recent study, Silvio Waisbord (2020) wonders if the simultaneity of political polarization and the rise of digital politics is mere coincidence or if, on the contrary, it is possible to establish a causal relationship between communicational and political factors. I agree with Waisbord (2020) that

N. Aruguete (✉)
CONICET, Universidad Nacional de Quilmes, Buenos Aires, Argentina

© The Author(s), under exclusive license to Springer Nature Switzerland AG 2024
M. Goyanes, A. Cañedo (eds.), *Media Influence on Opinion Change and Democracy*, https://doi.org/10.1007/978-3-031-70231-0_13

polarization responds to factors that go beyond the processes predetermined by digital politics and, in particular, by social media (p. 55).

In this chapter, I analyze how the political and affective dimensions of polarization coexist in our interactions on social media. To do this, first, I propose a conceptualization of political polarization and affective polarization, considering the complementarity of both in the analysis of our political behavior. Second, I present a series of cases (some of which include disinformation strategies) to analyze the role that polarization plays in our perceptions; specifically, the circulation of messages on social media. Several questions guide this journey: How do our mood and our preconceptions about others affect our interpretation of content? How does the way a message is presented influence our anger or motivate our joy? What happens when someone tells us we are right or, on the contrary, challenges our beliefs? Finally, I propose some final thoughts, not with the aim of closing the debate but of opening new questions.

Polarization

The literature in political science had focused on a classic and consolidated conception of polarization: that which divides those who adhere to certain ideas and policies from those who reject them. Recent studies of polarization have extended beyond strictly political considerations to areas such as marital decisions and scientific evaluations. This new form of polarization, which is increasingly influential and powerful, is characterized by the intensity of attachment to in-group members and hatred towards out-group members, who are perceived as enemies. This dynamic creates a sense of living in different, opposing worlds when it comes to perception about the out-group (Mason, 2016, 2018).

In its current form, polarization tends toward "sorting" (Mason, 2016), a process wherein various attributes of our social and political lives realign so that political-party divisions coincide with social, religious, and racial differences. Partisan identification groups identity attachments while organizing the views of supporters (members of the in-group) towards adversaries (members of the out-group) (Iyengar et al., 2019).

A careful examination of polarization will help us to understand why the concern and study of affective polarization have expanded so significantly. The instrumental and expressive perspectives have been competing for decades to provide comprehensive explanations for party identities and political commitment. According to the instrumental approach, there is an ideological agenda based on solid issues around which politicians and citizens express precise differences. Party identity encompasses the interests, ideology, and preferences of citizens regarding matters of interest (Fiorina, 1981).

The expressive approach, on the other hand, posits that partisan ties are not closely linked to the evolution of specific agenda items but have become independent of short-term economic and political priorities. This perspective has gained prominence in the academic field and has given rise to a line of research called "affective polarization" (Mason, 2018; Iyengar et al., 2019). Affective polarization measures the emotional temperature—the degree of liking, hatred, disgust, or joy—that voters report feeling towards opposing parties when exposed to a political message (Webster & Abramowitz, 2017).

Closely related to this perspective, Liliana Mason (2018) distinguishes between *issue position polarization* and *social* or *behavioral polarization*. The former refers to political preferences based on individuals' evaluations and positions on specific issues. The latter explains the intensity of the emotional distance between opposing groups through emotional bias. Social polarization accounts for the inclination of citizens—particularly those with more extreme identity positions—to view members of the opposing group in a stereotyped, prejudiced, and emotional manner, irrespective of agreements or disagreements on policy offerings or agenda items. This perspective also recognizes that hostility towards the out-group has deepened even though citizens may express only moderate discrepancies in their evaluations of public policies.

According to Druckman and his colleagues (2021), there is no such independence between these two dimensions of polarization. These authors criticize the focus of affective polarization on apolitical ramifications and, at best, on its implications for social behavior (such as family relationships, work colleagues, and marital choices). Little research has been conducted on the relationship between affective polarization and individuals' positions on issues. In their study on COVID-19, they found a strong association between interparty animosity and pandemic response behaviors (Druckman et al., 2021). This link between partisanship and health response was also observed in a series of studies on risk perception during the pandemic in various South American countries, where voters from ruling and opposition parties reported different probabilities of infection (Aruguete & Calvo, 2020; Aruguete et al., 2021; Calvo & Ventura, 2021).

Polarization and Risk

In response to the need to manage the social, health, and political costs of the pandemic, governments and oppositions worldwide focused on presenting responses to the uncertainty generated by a novel situation for which there were no established answers. Without empirical evidence, predictions of contracting coronavirus became associated with citizens' partisan identities. During the pandemic, voters aligned with ruling party leaders Donald Trump in the United States and Jair Bolsonaro in Brazil, downplayed the risk of contagion, while the opposition in both countries accused their governments of irresponsibly endangering public health. In Argentina, government supporters emphasized health risks, whereas the opposition criticized Alberto Fernández's administration for downplaying the economic costs of its health policies. In all these cases, people echoed their leaders' stances, tying the perceived probability of contagion to their political affiliations.

In this section, I analyze the individual perception of health risk during the pandemic in Argentina, aiming to understand how citizens evaluated such risks based on affective intuitions and cognitive shortcuts when information was scarce, and political polarization was high. Given that the probability of contracting COVID-19 was an impossible-to-calculate estimation, responses were based on "intuitive heuristics." Intuitive heuristics suggest that when faced with a difficult question for which we have no answer, we subconsciously replace it with an easier one (Simon, 1992).

Before making decisions among different alternatives, individuals evaluate the potential implications of their actions and the responsibilities attributed to the actors involved. "How likely are you to get sick with COVID-19/lose your job?" were two central questions in the national-electoral survey conducted with 2400 Argentine voters between March 23 and May 6, 2020, and replicated during the same period in Brazil and Mexico. Since Argentine voters could not determine the actual likelihood of infection, they substituted that question with a framing of responsibility, which accounted for the effect of polarization on risk perception (Aruguete & Calvo, 2020).

Figure 13.1 depicts that the perceived risk among Peronist voters (supporters of the government during the pandemic) and those affiliated with Juntos por el Cambio (aligned with the political opposition during the pandemic) was correlated more strongly with emotional attachments and aversions rather than rational deliberation mechanisms.

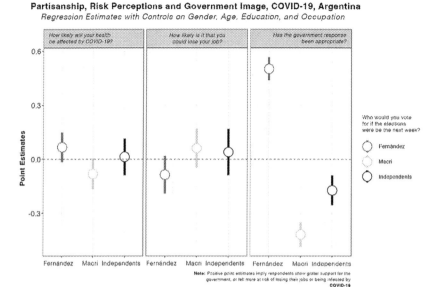

Fig. 13.1 COVID-19 and risk perception in Argentina. (Note: Least squares model describing differences)

Party identities and political affiliations emerged as primary predictors of the outcomes under examination. The regression model, incorporating controls for age, gender, and education, reveals that supporters of Alberto Fernández exhibit a heightened probability of contracting Coronavirus and express less certainty regarding potential job loss compared to adherents of Mauricio Macri. These disparities align with the narrative promulgated by Fernández's administration, which underscores the imperative of prioritizing public health, or with arguments articulated by the then-opposition, advocating for safeguarding the economy.

The differences in risk perception among voters from different parties are statistically significant, even amid initial widespread consensus regarding the healthcare strategies of Alberto Fernández's government at the onset of the pandemic. Furthermore, the favorable perception of the Peronist leader, relative to counterparts such as Jair Bolsonaro and Andrés Manuel López Obrador in Brazil and Mexico respectively, resulted in diminished polarization and heightened support in Argentina. Although the disparities observed within Argentina were less pronounced than those in Brazil and Mexico, the findings underscore the subjective nature of risk perception, wherein political loyalties, beliefs, and affiliations appear to influence the likelihood of contracting illness. Resonating like an echo chamber, the perception of health and labor-related risks consistently mirrors the political frameworks espoused by both ruling and opposition factions of voters.

Pandemic and Disinformation

The pandemic was rife with falsehoods, distinguished by content and political intentionality. Two major stages marked the trajectory of information circulation. The first was characterized by the subjective need to fill gaps in information with assumptions and prejudices to alleviate the perplexity of the initial moments. The second, marked by increasing political and identity polarization, shaped a dichotomous understanding of health, political, and socioeconomic events, leading to a consequent rise in levels of intolerance and incivility. One wonders whether the harm caused by these fallacies has been more or less severe than that generated in electoral campaigns, overthrow scenarios, or generalized political crises. There is no conclusive answer. Primarily because a significant number of misinformation did not result from widespread political operations but from activities driven by intense groups, often located on the periphery of politics, such as medical celebrities or anti-vaccine and anti-quarantine collectives. But at the same time, the convergence of lies about clinical issues and deep political conflicts has been a dangerous conjunction due to its health implications.

During the peak moments of virus spread, when the response of Alberto Fernández's government focused on circulation restrictions, disinformation strategies found a favorable context. The high levels of polarization in Argentine society not only resulted in disparate risk perceptions but also eroded confidence in the vaccination campaign as a solution to reduce virus spread, fueled by extremist groups aligned with anti-vaccination sentiments. In this context of uncertainty and distress, the circulation of disinformation had social media as the primary arena (Nieves-Cuervo et al., 2021). And it was precisely in the digital ecosystem where fact-checkers intervened most actively, both to reduce the spread of falsehoods and to increase the circulation of information endorsed by health authorities and professional associations (Walter & Tukachinsky, 2020).

My interest in this essay is not only centered on the process of creating fake news but above all on its communicative effects. I focus on two types of responses. On the one hand, observing how fake news activates forms of communicative intolerance (anger, disgust, stress). On the other hand, confirming the capacity of fact-checkers to establish themselves as authoritative voices and thus limit the circulation of spurious information.

The Political Cost of Verifying False News

The efficacy of fact-checking interventions hinges upon their capacity to reach a broader audience and mitigate the proliferation of false information on digital platforms. To accomplish this objective, it is imperative that the fact-checker maintains an appearance of impartiality and avoids incurring reputational costs. This necessitates ensuring that users do not perceive the fact-checker as possessing ideological biases or displaying favoritism towards particular groups. In this segment, I present a case study involving the correction of misinformation during the pandemic to evaluate the political ramifications—specifically, the perception of bias— associated with rectifying falsehoods. Through a survey experiment conducted among 5,757 adult voters in Argentina in November 2022, we assessed shifts in attitudes subsequent to the correction of news content classified as either 'true' or 'false' (Aruguete & Calvo, 2022).

The experiment was structured as follows: participants were initially exposed to a post disseminated by the Argentine media outlet *Infobae*. Various components of this tweet were manipulated; the authorship was alternated among media outlets such as *La Nación*, *Clarín*, *Infobae*, or *Página/12*, while the hyperlinks directed to two distinct news articles published in *Infobae* with a six-month interval. The article from October 2020 contained false information, whereas the May 2021 counterpart presented accurate information. Subsequently, the sample was divided into different groups, subjected to a series of inquiries, and presented with a fact-check by Chequeado, which either validated or refuted the veracity of the original tweet (see Fig. 13.2).

This experiment seeks to elucidate the impact of verification mechanisms on both the inclination to disseminate messages via social media and the perception of ideological bias attributed to the fact-checker subsequent to correction. In addition to assessing sharing tendencies, respondents were queried regarding their ideological self-positioning and the ideological stances of various politicians, some media outlets, and

222 N. ARUGUETE

Fig. 13.2 Original Tweet (*left*) and Correction as "True" or "False" (*right*). (Note: The figure shows the treatment when the authority issuing the original tweet is Infobae. Other rotations used the same tweet but alternated (rotated) the authorities of that post among Página|12, La Nación, and Clarín)

Chequeado. The decision to gauge the ideological disparity between respondents and the fact-checker both pre- and post-verification facilitates examination of whether corrections—whether congruent or incongruent with the user's standpoint—affect perceptions of the fact-checker's ideological orientation.

The findings of this study indicate that information affirming the respondent's beliefs heightens the likelihood of sharing, whereas messages perceived as challenging prompt a decrease in sharing propensity. Within the realm of social media, expressions of affinity with a message typically manifest through liking and retweeting without commentary, whereas quoting a post accompanied by a comment or replying suggests a lesser degree of acceptance. However, the affective impact extends beyond mere sharing intentions; exposure to verifications also influences perceived ideological bias. Favorable (pro-attitudinal) corrections correspond to diminished perceptions of ideological bias, whereas corrections that challenge one's position result in heightened ideological disparity. As noted by Aruguete and Calvo (2022, p. 761), "these findings underscore the prevalence of pro-attitudinal exchanges, both in the original publication and in Chequeado's interventions."

Resistance to sharing counter-attitudinal fact-checks is more pronounced on social media where toxic language and hate speech are perpetuated through oversimplified message labels. This phenomenon is particularly notable on X (formerly known as Twitter) and Facebook, where misinformation proliferates due to horizontal integration strategies facilitating widespread dissemination. Ultimately, akin to messages that engender polarizing political events, verification interventions are marked by conflict.

Affective Activation

The efficacy of a misinformation campaign is not solely contingent upon its creation; rather, it hinges on its resonance with other users to ensure widespread dissemination. Specific messages resonate with users within virtual communities by aligning with their ideologies and worldviews. This constitutes a crucial aspect of fake news circulation, as it aims to affectively engage users who share affinity with these narratives, thereby motivating them to disseminate such information. This affective engagement holds considerable sway, particularly in contexts of heightened polarization, such as during election cycles, owing to the vast volume of information circulating and the rapid amplification of political messages.

To elucidate the role of misinformation in highly polarized environments, I will analyze a case study from the 2019 presidential election campaign. In this instance, the then-candidate for vice-governor of the province of Buenos Aires, the largest electoral district in Argentina, became the target of a digital attack involving false information. I will employ the term "fake-fake news" to denote a specific case of misinformation deliberately crafted and disseminated on social media as a satirical yet derogatory piece of news, intended to evade verification of its content.

"The Gardens of Magario"

In Argentina, a majority of the population associates public education with universal principles of access and gratuity, which have been established since the mid-nineteenth century with the aim of improving socioeconomic disparities in the educational sphere. However, in recent years, education has also become enmeshed in political polarization, emerging as a contentious issue that divides political parties and their supporters. Anti-Peronist factions have characterized Peronism as an anti-education party, while from the Peronist perspective, both Radicalism and PRO have been portrayed as anti-secular and elitist parties.

On September 25, 2019, a few days before the national and provincial elections in Argentina, the satirical outlet @INFOen140 published a journalistic note that rapidly went viral on social media platforms. On Twitter, the spurious news article purported that the then-candidate for vice-governor, Verónica Magario, had made the statement: "Queremos un pueblo Peronista, y si escolarizamos a los nenes nunca van a ser Peronistas" (We want a Peronist people, and if we school the kids, they will never become Peronists). Within a few hours, the article garnered over 1400 retweets and more than 1800 likes (see Fig. 13.3). This false assertion alluded to the phrase "Alpargatas sí, libros no" (Espadrilles yes, books no)—incorrectly attributed to Juan Domingo Perón and his wife, Eva Duarte—which encapsulates the perceived anti-education sentiment among those opposed to Peronism.

13 CONTENT SHARING DYNAMICS AND POLITICAL POLARIZATI... 225

Fig. 13.3 Original post by @INFOen140, verification by Chequeado, and responses to the fact-check. (Note: The figure shows the treatment when the original tweet is issued by Infobae. Other rotations used the same tweet but alternated (rotated) the sources of the post among Página|12, La Nación, and Clarín)

The Dilemma for Chequeado

The publication by @INFOen140 posed a dilemma for Chequeado. Despite being explicitly labeled as political satire, the news quickly gained traction as a genuine story just weeks before the elections in the Province of Buenos Aires (Aruguete & Calvo, 2023). On social media, the then-vice-governor Verónica Magario (2019–2027) faced accusations stemming from this false news. Chequeado's decision to classify the news from @INFOen140 as false elicited a sarcastic response from the @INFOen140 account, initiating a discourse wherein @Chequeado was criticized for its purportedly "ineffective" attempt at rectifying information disseminated by a satire outlet (see Fig. 13.3). @INFOen140 posted: "Buenas tardes, @Chequeado, nuestros empledos inventaron la noticia mientras escupían semillas de sandía en la vereda" (Good afternoon @Chequeado, our employees invented the news while spitting watermelon seeds on the sidewalk). Describing itself as a producer of "Noticias a la carta sobre temas de interés general" (News on demand about topics of General Interest,) the @INFOen140 account effectively generated a fake-fake news item, which, after being labeled as false, garnered increased exposure.

The efficacy of such messages lies in the fact that the @INFOen140 account disseminates ostensibly false information under the guise of political satire. This mechanism yields several consequences. On the one hand, it precludes intervention by fact-checkers since the information is presented not as fake news but as sarcasm. On the other hand, in contexts characterized by high polarization, low political tolerance, and heightened toxicity on social media, such messages often become viral. Ultimately, it proves challenging to curtail the circulation of such content and alert audiences to its falsehood, particularly when the audience identifies with a specific political ideology, as correction of a message recognized as "false" may offend them and further exacerbate polarization rather than foster constructive debate.

For a narrative to resonate and gain visibility, it must activate shared interpretations. The fake-fake news disseminated by @INFOen140 is more than a mere falsehood; it triggers latent perception schemas within a segment of Argentine society, prompting individuals to share it as it reinforces preexisting prejudices cultivated and perpetuated over decades, such as the portrayal of a Peronist official. Data gathered from the X account regarding the interactions generated by this fake news corroborate this assertion. The initial post, as well as the @INFOen140 account, elicited engagement predominantly from users affiliated with Juntos por el Cambio (JxC), owing to the cognitive alignment and enthusiasm it elicited. Notably, the @Chequeado account also garnered heightened engagement within the JxC community, as the sarcastic rejoinder from @INFOen140 to @Chequeado's intervention spurred intense criticism of the fact-checker, which circulated widely among a community that reacted antagonistically (see Fig. 13.3).

"The Gardens of Magario" serves as a poignant illustration of how identity sentiments are activated within a predisposed sector, encouraging individuals to consume, accept, and propagate content that denigrates their adversaries. Partisan allegiance does not necessarily align with an objective assessment of public policies. Particularly in electoral contexts, exposure to information that denigrates and undermines opposing parties reinforces individuals' biased perceptions of their adversaries (Iyengar et al., 2012).

Final Thoughts

The reactions observed on social media do not solely stem from cognitive alignment following a logical interpretation of an event; they also serve as a defense of our convictions against what we perceive as the communicative objectives of others. Beyond comprehensive arguments, political information provides both an emotional and ideological framework (Calvo & Aruguete, 2020). Within this context, users' affective reactions to messages are not markedly different when they encounter verified information compared to when they share false content.

In recent times, the proliferation of falsehoods has further eroded the institutional stability of democracies. Fake news not only disseminates false information but also serves as a strategic attack to undermine adversaries. It posits the existence of an enemy rather than an interlocutor, suggesting that this adversary seeks not to engage in discourse but rather to inflict harm and achieve a political outcome. Challenging the communicative intent of this "other" erodes the trust necessary for democratic dialogue to flourish.

Both false information devoid of political intent and "weaponized" falsehoods—employed as a tool to inflict harm—undermine belief in the communicative intent of our interlocutors. Wardle and Derakhshan (2017) posit that fake news constitutes political operations, distinguishing them from false news arising from validation errors or inadvertent mistakes. While false news may aim to challenge underlying beliefs, fake news renders dialogue unviable, as it lacks a communicative intention aimed at fostering discourse and instead seeks to toxify the public sphere.

Disinformation strategies are not isolated phenomena and hold greater sway in polarized environments. Such polarization manifests in our perception of what distinguishes us from others. Among its myriad consequences, discursive violence on social media—of which misinformation is only one type of violence—undermines cognitive, political, and civic consensus. The breakdown of cognitive consensus manifests in motivated reasoning, which prompts individuals to accept evidence that aligns with their beliefs while disregarding contradictory information. The erosion of political consensus aims to provoke a political effect, with the objective being to harm opponents or elevate the visibility of certain issues where a comparative advantage exists. Finally, when civic consensus deteriorates, political narratives become fragmented and extreme. Affective polarization plays a pivotal role in this dynamic, as the emotions evoked by political discourse contribute to the distancing between parties and their leaders, transcending mere agreement or disagreement on public policies.

In certain countries, political elites have explicitly sought to distort the communicative space, either as a defensive mechanism when reality contradicts their political ambitions or as a means of constructing in-group identity in opposition to the out-group. Figures such as Donald Trump Jr., Jair Bolsonaro, and more recently, Javier Milei, serve as illustrative examples of both communicative intentions: downplaying the threat of COVID-19 when politically inconvenient and disseminating intentionally false information or launching consistent attacks on adversaries as a means of cultivating loyalty among their electorates and supporters.

Today, we are witnessing the erosion of the preconditions for tolerant, consensus-oriented democratic debate. In this context, it is imperative to analyze the strategic deployment of fake news and question whether democratic deliberation remains feasible when trust in the communicative intent of our interlocutors is undermined within the digital public sphere.

Viewed through this lens, fake news emerges as a primary instrument in the erosion of democratic debate. Faced with the perception that our adversaries propagate falsehoods, filter bubbles cease to be spaces that arise from affective intolerances but rather serve as defense mechanisms. Individuals retreat within their ideological boundaries in response to the strategic encroachment of those who engage in discursive violence. Consequently, if consensus cannot be reached on what constitutes factual information, political dialogue and deliberative democracy lose their normative significance.

References

Aruguete, N., & Calvo, E. (2020). Coronavirus en Argentina: Polarización partidaria, encuadres mediáticos y temor al riesgo. *Revista Saap*, *14*(2), 280–310. https://doi.org/10.46468/rsaap.14.2.a2

Aruguete, N., & Calvo, E. (2022). La sustentabilidad del fact checking en tiempos de polarización. Estudio de caso de Argentina durante la pandemia. *Estudios sobre el Mensaje Periodístico*, *28*(4), 751–764. https://doi.org/10.5209/esmp.82831

Aruguete, N., & Calvo, E. (2023). *Nosotros contra ellos. ¿Cómo trabajan las redes para confirmar nuestras creencias y rechazar las de los otros?* Siglo XXI.

Aruguete, N., Calvo, E., Cantú, F., Ley, S., Scartascini, C., & Ventura, T. (2021). Partisan cues and perceived risks: The effect of partisan social media frames during the COVID-19 crisis in Mexico. *Journal of Elections, Public Opinion and Parties*, *31*(sup1), 82–95. https://doi.org/10.1080/17457289.2021.1924740

Calvo, E., & Aruguete, N. (2020). *Fake news, trolls y otros encantos: Cómo funcionan (para bien y para mal) las redes sociales*. Buenos Aires: Siglo XXI.

Calvo, E., & Ventura, T. (2021). Will I get COVID-19? Partisanship, social media frames, and perceptions of health risk in Brazil. *Latin American Politics and Society*, *63*(1), 1–26. https://doi.org/10.1017/lap.2020.30

Druckman, J. N., Klar, S., Krupnikov, Y., Levendusky, M., & Ryan, J. B. (2021). Affective polarization, local contexts and public opinion in America. *Nature Human Behavior*, *5*(1), 28–38. https://doi.org/10.1038/s41562-020-01012-5

Fiorina, M. P. (1981). Some problems in studying the effects of resource allocation in congressional elections. *American Journal of Political Science*, *25*, 543–567.

Iyengar, S., Sood, G., & Lelkes, Y. (2012). Affect, not ideology: A social identity perspective on polarization. *Public Opinion Quarterly*, *76*(3), 405–431. https://doi.org/10.1093/poq/nfs038

Iyengar, S., Lelkes, Y., Levendusky, M., Malhotra, N., & Westwood, S. J. (2019). The origins and consequences of affective polarization in the United States. *Annual Review of Political Science*, *22*, 129–146. https://doi.org/10.1146/annurev-polisci-051117-073034

Mason, L. (2016). A cross-cutting calm: How social sorting drives affective polarization. *Public Opinion Quarterly*, *80*(S1), 351–377. https://doi.org/10.1093/poq/nfw001

Mason, L. (2018). *Uncivil agreement: How politics became our identity*. University of Chicago Press.

Nieves-Cuervo, G. M., Manrique-Hernández, E. F., Robledo-Colonia, A. F., & Grillo, A. E. K. (2021). Infodemia: noticias falsas y tendencias de mortalidad por COVID-19 en seis países de América Latina. *Revista Panamericana de Salud Pública, 45*, e44. https://doi.org/10.26633/RPSP.2021.44

Simon, H. A. (1992). What is an "explanation" of behavior? *Psychological Science, 3*(3), 150–161. https://doi.org/10.1111/j.1467-9280.1992.tb00017.x

Waisbord, S. (2020). ¿Es válido atribuir la polarización política a la comunicación digital? Sobre burbujas, plataformas y polarización afectiva. *Revista saap, 14*(2), 248–279. https://doi.org/10.46468/rsaap.14.2.A1

Walter, N., & Tukachinsky, R. (2020). A meta-analytic examination of the continued influence of misinformation in the face of correction: How powerful is it, why does it happen, and how to stop it? *Communication Research, 47*(2), 155–177. https://doi.org/10.1177/0093650219854600

Wardle, C., & Derakhshan, H. (2017). *Information disorder: Toward an interdisciplinary framework for research and policymaking.* Council of Europe. https://edoc.coe.int/en/media/7495-information-disorder-toward-an-interdisciplinary-framework-for-research-and-policy-making.html

Webster, S. W., & Abramowitz, A. I. (2017). The ideological foundations of affective polarization in the US electorate. *American Politics Research, 45*(4), 621–647. https://doi.org/10.1177/1532673X17703132